EAST AFRICA:
A Century of Change 1870–1970

W. E. F. WARD
and
L. W. WHITE

Maps by Peter Shrives

AFRICANA PUBLISHING CORPORATION · NEW YORK

Published
in the United States of America 1972
by Africana Publishing Corporation
101 Fifth Avenue
New York, N.Y. 10003

Library of Congress Catalogue Card No. 70–161232

ISBN 0–8419–0079–5 (hc)

1 - 19 - 73

Printed in Great Britain

Contents

56342

Illustrations

Nos 1–3 and 5–12 inclusive are by courtesy of Camera Press; No. 4 is by courtesy of the Radio Times Hulton Picture Library. Both sources are gratefully acknowledged.

Maps

Preface

This book is intended in the first place for African students who are preparing for the East African School Certificate or the East African Certificate of Education examination, but we hope that it will be useful to readers in Africa and elsewhere who have no examination in view.

The century which began with the accession of Sultan Barghash to the throne of Zanzibar has seen the partition of East Africa, the development of the colonial system, and the establishment of the former colonies as independent states. In 1870, East Africa was almost untouched by European influence; it has long since become part of the modern world. This century of change has been full of controversy, and different interpretations are possible of many events. In telling the story, we have borne in mind the saying of a great historian that to know what happened is less important than to understand why it happened; and we have tried to understand and explain the motives of those who took part.

We hope that the questions and exercises and the other appendices will be convenient not only for school use, but also for readers who cannot call on the help of a specialist history teacher.

Chapter 1

EAST AFRICA IN 1870

In the year 1870, all the peoples of East Africa, from the swamps of the Nile right down to the river Limpopo, were independent of any European control. They governed themselves as they pleased, whether through powerful chiefs or kings like the Baganda or through clan elders like the Kikuyu. They lived by growing crops or herding cattle, they stayed in one place or they wandered with their herds, they made war and peace as they thought fit. Africa was large; there was plenty of land for all. Far away down the Nile was the kingdom of Egypt, far away in the south there were the British and Afrikaner settlers in South Africa. Both Egypt and South Africa were too far off to trouble the East African peoples. Along the coast there was a string of Arab trading settlements, and the Arab trading caravans penetrated deeply into the country, bringing with them trade goods and taking out slaves and ivory, sometimes honestly bought, sometimes captured by violence. Zanzibar was the most important place in this trade, and the Sultan of Zanzibar had authority over the other Arab towns on the coast. So important was Zanzibar that the saying ran, 'When they whistle in Zanzibar, people dance on the shores of the great lakes.'

The Arab traders were foreigners in East Africa, but everyone knew where they came from; they had their homes on the coast, in Kilwa and Mombasa and Malindi and other towns. They had been there for hundreds of years, living among the African peoples and mixing with them; the Swahili language, half-Bantu and half-Arab, was spoken and understood as a useful trade language all along their caravan routes far into the interior.

But the Europeans were a new kind of foreigner, coming from nobody knew where; some people indeed thought that they had no home of their own and were constantly wandering to look for a home. So they came to be called *wazungu*, the wanderers.

They were of two kinds. The name *wazungu* was specially suitable for the first kind. These were men who came wandering through the country asking to be shown rivers and lakes and mountains, and asking their names. They carried enough trade goods to be able to buy food and to give the necessary presents to a chief when they asked his permission to travel through his territory. But they did not seem to want ivory or slaves; they never stayed still in one place, but must be always on the move.

1

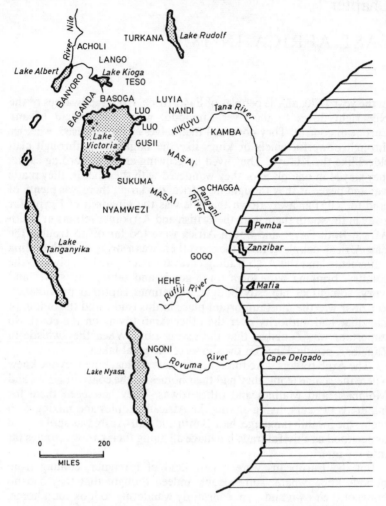

THE PEOPLES OF EAST AFRICA

The other Europeans were different; they stayed in one place. They seemed to be kind and well-meaning. They greatly disliked the slave trade, and set up settlements for freed slaves; but they would never sell firearms so that Africans could defend themselves against the slave raiders. They had strange ideas: they seemed to condemn many good old African customs almost as much as they condemned the slave trade. They preached a new religion which seemed to regard such customs as evil.

These men, the explorers and the missionaries, were regarded by the Africans with wonder and pity. They seemed so wise, and yet so ignorant; so strong, and yet so helpless. Above all, they seemed to have no home or land of their own, and one should always pity the homeless stranger.

Europeans later in East than in West Africa

In East, as in West Africa, the first Europeans to arrive were the Portuguese. But in West Africa, the Portuguese empire was overthrown by other Europeans, and European trade continued without a break. The Portuguese empire in East Africa was overthrown by the Arabs, and the Portuguese footing in East Africa was restricted to a few towns in Mozambique. From about 1700 onwards, no more European ships came to trade at the old Arab seaports along the East African coast. Thus, certain developments which took place in West Africa did not take place in East Africa. There were small missionary schools in the European settlements on the West African coast, and in the eighteenth century a few West Africans received higher education in Europe. At the beginning of the nineteenth century, there was an expansion in West Africa both of missionary education and of European exploration. By 1830, the whole course of the river Niger had been explored, and Europe knew that it had no connection with the Nile, as Arab geographers believed.

The first European missionary, Johann Krapf, did not arrive in East Africa until 1844, almost at the same time that David Livingstone set out from his mission station in Cape Colony to carry the Gospel farther inland. Krapf and his colleagues, working for the Church Missionary Society, made their base near Mombasa and settled down to study, to preach, and to travel. Their study of the Swahili language and of the customs of their African neighbours, their travels to Kenya and Kilimanjaro and the surrounding region, were all preliminary steps to their great aim, which was the effective preaching of the Christian Gospel. In 1848, Krapf's fellow-missionary Johann Rebmann became the first European to see Kilimanjaro, and next year Krapf himself saw Mount Kenya. The Arabs had reported the existence of snow mountains in East Africa, but no one in Europe believed them; and even Krapf and Rebmann had difficulty in convincing Europe that perpetual snow existed on the Equator. Why, then, was Europe so ignorant of East Africa?

One reason is that East Africa lay much farther off from Europe. There was then no Suez Canal, and the journey from Britain to Zanzibar

1 FORT JESUS AT MOMBASA
   A relic of the Portuguese empire

round the Cape was twice as long as the journey from Britain to Lagos.
The main trade route round the Cape went to India. East Africa would
have been better known if ships had been able to call there on the way to
and from India. But this would have meant going far out of their way, so
British and other European ships seldom troubled to visit East African

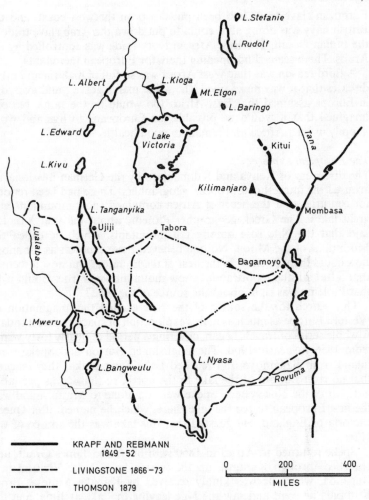

L.Stefanie
L.Rudolf
L.Albert
L.Kioga
Mt.Elgon
L.Baringo
L.Edward
Lake Victoria
Kitui
Tana
L.Kivu
L.Tanganyika
Ujiji
Tabora
Kilimanjaro
Mombasa
Lualaba
Bagamoyo
L.Mweru
L.Bangweulu
L.Nyasa
Rovuma

	KRAPF AND REBMANN 1849–52
	LIVINGSTONE 1866–73
	THOMSON 1879

0   200   400
MILES

EUROPEAN EXPLORERS

ports. What little trade there was along the Somali coast and in the Persian Gulf was left to the Arabs. The internal-combustion engine had not been developed, so there was no demand for petroleum oil; there were no oil-wells in Bahrein or Kuwait, and no fleets of oil-tankers on the high seas.

A second reason for European ignorance is that as far as Europe then knew, East Africa produced nothing but slaves and ivory. The

European slave trade had been put down on the west coast, and the British navy was doing all it could to put down the Arab slave trade in the Indian Ocean. The East African ivory trade was controlled by the Arabs. There seemed no opening there for European merchants.

A third reason was that West Africa was so full of malaria and other diseases that it was nicknamed 'the white man's grave'; and everyone in Europe assumed that East Africa too would be the same. No one imagined that it would be possible for Europeans to live and work happily in East Africa and remain in good health.

The European explorers

The discovery of Kenya and Kilimanjaro by the German missionaries aroused the interest of European geographers. There had been reports for centuries that the heart of Africa contained snow mountains and great lakes. The Greek geographer Ptolemy about the year A.D. 150 said that the Nile rose among tall mountains, which he called the Mountains of the Moon. No one believed these reports; as for snow, how could there be snow in the heat of the Equator? But now it seemed that, after all, the report about snow mountains was true. Could it be that Ptolemy was right about the source of the Nile?

This search for the source of the Nile excited the imagination of Western Europe as much as man's exploration of space excites it today. A whole series of travels began, covering a period of nearly forty years, from 1856 to nearly 1900. The Englishmen Burton and Speke went inland from Bagamoyo and reached Lake Tanganyika; they learned that no river ran out of the lake to the north, so that it was probably not part of the Nile system. Speke went on alone to Mwanza and was the first European to see the lake there, which he named after Queen Victoria of England. He guessed that this lake was the source of the Nile.

Speke returned to Africa in 1860 with his friend James Grant, and travelled through Karagwe up the west side of Lake Victoria into Buganda, where he was kindly received by Kabaka Mutesa. From Kampala he went and saw the Nile leaving the lake at Jinja, and the two men returned to England down the Nile valley.

Others followed. Samuel Baker came up the Nile from Egypt and explored Lake Albert. Henry Stanley explored the whole coastline of Lakes Victoria and Tanganyika, proving that they were two separate lakes, unconnected, and that each was one large lake and not a string of smaller ones; then he crossed to the Lualaba river and went down the Congo to the sea. The Hungarian Count Teleki discovered and named Lake Rudolf. Much of the exploration of modern Kenya was carried out by the Scotsman Joseph Thomson. He left the east coast in

EUROPEAN EXPLORERS

March 1882 and went to Taveta; he climbed some way up Kilimanjaro, and in September reached Lake Naivasha. Then he went through the Masai country farther north, discovering and naming the Aberdare mountains and visiting Mount Kenya and Lake Baringo; he visited Mount Elgon and Lake Victoria, and returned through Teita to Mombasa.

EUROPEAN EXPLORERS

The greatest explorer of all was David Livingstone, though only the last of his journeys covered East Africa. He was the greatest because he was the pioneer; because he depended entirely on the help and friendship of the Africans among whom he moved; because he was able to arouse their love and devotion to an extraordinary degree; and because he was not interested merely in geographical discovery but was first and foremost a missionary, hoping to stop the slave trade and replace it by Christianity and healthy commerce.

Livingstone's last journey lasted from 1866 to 1873. He went up the Rovuma river, round the southern end of Lake Nyasa, and across modern Zambia to Lake Mweru, and so up to Lake Tanganyika and across to the Lualaba river. He was asking himself whether the Lualaba flowed into Lake Victoria (and so was the true beginning of the Nile) or into the Congo. He turned upstream, meaning to follow the Lualaba all the way to its source, and then to go downstream to the river's end in Lake Victoria or the ocean. But near Lake Bangweulu he died; and his African friends carried his body several weeks' journey to Tabora and down to the coast so that it might be buried in England. The question about the Lualaba river, which Livingstone left unanswered, was soon afterwards settled by Stanley's journey.

The details of these explorations may not be of great importance. The important fact is that within a few years the profound European ignorance of East Africa was removed. In 1848, Europeans knew nothing about the interior of East Africa. By 1880, they were familiar not only with the general outlines of the river, lake and mountain systems of East Africa, but also with the climate and—most important—the peoples of the region. They had seen the Masai herds travelling over the vast pasture, and the Kikuyu homesteads in the thick forest. They had been received as guests in the stately courts of Buganda and Bunyoro. They had found that it was possible for Europeans to travel for months or even years at a time over East Africa in good health and in reasonable safety. They had lost not only their ignorance but also their fear: their fear of disease, of lions and snakes, of spears and poisoned arrows.

The Suez Canal

In November 1869, in the middle of this period of active exploration, the whole geographical position was changed by the opening of the Suez Canal. Mombasa and Zanzibar were at once brought six thousand miles nearer to Europe. They lay as far off the new route to India through the Canal as they did off the old route round the Cape; but now, if anyone wished to go there, the journey was much shorter. Steamers from Europe going to India through the Canal used to call at Aden; and within three years after the Canal was opened, a branch line of steamers was set up with a regular service from Aden to Zanzibar.

Zanzibar to 1870

Zanzibar became an important place in 1840, when Sultan Seyyid Said of Oman made it his capital. Although the British had inconvenient ideas about restricting his extremely profitable trade in slaves, Seyyid Said remained steadfastly their friend, and he was accustomed to rely on the advice of the British consul at Zanzibar. An American consulate was opened at Zanzibar in 1837, and a British consulate four years later. Seyyid Said was a man of large ideas. He introduced the clove industry, he made commercial treaties with France as well as with the United States, and he conceived the idea of establishing a series of trading posts all the way from Zanzibar to the Congo. The history of East Africa might have been very different if this last idea had been carried out. It was not carried out. The Arab caravans travelled far and wide through East Africa buying or capturing ivory and slaves, and many of them carried a flag from the Sultan to show that they were under his protection. But the trading settlements (such as Tabora) which they established in the interior were never organized into a solid state and governed from Zanzibar. The caravan leaders, and many of the African chiefs with whom they did business, would readily agree that the Sultan was a great man, and was in some vague sense their master. But he had no power to give them orders and see that they carried them out. The Sultan's real power extended only over the region near the coast. Once a caravan had disappeared from Bagamoyo into the bush, it was out of the Sultan's reach. East Africa became Zanzibar's sphere of influence; but it never became Zanzibar's dominion.

Seyyid Said died in 1856, leaving several sons. Oman and Zanzibar were still united; one of Seyyid Said's sons, Thuwain, ruled Oman, and another, Majid, ruled Zanzibar. A third son, Barghash, attempted to seize power from Majid in a palace revolt, but the British stepped in; they arrested Barghash and exiled him to Bombay. The British then turned to deal with the danger that Thuwain might make war on Majid, and they persuaded the two brothers to submit their dispute to the arbitration of Lord Canning, the governor-general of India.

Lord Canning's decision was announced in April 1861. Oman and Zanzibar were to be separated. Thuwain was to rule Oman and Majid to rule Zanzibar; and since Zanzibar was the richer, Majid was to pay his brother an annual compensation of about £9,000. On this basis, Zanzibar was recognized as an independent state in 1862 by Britain and other countries. In that same year, Britain and France came to an agreement not to make difficulties for each other in East Africa: France agreed to leave Britain a free hand in Zanzibar, and Britain agreed not to interfere in Madagascar.

Beyond the great lakes, even the Sultan of Zanzibar would not claim any authority. West of Lake Victoria was the kingdom of Karagwe, under its great king Rumanika, who died in 1878. To the north and north-west lay the kingdoms of Buganda and others. In the 1870s,

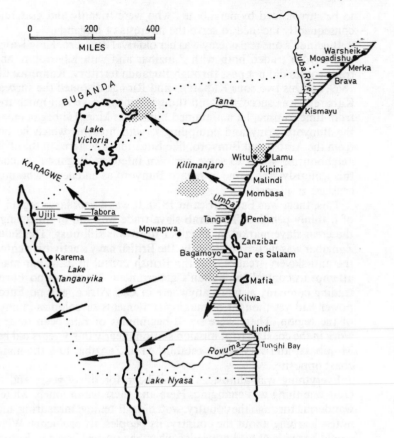

LAND CLAIMED BY THE SULTAN OF ZANZIBAR

Arrows show main trade routes. Area shaded shows where the Sultan's
authority was intermittently acknowledged. Dotted line shows (roughly)
the limit of the Sultan's claims.

Areas of Karl Peters's treaties

Buganda was the strongest kingdom in that region, but she made no
attempt to rule her neighbours. What Buganda did do was to take every
chance that came of getting some advantage out of any civil dissension
in a neighbouring country. In such a case, the Kabaka might send
Baganda troops to help one side against the other; or he might wait in
the hope that both sides would bid for his support. Buganda's aim was

to be surrounded by neighbours who were friendly and grateful, and consequently inclined to serve the interests of Buganda.

Buganda's one real enemy was her old rival Bunyoro. King Kamurasi of Bunyoro traded both with Zanzibar and with Khartoum, and his trade routes did not pass through Buganda territory. Kamurasi died in 1869, and his two sons Kabarega and Rionga disputed the succession. Kabarega was successful, and though Rionga gave him much trouble from time to time, he maintained himself as king. He began enlarging the Bunyoro army and equipping it with firearms which he bought from the Arabs; and Bunyoro, like Buganda, interfered in the affairs of neighbouring states to serve her own interests. Buganda watched all this jealously, and came to regard Bunyoro as an enemy who must be crushed at all costs.

This, then, was East Africa in 1870. It was a very large region, most of it thinly peopled. The Arab slave trade was still in full swing, and the great slave market in Zanzibar town was still busy. The Sultan of Zanzibar was inconvenienced by the British navy's activity in enforcing the anti-slavery treaties, but the British consul in Zanzibar made no attempt to control the Sultan's government. There was no European trading company at work anywhere in East Africa, and no European power had yet thought of making settlements or colonies in any part of the region. There were small beginnings of European missionary work in the coastal strip: mission stations nearly thirty years old behind Mombasa, and very newly established in Zanzibar and the mainland coast opposite.

Everything was almost as it had been for thirty years and more. Only one thing was changing. Here and there was a lonely white man wandering through the country, watching, listening, measuring, making notes, learning about the country, its peoples, its problems. What use would be made of his knowledge when he returned home to Europe?

Chapter 2

THE PARTITION OF EAST AFRICA

Until the 1880s, no European power thought of establishing large colonies in East Africa. The Portuguese settlements in Mozambique and Angola at that time were of no importance. Even in West Africa, where European trading posts had been established so long, there was hardly any direct European authority inland. The French ruled a few miles inland from the Senegal coast. There were a few Spanish and Portuguese coastal settlements. The British had settlements in Sierra Leone and the Gold Coast; a shadowy sort of British protectorate on the Gold Coast was converted in 1874 into a colony, running about forty miles inland. The British had also annexed Lagos island, mainly for the purpose of stopping the slave trade; but they had so far made no attempt to enlarge this tiny colony. The only places in Africa where Europeans had made a serious attempt to take and hold a large area were in Algeria and in South Africa.

As we have said, until about 1870 Europe was very ignorant about the interior of Africa; but there were other reasons, besides ignorance, for Europe's neglect of its colonial opportunities.

Two of the great colonial powers of the twentieth century, Germany and Italy, did not exist until the second half of the nineteenth. Each was a group of independent or semi-independent states. The Italian states joined together between 1860 and 1870, the German states in 1871. After two hundred years of intense activity in exploring and colonizing the tropical world, Portugal lay exhausted and passive, holding her African seaports but making no attempt to extend her rule far inland.

There remained Belgium, France, and Britain. Belgium was a tiny country and would never have thought of becoming a colonial power had it not been for the energy and ambition of one man, her king, Leopold II. In the 1850s, France made some progress in extending her rule in the Senegal valley, but her effort died away again.

And what of Britain? If she had chosen to do so, during the first three-quarters of the century Britain could have occupied almost any part of the African coast and established colonies there. But Britain was not interested in the idea of African colonies.

There were special reasons for this. One reason was that Britain had already lost the colonies which became the United States of America, and tended to assume that sooner or later she would lose Canada, Australia and New Zealand as well. This feeling was strong in Britain until the 1870s. If even colonies settled by British people were likely to declare themselves independent, what would be the good of establishing British rule over the peoples of tropical Africa?

A second reason was that Britain did not need colonies for trade purposes, for British trade was flourishing without them. Britain led the world in the invention of new machinery and new industrial techniques. Until 1875 or thereabouts, no other country could compete with British goods. Thus, as long as Africa was free to buy wherever it

wished, Africa would buy British goods, since they were the cheapest and best. It was in British interests to keep Africa open freely to European trade; then British goods would sell freely in Africa, and British manufacturers would obtain all the African raw materials they wanted. Why take on the risk and responsibility of governing Africa?

A third reason was that British capital and skill had plenty of openings in North and South America, as well as in India, Australia and New Zealand. All these countries had great trading possibilities; Africa was unknown, and seemed to have little to offer.

There was a fourth reason: a more personal reason, but a strong one. For many years during the nineteenth century, the British government was headed, or strongly influenced, by William Gladstone. Gladstone was four times prime minister, and for many years before becoming prime minister he held important cabinet posts. It so happened that Gladstone took no interest in Africa. He took a great interest in some countries: in Italy, for example, and in Turkey. But Africa never touched his imagination as these countries did. He thought it no business of Britain to interfere in any way on the African mainland, even for such a good purpose as putting down the slave trade. If British missionaries or explorers or traders went to Africa, they must go at their own risk. All Gladstone's influence was used to keep Britain out of any political responsibility in Africa.

For these reasons, Britain steadily refused to increase her colonial responsibilities in Africa. In 1865, a committee of the British parliament resolved that the government should give up all its West African possessions as soon as it could safely do so without causing the slave trade to start up again; and the resolution added that no new British settlements must be made in Africa. The first part of the resolution was not carried out; for various local reasons the British stayed where they were in West Africa. But both the government and the people were determined not to be enticed into fresh African adventures. During the greater part of the nineteenth century, Britain was the only country with the power to occupy and colonize Africa, and Britain was determined not to do so.

Curiously enough, it was Gladstone who reluctantly decided to send British troops into Egypt and occupy the country, and the British occupation of Egypt was one of the events which set the European powers off on the process of partitioning Africa. But five years before this happened, the first Christian missionaries arrived in Uganda, and thus the people of Uganda came into contact with Europeans. To the results of this contact we must now turn.

The missionaries in Uganda

The missionaries were not the first Europeans to visit Uganda. Speke and Stanley and Baker and other explorers had seen the country. Baker was not merely an explorer; he was an officer of the Egyptian government. The Khedive Ismail of Egypt, who ruled his country in the 1870s, had plans for building an Egyptian empire. He conquered the Red Sea coast, and he sent Baker to establish the Egyptian power to the southernmost parts of the Nile valley. In April 1872, Baker in carrying out this mission entered Bunyoro and made contact with Kabarega, who proposed that Baker should help him against his rival Rionga. Baker was willing to help him but proposed that, in return, Kabarega should accept Egyptian protection. Kabarega refused, whereupon Baker did just what Kabarega himself would have done: he offered his help instead to Rionga on the same condition. But Kabarega was too strong for them, and Baker had to retreat northward; he spread the report in Egypt and in Europe that Kabarega was hostile to Europeans and other foreigners, a report which Kabarega had cause to regret later on.

Buganda watched all this with much interest, and when in 1874 Baker's successor, the Englishman Charles Gordon, arrived at Gondokoro, he was met there by envoys from Buganda, who invited him to join with Buganda in overthrowing Kabarega. Gordon did not accept this invitation, but it seemed to him that Buganda was more ready than Bunyoro to enter into friendly relations with Egypt. He sent a detachment of troops to hoist the Egyptian flag on the shores of Lake Victoria; but the Kabaka Mutesa would have none of this, and Gordon had to withdraw the troops again. Gordon still did not give up hope of establishing Egyptian power in East Africa. In 1875, the Khedive sent an Egyptian force to occupy Brava and Kismayu, and Gordon had the idea of setting up a line of Egyptian posts all the way up the Tana river to Lake Victoria. But Brava and Kismayu belonged to the Sultan of Zanzibar, and Britain decided that the Sultan's authority must be maintained. Under British pressure, the Egyptian force was withdrawn, and Gordon's ambitious plan fell to the ground.

Nevertheless, the peoples of Uganda were becoming exposed to foreign influences. Gondokoro in the Sudan was a centre of Arab slave traders, and other slave traders from the east coast were beginning to come round the western side of Lake Victoria and enter Uganda from the south. In 1875, the year of the unsuccessful Egyptian expedition to Kismayu and Brava, Stanley visited Buganda, and suggested to Kabaka Mutesa that he should receive Christian missionaries. Like other African rulers then, Mutesa perhaps had no very clear idea of what missionaries did; but he was attracted by the idea of having Europeans

Khartoum

Massawa

Adowa

Zeila

Berbera

Fashoda

Addis Ababa

ETHIOPIA

Juba

Gondokoro

Warsheik
Mogadishu
Brava

Tana

Kismayu

SEAPORTS OCCUPIED BY EGYPT
BRAVA

ARROWS SHOW LINES OF
EGYPTIAN ADVANCE

0   200   400
MILES

THE EGYPTIAN PLAN
FOR AN EAST AFRICAN
EMPIRE

resident at his court, where their wisdom and strength might be useful to him in his struggles against Arab slave traders, Egyptian generals, and his rival of Bunyoro. He agreed, and Stanley wrote to England to invite missionaries to come to Buganda.

The invitation was timely, for it was in line with the advice which Livingstone had given the missionary societies. He had warned them that Islam and the slave trade were marching into the interior of Africa much faster than Christianity. If they wished the Church to play an effective part in stopping the slave trade and winning Africa for Christ, it was not enough to plant mission stations in the coastal strip; they must plunge boldly into the heart of Africa and plant their mission stations where the slavers were at work. The Church Missionary Society took up Stanley's challenge, and its first missionaries arrived at Kampala in July 1877. A second party arrived in 1879, and hard on their heels came the first Roman Catholic missionaries, a party of White Fathers from France.

It was unfortunate that when Christianity came to Uganda, it should be brought by two rival Churches; it was still more unfortunate that one set of missionaries should be British and the other French. The Kabaka kept the missionaries close to his court, and soon a number of his court officers and senior chiefs became Christians. It happened in Buganda as it happened in Europe when Protestantism first began: the Protestants and Catholics in Buganda became not merely rival Churches but rival political factions, intriguing against each other for power and office. By the time that Kabaka Mutesa died in 1884, Buganda was deeply divided: there were the Fransa (the Catholics), the Ingleza (the Protestants) and the Muslims, as well as those who still followed the traditional religion of the country. From the Kabaka's point of view, Fransa, Ingleza and Muslims had one fault in common: they claimed the right to decide for themselves whether his decrees were righteous and whether they should obey him or not, a right which no Muganda had ever claimed before. These new religions had brought to Uganda a great and increasing danger of civil war.

Zanzibar under Sultan Barghash, 1870–1888

In 1870, Sultan Majid of Zanzibar died, and the British allowed his brother Barghash to succeed him. Zanzibar was nominally independent, but in reality the British kept a close watch on Zanzibar affairs. At that period, the British and Foreign Anti-Slavery Society was very strong in Britain and had great influence with the government, and the British government's only interest in Zanzibar was in putting down the slave trade. The West African slave trade had at last been stopped, and the British navy was still struggling (with too few ships) to put down the Arab slave trade in the Indian Ocean. The Sultan of Zanzibar had already accepted two treaties which together made the export of slaves from Africa by sea completely illegal. Under the Moresby treaty of 1822, the Sultan forbade slave ships from Zanzibar to sail south of

Cape Delgado, or east of a line drawn from the island of Socotra to Diu in India. He agreed moreover that his people should not sell slaves to any Christian. The effect of this treaty was that the traders of Zanzibar could carry slaves only to other East African ports, to Arabia and Persia, and the extreme west of India, the country now known as West Pakistan; in addition, they could not evade this restriction by selling slaves in

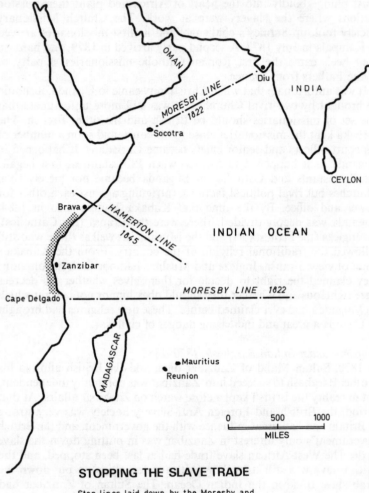

STOPPING THE SLAVE TRADE

Stop lines laid down by the Moresby and Hamerton Treaties ·—·—·—·

Coast open to slave trade from 1845 to the closing of the market in 1873

Zanzibar to European dealers for export to other markets. The trade was still more restricted by the Hamerton treaty of 1845, which stopped Zanzibar slave ships from sailing north of Brava. This excluded all the Asian ports, and after 1845 slaves could legally be moved by sea only up and down the East African coast within the Sultan's dominions. These two treaties were unpopular among the Sultan's Arab subjects. Slaves were the most profitable commodity that East Africa produced, and Arab society in Zanzibar and the coastal strip was built on slavery. Even if he wished to enforce the treaties, the Sultan would have been unable to do so. Enforcement of the law depended on the British navy.

Sultan Barghash thus began his reign under difficulties. Though nominally independent, he was plainly under British control, and British control was used mainly to bring pressure on him to stop his Arab subjects' most profitable trade. In 1871 the British government, under pressure from the Anti-Slavery Society, set up a commission to consider how the slave trade could more speedily be brought to a complete stop. The British navy's nearest base was at Simonstown, nearly 2,500 miles away at the Cape; the navy had not enough ships to patrol the East African coast closely. The commission advised that the best way of stopping the trade was to close the slave markets and make it illegal to buy and sell slaves even in Zanzibar itself.

The Sultan and his people would of course resist such an extreme proposal. In 1872 the whole clove crop on Zanzibar island (though not on Pemba) was destroyed by a cyclone. The planters set to work to rebuild and replant, and they needed more labour than ever. Their demand for slaves rose, and it was not a suitable moment for asking them to close the slave market and give up all hope of buying new slaves. In 1873 a special mission was sent from England, led by Sir Bartle Frere, to invite the Sultan to sign a fresh treaty. It was still permissible to send slaves over land, and there was a good deal of trading done in this way, slaves being sent north by land and sold in the coastal strip, or being put across the narrow channel in ships for sale in Zanzibar and Pemba. Frere carried out his mission without any attempt at tactful persuasion; he told the Sultan bluntly that this overland trade too was now to be stopped, and the slave markets were to be closed. In return, the British offered Barghash the concession that he need no longer make the annual payment to the Sultan of Oman.

Sultan Barghash was in despair. Zanzibar had already given up the profitable export trade in slaves. But his Arab people in the islands and in the coastal strip needed to import fresh slaves to cultivate their estates. Like slave-owners all over the world, they found it cheaper to import slaves than to breed them. To the Sultan, this new restriction on the trade seemed quite unreasonable. He thought of inviting France to take his dominions under her protection, for the French were less strict than the British in the matter of slave-trading. But France was faithful to the Anglo-French declaration of 1862, and would give him no help. Still Barghash refused to sign the new treaty, and Frere had to leave Zanzibar with his mission unfulfilled.

Sir John Kirk

But the British were determined, and Sultan Barghash had no hope of escape. In June 1873 the navy blockaded the islands and cut off all trade. Then at last Barghash consented to sign the treaty. He did so not only because of the naval blockade but because he listened to the advice of the new British consul-general. This was Dr John Kirk, later Sir John Kirk.

Kirk came to Africa as a young doctor, and from 1858 to 1863 he was with Livingstone on his exploration of the Zambesi and Shiré rivers and Lake Nyasa. On this journey Kirk saw the slave trade being carried on in all its horror. In 1866, when Livingstone began his third and last journey, Kirk was appointed doctor to the British consulate in Zanzibar, and next year he became vice-consul; in this difficult year 1873 he became consul-general. Kirk was a man who could see other people's points of view, and he and the Sultan got on well together. Kirk was just as strongly opposed to the cruelty of the slave trade as Livingstone or any of the Anti-Slavery Society members in England. He agreed that the trade must be stopped. But he could see that to go further and abolish the status of slavery altogether, as the society in England desired, would cause complete dislocation of Zanzibar's economy. Abolition could only be brought about very gradually.

The Sultan accepted Kirk's advice that it would pay him much better in the long run to accept this new treaty and entrust the fortunes of his country entirely to the goodwill of Britain. He signed the treaty; the great slave market in Zanzibar town was closed, and to the joy of the missionaries a Christian cathedral was built on the site.

Having accepted Kirk's advice, the Sultan acted upon it to the full. In 1876 he issued fresh decrees to stop any slave caravans from the interior from entering the coastal strip under his rule.

So far, his connection with the British had merely weakened the Sultan; it was only natural that he should look for ways of strengthening his position. He obtained the services of a young British naval officer, Lloyd Mathews, to train and command a disciplined army, some 1,800 strong. With this force, Mathews attacked the Arabs in Pemba, who were ignoring the Sultan's authority and were carrying on the slave trade whenever the British warships were out of sight. After heavy fighting, Pemba surrendered and submitted to the Sultan. The victory greatly diminished the chance of any revolt in Zanzibar, or of an attack from Oman.

Sir William Mackinnon

Seyyid Said, years before, had thought of a chain of Zanzibari trading posts inland; could not this idea be revived, and the authority of the Sultan of Zanzibar made effective over the East African mainland? There were two men in Zanzibar who thought this was possible. One was Kirk, who agreed with Livingstone that the slave trade could never be stopped merely by police action, and that it would die naturally if healthy commerce grew up to replace it. Moreover, Kirk thought that, having given up the profitable slave trade, the Sultan was entitled to some compensation for his losses.

Any talk of opening up new commerce routes aroused the interest of the British shipowner Sir William Mackinnon. Mackinnon had been running steamship services in the Indian Ocean for twenty years. The opening of the Suez Canal in 1869 gave him fresh opportunities. As a businessman, Mackinnon was eager to open up the interior of East Africa, and both he and Kirk encouraged the Sultan to hope for great things in this way. The Sultan went so far as to offer to lease to Mackinnon the whole of the coastline from Warsheikh in the north to Tunghi bay in the south, a distance of over a thousand miles, together with the whole of the country behind it as far inland as Mackinnon could penetrate. Mackinnon was to form a company to open up this vast area, and his company and the Zanzibar government were to share the profits. It was a glittering scheme, and Mackinnon and Kirk were eager that it should be carried out. Mackinnon began building a road, suitable for wheeled traffic, from the new harbour which Sultan Majid had built at Dar-es-Salaam in the direction of Lake Nyasa, and he had completed seventy-three miles before abandoning the work.

This scheme for opening up East Africa would need very large sums of money, and the money could be provided only by British and other foreign investors who were hoping for a profit. But the risks were great. There was certain to be opposition from all the powerful African chiefs, and many Arab merchants who were glad enough to carry the Sultan's flag would object to coming under the Sultan's control. The scheme could not succeed without the backing of the British government. The British government refused to have anything to do with it, and it all came to nothing.

Mirambo and Tippoo Tib

As long as the British government maintained this attitude, the Sultan had no hope of establishing direct rule over East Africa. Failing this, he might still hope to govern East Africa by a system of indirect rule. Some of the powerful men in the region might perhaps find it worth their while to acknowledge the Sultan's authority, to govern in his name, and to send their trade eastwards to Zanzibar, where it would provide the Sultan with revenue.

Two men whom the Sultan thought of using in this way were Mirambo and Tippoo Tib. The two men were very different. Mirambo was an African; during the 1860s he was a minor chief among the Nyamwezi, with his headquarters some forty miles west of Tabora. He set out to increase his power, using the methods that were commonly used, both in East and West Africa, by ambitious chiefs in his position. He raided neighbouring tribes for slaves, and used the proceeds of the sale to form an army of Masai and Ngoni warriors and to equip them with firearms. By 1870 he was strong enough to attack the Arabs of Tabora, who were his nearest commercial rivals. Commerce and empire went together; these Arabs wished to conquer the surrounding peoples and so compel them to trade on terms favourable to the Arabs. Mirambo wished to compel the Arabs to give his people easier terms. After six years' fighting, Mirambo's army had put an end to his difficulties with the Tabora Arabs, and he then began to extend his control over the surrounding country. By 1880 he controlled the roads to Ujiji and Karagwe, and his influence extended southward all down the eastern shore of Lake Tanganyika.

Tippoo Tib was a half-Arab from the Tabora district, a great trader in slaves and ivory. Like Mirambo, and like all big men in the slaves-and-ivory business, he had his own army. His method was to conquer a wider and wider area, in which he would control all the trade: either driving his competitors out of business altogether, or compelling them to share their profits with him. While Mirambo was fighting to extend his power east of Lake Tanganyika, Tippoo Tib was pushing farther west into the Congo basin, and he made his headquarters between the Lualaba and Lomami rivers. At the southern end of Lake Tanganyika, the dominions of Mirambo and of Tippoo Tib met, and the two men formed an alliance. Mirambo was willing to acknowledge the Sultan's authority, and he suggested that the Sultan should appoint Tippoo Tib as governor of Tabora, so that the Arabs there could be brought under control and the trade route to the coast could be made more secure.

Sultan Barghash hesitated, and he lost his chance. King Leopold II of Belgium had just formed an international Association to explore the Congo. One of the Association's Belgian officers found Tippoo Tib in control of the Lualaba and Lomami rivers, and made him an offer: he

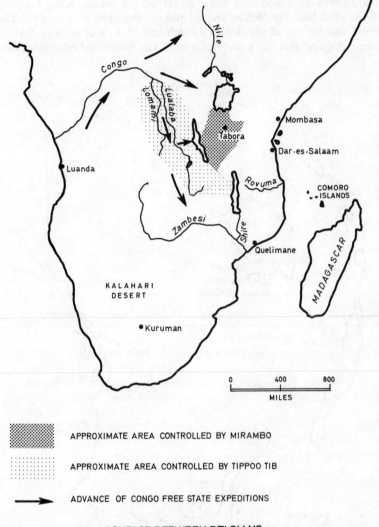

APPROXIMATE AREA CONTROLLED BY MIRAMBO

APPROXIMATE AREA CONTROLLED BY TIPPOO TIB

ADVANCE OF CONGO FREE STATE EXPEDITIONS

CONTACT BETWEEN BELGIANS
AND ZANZIBARI IN CENTRAL AFRICA

should be recognized by the Association as ruler of this area if he would send all his ivory down the Congo to be marketed by the Association in Europe. About the same time, another of the Association's exploring parties came into the Nyamwezi country; it was attacked by some of

Mirambo's men and had some of its people killed. King Leopold demanded that the Sultan should punish the chief responsible. The chief was far out of the Sultan's reach and there was nothing that he could do; and this was noted in Europe. The Sultan did establish a new

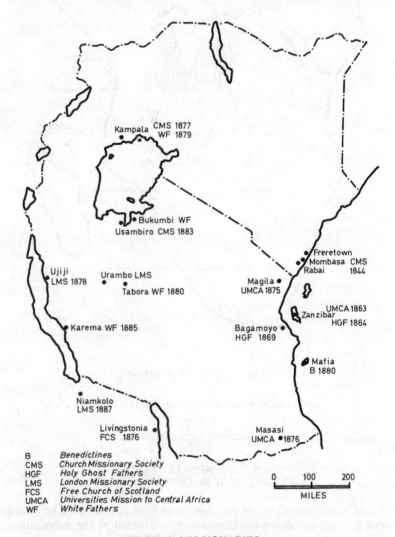

Kampala CMS 1877
WF 1879

Bukumbi WF
Usambiro CMS 1883

Freretown
Mombasa CMS
Rabai   1844

Ujiji
LMS 1878

Urambo LMS
Tabora WF 1880

Magila ●
UMCA 1875

UMCA 1863
Zanzibar   HGF 1864

Karema WF 1885

Bagamoyo
HGF 1869

Mafia
B 1880

Niamkolo
LMS 1887

Livingstonia
FCS 1876

Masasi
UMCA ●1876

B	Benedictines
CMS	Church Missionary Society
HGF	Holy Ghost Fathers
LMS	London Missionary Society
FCS	Free Church of Scotland
UMCA	Universities Mission to Central Africa
WF	White Fathers

0   100   200
MILES

CHRISTIAN MISSIONARIES
IN EAST AFRICA BEFORE 1890

fortified post on the Tabora road, 120 miles from Bagamoyo; but he could do no more.

After this unfortunate incident, Sultan Barghash lost confidence in Mirambo and turned to Tippoo Tib, who came to Zanzibar in 1882 and reported the offer the Belgians had made him. What was he to do? If he went to be the Sultan's governor at Tabora, he could not administer his territory in the Congo; and if he stayed in the Congo, he must choose between sending his ivory westward to the Belgians or eastward to Zanzibar. The Sultan begged him to go back to the Congo and to send his ivory eastward, and this is what Tippoo Tib did. But with the Belgian pressure increasing, his position became impossible. About ten years later he was driven out by the Belgians and retired to Zanzibar. Mirambo died in 1884 and was succeeded by his son Siki. Siki had little chance of showing whether he could continue his father's work, for he found himself facing a more formidable enemy than the Tabora Arabs: he was defeated by the Germans.

The Sultans of Zanzibar had left their empire-building until it was too late. If they could have asserted their authority over the Arab caravans in the interior, they might have made Tabora and other places into provincial capitals of their dominions. If they had done this about 1840, when the first Arab settlement was made in the Nyamwezi country, Mirambo might have been glad in 1870 to be appointed the Sultan's governor of the country between Lake Victoria and Lake Tanganyika, and Tippoo Tib might have been strong enough farther west to make the Belgians respect his Sultan's authority. But by 1880 it was too late for anything like this. The Europeans were beginning to arrive.

THE INTERNATIONAL AFRICAN ASSOCIATION

We have already mentioned King Leopold II of Belgium and his Association. In more ways than one, the explorer Stanley's great journey of 1874–76 from Bagamoyo to the Atlantic, via Lake Victoria, Lake Tanganyika, and the river Congo, was a turning-point in the history of East Africa. As we have seen, his visit to Kabaka Mutesa led to the settlement of Christian missionaries in Kampala. His journey also attracted the interest of King Leopold. There was a vast area of Africa untouched by European influence, unknown to European geographers and scientists. If it could be opened up, the material there would keep scientists occupied for many years, and perhaps it would also bring in good profits to businessmen. Leopold thought that a scientific association for the study of Africa would perhaps arouse less suspicion in other countries than a commercial company. He founded what he called the International African Association,[1] and Stanley accepted an invitation to return to the Congo on the Association's behalf and make treaties with the African chiefs there so that European scientists and others might travel in the Congo basin. From 1878 onwards, Stanley and others led a series of expeditions; in 1880 one of them, as we have seen, got into trouble with Mirambo's people.

It was not long before other European countries began to suspect that Leopold's interest in the Congo basin was not purely scientific; they feared that his real aim was to gain control of the region for himself and keep away all traders and travellers from other European countries. Portugal felt especially sensitive, for she had old connections with the Congo region. The Portuguese who first came to the kingdom of Kongo in 1482 were greatly impressed with its high degree of civilization. It seems to have been somewhat like Buganda under the Kabakas: it had a regular organization of provincial governors and lesser chiefs and a system of revenue. The king of Kongo became a Christiàn in 1491; for many years he exchanged ambassadors with the king of Portugal and the two countries remained on friendly terms. In the middle of the sixteenth century the kingdom of Kongo was conquered by invaders from farther inland, and its great days were over. But it lingered on, and still existed in King Leopold's day; and Portugal still felt that she had a special interest in the region.

The kingdom of Kongo had formerly ruled both north and south of the Congo mouth. From 1875 onwards, the French explorer De Brazza had been travelling in its territory north of the river and crossing some of Stanley's routes. French traders were beginning to establish themselves along the coast north of the Congo mouth, and the French government was taking a special interest in this part of the coast. Later on, this special French interest was to lead to the establishment of the French colony of Gabon or French Congo, whose capital of Brazzaville was named after the explorer. Thus, both Portugal and France felt uneasy when the Belgian officers of the International African Association seemed likely to claim the whole of this region for King Leopold.

During 1880 and 1881, these suspicions about Leopold and his Association became stronger. A Frenchman named Rabaud offered Sultan Barghash a large loan if he could be allowed to build a railway from Bagamoyo to Ujiji and have exclusive trading rights along it. Kirk suspected that Rabaud was not asking for himself, but was really an agent of the Association, and he persuaded Barghash to refuse the

---

[1] This has no connection with the International African Institute of today, which is a purely scientific body founded in 1926 for the study of African languages and cultures.

concession. During 1880, Belgium actually asked Britain what the British view would be if Belgium were to establish a colony in East Africa. The question was becoming urgent, for it soon became known that the Association had already acquired land at Tabora and at Karema on the east shore of Lake Tanganyika. The air was becoming full of suspicions and talk of colonization.

Britain and Portugal had been allies in Europe for more than 250 years, so it was natural that Portugal should turn to Britain and ask for her support in her complaints against Leopold and his Association. Britain too was nervous, for there were already some British traders and missionaries in the Congo basin, and Britain feared that Leopold's men would drive them out. So in 1884 Britain and Portugal made a treaty, by which Britain recognized Portugal as the ruler of the lower part of the Congo basin, and in return Portugal promised to allow British traders and missionaries to travel and work there freely. Gladstone's government in Britain was still trying to keep the door open for trade but to avoid the expense and responsibility of colonization.

THE BRITISH IN EGYPT

Meanwhile, in spite of wanting to keep out of African responsibilities, Gladstone was in trouble in Egypt. Khedive Ismail of Egypt was in some ways a great man. He did much to modernize his country and, as we have seen, he had ambitious schemes for an Egyptian empire in East Africa. But he had one great weakness: he did not know how to manage money. He borrowed right and left, he taxed his people harder and harder, he sold everything he could sell, even his shares in the new Suez Canal; but nevertheless the day came when he could no longer pay his European creditors the interest on their money. The creditors asked Britain and France to act on behalf of all of them, and Khedive Ismail was compelled to accept British and French advisers to handle his financial affairs. This 'Dual Control', as it was called, was set up in 1876, the year in which King Leopold set up his International Association. It was naturally unpopular in Egypt, and three years later Ismail dismissed his foreign advisers and declared the Dual Control at an end. The reply of Britain and France was to persuade the Sultan of Turkey (who was nominally the Khedive's master) to depose him and appoint his son Tewfik to succeed him. The Egyptian army—under the leadership of Colonel Arabi and with the cry of 'Egypt for the Egyptians'—speedily revolted against Tewfik.

The British and French would have been wiser to cooperate with Arabi, but for various reasons of finance and European politics they chose to support Tewfik. In May 1882 the two governments agreed to send troops into Egypt to overthrow Arabi and restore the Khedive's authority, and an Anglo–French fleet gathered off Alexandria. At the last moment, however, there was a general election in France, and the new government had a different policy. The French fleet outside Alexandria received fresh orders and steamed away, leaving the British to act alone if they chose. There was rioting and bloodshed in Alexandria, and, much as he hated the idea of military intervention, Gladstone thought he had no other choice. If Britain did nothing, Arabi would run Egypt in his own way, there would be no Dual Control, the Canal might perhaps be blocked, and Egypt's European creditors would never see their money again. If all this happened, some European power would have to intervene in Egypt sooner or later. British forces were on the spot, and Arabi had not yet had time to consolidate his power. If Britain intervened now, the affair, thought Gladstone, should not take long; a few weeks should see Arabi overthrown and Egyptian finances put under proper supervision. In a few months the British troops could be withdrawn.

In this frame of mind, Gladstone sent the British troops into Egypt, in order, as he said, 'to restore the Khedive's authority'. True enough, in a few weeks Arabi was defeated and a prisoner. But to restore the Khedive's authority meant, in practical terms, making the Khedive's government able to pay its way; and this involved reforming land tenure and the taxation system, damming the Nile and extending irrigation, and taking complete control of the country. Though Gladstone meant the British occupation of Egypt to be purely temporary, months and years went by and the British were still there. Though France herself had occupied Tunis in just the same way in 1881, she felt that Britain had cheated her in Egypt; she became bitterly hostile to Britain, and began to look for compensation at Britain's expense in other parts of Africa.

By the end of 1882, these two men, King Leopold of Belgium and the British prime minister Gladstone, though very different in character and motive, had involved their countries in Africa, and had incurred the jealousy of France in doing so.

Changed European attitude to Africa

Thus the whole European attitude to Africa had changed. Africa was no longer regarded as a dark and dangerous continent into which Europeans had better not try to penetrate. It was now regarded as an exciting continent: penetration was no doubt risky, but it might be extremely profitable.[2] The British policy of leaving Africa to itself and

---

[2] The diamond deposits of Kimberley were discovered in 1870, the gold-field of the Rand in 1886. Who could tell what more might be awaiting discovery in tropical Africa?

trusting the efficiency of British businessmen to bring home the biggest share of the profits was out of date in the new circumstances. Britain's competitors would no longer accept this position. If free trade in Africa benefited Britain at their expense, then African trade, they thought, must be controlled; and the only way was to hoist their own flag and take political control of the soil and the people. This was Leopold's idea, and it was also that of the French government. In 1884 a new and dangerous competitor appeared in East Africa. This was Germany.

GERMANY ENTERS AFRICAN POLITICS

In this situation, Germany had one great advantage over Britain and France. British and French foreign policy could sometimes be changed as a result of parliamentary elections—as with the French fleet off Alexandria. The German parliament had no control over foreign policy, and from 1871 to 1890 German policy was decided by one man, Bismarck. Bismarck sometimes changed his mind as to means, he never changed it as to ends; and so he was able to take advantage of French and British wavering and to further German interests.

In the Franco–German war of 1870–71, France had been defeated and a unified Germany had been created. One great object of Bismarck's policy for the rest of his career was to keep France weak and preoccupied so that she could never again attack Germany. He never lost a chance of arousing jealousy between France and her neighbours, Britain and Italy, so as to avoid all danger of an alliance between them.

Bismarck was no more of a believer in colonies than Gladstone. He would have preferred to leave Africa to Britain, for he knew that he could trust Britain to leave German trade unrestricted wherever the British flag flew. He encouraged Britain to occupy Egypt and supported her there afterwards: partly, it is true, because he knew that it would make France hostile to Britain, but partly also because he knew that the interests of the Khedive's German creditors would be safe in British hands. But if France and Belgium and Portugal were to colonize Africa, they would try to give their own traders a monopoly in their own colonies. In that case, Germany too must secure African colonies in the interests of German trade.

In 1883 and 1884, Bismarck had his own reasons for being annoyed with Gladstone's government. He had hoped that Britain would show some gratitude for the steady support he had given her in Egypt, but she had shown none. There was another irritation in South West Africa, where a German trader was trying to set up a series of trading posts. Bismarck asked Britain whether she had any claims in this region. For nearly a year he could get no answer, and at last he was told that Britain had no claims there, but that any other country colonizing the region would harm British interests.

Bismarck thought this unreasonable and determined to teach Britain a lesson. He suggested to France that she and Germany should work together to oppose British interests in Africa. France agreed; and Britain was told that the treaty she had just made with Portugal over the Congo would not be recognized by France and Germany. The Congo question, they said, was too big to be settled by this sort of private arrangement, and must be fully discussed at a conference of the European powers. This was a clever opening move on Bismarck's part, for the British government was known to support the principle that international disputes should be settled by peaceful talks round a conference table. The British and Portuguese governments accepted the idea and abandoned their Congo treaty, and the conference was invited to meet at Berlin in November 1884.

Harry Johnston and Karl Peters

Before the conference met, there were fresh developments in East Africa. In the spring of 1884, some learned societies in Britain, with no thought at all of politics or colonization, sent out a young scientist, Harry Johnston, to make a survey of the plants and animals of the Kilimanjaro region. As Johnston moved up and down the country collecting his specimens, he became more and more impressed with the place; and the idea came to him that it would make a splendid British colony. In July he wrote to the Foreign Office in London:

'Here is a land eminently suited for European colonization, situated near midway between the equatorial lakes and the coast. Within a few years it must be either English, French, or German.'

Not only did he write in this way; he made treaties with some of the chiefs, and he actually bought a few plots of land at Taveta and elsewhere.

The British government hesitated. Kirk did not approve, for the Sultan claimed the Kilimanjaro district as part of his dominion. Some members of the government in London were inclined to try to make some arrangement with the Sultan over the proposed colony. But Gladstone would have nothing to do with it, and no decision was taken.

While the British hesitated, the Germans acted. There were many people in Germany who disapproved of Bismarck's lack of interest in colonies. One of them, Karl Peters, determined to bring pressure to bear on his government. In November 1884, he and some companions arrived in Zanzibar. The German consul was expecting him, and showed Peters a telegram from Berlin warning him that he must expect no help from his government if he got into trouble. Peters and his companions were prepared to run the risk. They crossed to the mainland, and spent a busy five weeks travelling from place to place making treaties with African chiefs, by which they placed themselves under German protection. All the treaties were made in an area roughly 200 miles inland from the coast and from the Pangani river southward as far as Dar-es-Salaam. With his treaties in his pocket, Peters hurried back to Germany as fast as steamship and railway[3] could take him, and early in February 1885 the treaties were in Bismarck's hands.

When these African chiefs placed themselves and their people under German protection, they did not realize what they were doing. They did not know the Germans, and against whom did they think they needed protection? Against Arab slave raiders perhaps; against powerful rulers like Tippoo Tib or Mirambo who might threaten their independence; perhaps even against the Sultan of Zanzibar himself. Freedom from interference was all they wanted.

The Berlin conference

Bismarck had now made up his mind that Germany must become a colonial power, and he resolved to establish German colonies as close as possible to regions where British traders were well established. He annexed Togo and the Cameroons in July 1884, and next month he expanded the small German trading settlement on the coast of South West Africa into a large protectorate. The British delegates to the Berlin conference knew that their government had no objection to Germany's becoming a colonial power and had no wish to compete with her. They thought that the purpose of the conference was merely to draw up some sensible rules to avoid quarrels over Africa. They did not know France and Germany intended it to have a further purpose, to set limits to the expansion of British trade and influence, especially in the Congo and Niger basins. As regards the Congo, France and Germany successfully blocked the Portuguese claim and the British policy of trade without colonization. The conference approved of the colonization of the Congo basin by Leopold's Association but, as a concession to Britain, it declared that a vast region of equatorial Africa must be a free trade zone: a region including not only the Congo basin but modern Kenya, Uganda, Tanzania and more besides. This concession seemed satisfactory to Britain, but the Belgian

---

[3] There were no aircraft in those days. The journey from Zanzibar to Berlin took Peters about seven weeks.

authorities in the Congo ignored the free trade requirement. France and Germany then tried to squeeze Britain similarly out of the Niger basin, but there the British put up a strong resistance, and Bismarck gave way.

Having thus settled the thorny problems of the Niger and the Congo, the conference could agree on general principles for the partition of Africa. Its agreement is called the Berlin Act. Any European power was free to take possession of any part of the African coast not already under European occupation. Then it must notify all the other powers, so that they might have a chance of putting forward their own claims to the site, and any dispute would be settled in conference. When its claim was admitted, the occupying power must exert enough authority over the area to protect existing rights and the traders of all nations. If the European occupying power was not content with a protectorate but went further and annexed territory to form a colony, it must do more than merely protect trade; it must exercise effective political control.

France, Belgium and Germany assumed that the time had come for the European powers to colonize Africa; and on this assumption, the Berlin Act was a sensible arrangement for ensuring that the process of colonization should be carried out without quarrelling. The European powers did not think Africa worth fighting over. But the very terms of the Act made it certain that the whole of Africa would be speedily partitioned. The three energetic colonial powers (France, Belgium, Germany) might at any time send an expedition to hoist their flag in any village on the coast or inland. Unless Britain was prepared to allow her trade to be squeezed out of Africa, she must herself enter the competition and become an energetic colonial power. And so the partition of Africa began.

The German protectorate
Bismarck received Karl Peters' treaties on February 7, 1885, while the Berlin conference was still sitting. He kept them secret during the conference; the delegates left Berlin on March 2, and on March 3 the German government published the treaties and announced that the twelve chiefs and their peoples had been granted German protection. The action was typical of Bismarck.

The Sultan of Zanzibar and his British advisers were horrified, and Kirk protested to the Foreign Office in London. The new German protectorate blocked the main trade route from Bagamoyo to Tabora and Ujiji. It was plainly on land which the Sultan claimed as part of his dominion, and the German protectorate would need a seaport, and no doubt would soon be demanding one, probably Dar-es-Salaam itself.

But the British government would give the Sultan no support. It had no interest in Zanzibar now that the slave trade had at last been stopped there. The government already had enough trouble on its hands. Lord Cromer was at work reorganizing the Egyptian finances, and Britain was still hoping that in a few months, or perhaps a year or two, she would be able to leave Egypt. The Mahdi was rapidly conquering the Sudan, and his men had just killed Gordon in Khartoum. Gordon's death and the failure of the military expedition sent to save him caused a first-class political row in Britain. At the same time, the government was uneasy over events in South Africa and was facing serious difficulties in Asia; it was quite unable to interest itself in the troubles of the Sultan of Zanzibar. So the Foreign Office told Kirk firmly that they could give him no support, and told the German government that Britain would raise no objection to the establishment of the new German protectorate in East Africa.

The Germans at Witu and Zanzibar

Now that the German government had decided to enter African affairs, it acted energetically. Long ago, in 1862, Sultan Majid had had to send troops against a rebel chief named Simba, who had established himself on an island near Lamu. Simba was driven out of his island but escaped to the mainland and fortified himself at Witu, where he repelled a second attack by Majid's troops. Having made himself Sultan of Witu, Simba applied for German protection. His application lay neglected in Berlin for twenty years; and in 1884 the Germans thought the time had come for them to use it. If the German flag flew over Witu in the north, as well as over Peters' new protectorates in the south, Germany might hope to fill in the gap and take over the whole of the coast from Somaliland right down to Mozambique. They granted Simba their protection, and the Sultan of Zanzibar found his dominions threatened from two directions.

The Sultan saw that he could expect no help from Britain, so he determined to help himself. He sent Mathews with a force of troops to the Kilimanjaro region, and twenty-five chiefs in Taveta, Arusha, Pare and elsewhere recognized his authority. Mackinnon too became active. He hoped that even if the government in London would not help the Sultan, it might perhaps be prepared to support a strong British trading interest, as it had done in the Niger delta. He set himself to develop such an interest, and formed a company, the British East Africa Association, to develop trade in the region between Witu and the Umba river. His company confirmed some of Johnston's treaties north of Kilimanjaro, and made good use of the geographical discoveries which the British explorer Joseph Thomson had made on his travels in 1883 and 1884 between Mombasa and the Kavirondo gulf on Lake Victoria.

But the German government made sure that it should not lose what it had already gained. In August 1885 a German naval squadron arrived at Zanzibar, and the German admiral demanded that the Sultan should give his consent not only to a German protectorate over the chiefs who had accepted Karl Peters' treaties, but also over Witu and part of the Kilimanjaro region. Moreover, the port of Dar-es-Salaam must be freely available for German use. In return for these concessions, the German government promised to respect the independence of the Sultan's territories. In rage and despair, Sultan Barghash sought Kirk's advice; but Kirk, deserted by the government in London and broken-hearted at the ruin of his hopes for Zanzibar, could only tell him that he must submit. Barghash had to accept the German demands; and he never trusted the British again.

Delimiting the Sultan's territory

In promising to respect the independence of the Sultan's territories, the German admiral had brought the British government up against a difficulty which it had long foreseen but had hoped to avoid. What *were* the Sultan's territories? How far inland did his effective authority reach? In 1881 the government in London had told Kirk that he 'should avoid committing Her Majesty's Government to any policy entailing a definition of the extent of the Sultan's territory inland'. But this definition could no longer be avoided.

In 1886 Britain and Germany set up a commission to carry out this task; they thought it desirable to invite France to take part, though France had very little direct interest on the mainland of East Africa. It was not until the Sultan protested that they thought of inviting him to send a representative. Mathews attended on the Sultan's behalf.

It soon became clear that the Sultan's authority was effective all along the coastal strip, but not very far inland except at a few places like Tabora and the Kilimanjaro district, where the chiefs had so recently recognized Mathews as the Sultan's representative. The German delegates were instructed to keep the Sultan's territory as small as possible so as to leave as much land as possible free for German colonization. Mathews, who spoke fluent Swahili, was a great help to the British representative, who desired only to get at the truth; but the British government was not interested in upholding the Sultan, and was determined not to quarrel with Germany. The British representative proposed to leave the Sultan a coastal strip forty miles wide, and one or two blocks of country inland at Tabora and elsewhere. But the

Germans would not hear of this, and the commission broke up without reaching agreement.

In the end, the matter was settled by an Anglo–German agreement of October 1886. The Sultan's dominion was defined as a coastal strip ten miles wide from the mouth of the Tana to Tunghi bay. (As soon as the Sultan had reluctantly accepted this decision, the Germans, much to his annoyance, gave the Tunghi bay section to Portugal, moving the frontier up to the mouth of the Rovuma river.) In addition to this stretch of coast, the Sultan was to keep some towns north of the Tana: Kismayu, Brava and Merka with a ten-mile radius round them, and Mogadishu and Warsheikh with a five-mile radius. The islands of Zanzibar, Pemba,

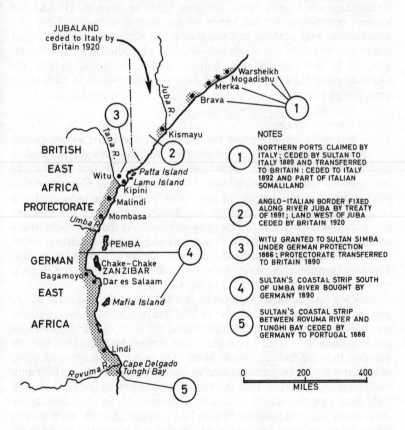

JUBALAND
ceded to Italy by
Britain 1920

Warsheikh
Mogadishu
Merka
Brava

③

②

Kismayu

NOTES

BRITISH

EAST

Tana R.

Witu
Patta Island
Lamu Island
Kipini

AFRICA

Malindi

PROTECTORATE

Umba R.
Mombasa

① NORTHERN PORTS CLAIMED BY ITALY; CEDED BY SULTAN TO ITALY 1889 AND TRANSFERRED TO BRITAIN: CEDED TO ITALY 1892 AND PART OF ITALIAN SOMALILAND

② ANGLO–ITALIAN BORDER FIXED ALONG RIVER JUBA BY TREATY OF 1891; LAND WEST OF JUBA CEDED BY BRITAIN 1920

③ WITU GRANTED TO SULTAN SIMBA UNDER GERMAN PROTECTION 1886; PROTECTORATE TRANSFERRED TO BRITAIN 1890

GERMAN

PEMBA

Chake–Chake
ZANZIBAR
Bagamoyo
Dar es Salaam

④

④ SULTAN'S COASTAL STRIP SOUTH OF UMBA RIVER BOUGHT BY GERMANY 1890

EAST

Mafia Island

⑤ SULTAN'S COASTAL STRIP BETWEEN ROVUMA RIVER AND TUNGHI BAY CEDED BY GERMANY TO PORTUGAL 1886

AFRICA

Lindi

Cape Delgado
Rovuma R.
Tunghi Bay

⑤

0   200   400
MILES

**THE DOMINIONS OF THE SULTAN
OF ZANZIBAR AFTER 1886**

Mafia and Lamu were left to the Sultan, but Witu was granted to Simba under German protection. Britain and Germany agreed that the coast south of the Umba river should be a German sphere of influence, and north of it, a British sphere. They agreed to settle their Kilimanjaro differences peacefully. Neither the British nor the German government wished to govern directly; both governments left the job of opening up and administering the country to commercial companies. One German company dealt with German East Africa and another with Witu; in the British sphere, Mackinnon's British East Africa Association was the responsible firm.

So there was an end of the dreams that Sultan Barghash had had of establishing his empire up to the great lakes or beyond. He had put himself completely in the hands of his British advisers, Kirk and Mackinnon, and nothing had come of it. To please the British he had risked the wrath of his Arab subjects and abolished the slave trade; and the British had left him helpless and unprotected to face the German guns. Kirk, ashamed and disappointed, retired in 1887; next year, Barghash died.

Anglo–German rivalry
There was still plenty of room for the British and German companies to meet and quarrel. The British East Africa Association pushed rapidly inland along the Tana river and along the line later to be traversed by the Uganda railway. The German Witu Company also pushed up the north bank of the Tana towards Uganda, and the German East Africa Company was busily occupying the country along the old trade route to Karagwe and Ujiji. At the same time, there was another British company, based on Lake Nyasa, which was eager to extend its field northward and occupy the shores of Lake Tanganyika. The two German companies hoped to join hands behind the British, the two British companies behind the Germans.

Italy too had colonial ambitions. In 1885 she took advantage of the weakness of Ethiopia to occupy the Red Sea port of Massawa, and she was building up an Italian empire round the horn of Africa, much as the Egyptians had tried to do ten years earlier. In May 1888 she demanded that the Sultan should hand over to her Kismayu and other northern ports to be incorporated in Italian Somaliland. Both Britain and Germany told Italy that this could not be allowed; but Britain and Italy were able to come to a friendly arrangement. By that time, as we shall see in the next section, Britain had realized that she must stay in Egypt for many years yet, and must one day reconquer the Sudan from the Mahdi. It thus became a matter of importance to her that the Sudan should have neighbours who were friendly to Britain; and Italy was traditionally friendly to Britain, whereas France was hostile. Britain and Italy therefore came to an understanding by which Britain undertook to raise no objection if Italy occupied Ethiopia and made it an Italian protectorate, Italy in return undertaking not to interfere with the waters of the Blue Nile. The Sultan formally ceded his northern ports to Italy, who transferred them to Britain; and Britain administered them as part of the Sultan's dominions, paying him a rent for them.

THE STRUGGLE FOR UGANDA

In 1887 a significant change occurred in British policy. Gladstone was out of office, and the Conservatives under Lord Salisbury were in power. The British had now been busy in Egypt for five years, hoping all the time that they would soon have finished their work there and would be able to leave the country. But in 1887 Salisbury abandoned this hope, and made up his mind that Britain must stay for many years yet.

There were several reasons for this change. The work of building up the Egyptian finances and reorganizing the administration was taking longer than had been expected. The Suez Canal was becoming more and more important to British shipping interests; the British merchant navy in those days was by far the biggest in the world, and Britain could not bear the thought of the Canal's falling into hostile, or even merely careless hands. Moreover, the Mahdi's successor in the Sudan was trying to extend his empire. He sent armies to invade Ethiopia, Eritrea and Egypt. It seemed probable that if the British left Egypt it would be conquered by Sudanese troops, and the work that Britain had been doing there since 1882 would have to be begun all over again by Britain or some other power.

Even so, in 1887 Salisbury made a last attempt to abandon Egypt. He persuaded the Sultan of Turkey to sign an agreement which provided that Britain should withdraw from Egypt and the Sultan should resume his control, but that Britain should have the right to reoccupy the country to defend the Suez Canal against attack. When France and Russia saw the treaty they protested and persuaded the Sultan not to ratify the treaty. Salisbury's attempt to withdraw from Egypt on what seemed to him reasonable conditions had failed; and so he decided Britain must stay. As soon as this decision was taken, its consequences became plain. Whoever rules Egypt must try to control the Nile, for without the Nile there would be no Egypt. Any plan which takes water from the Nile to irrigate any part of Uganda or the Sudan is of the greatest concern to the government of Egypt. So immediately Salisbury's government had to ask itself: What about Uganda and the Sudan?

For the moment, the Sudan could be ignored. It was controlled by the Mahdi's successor (the Khalifa), and its government did not threaten the Nile water. But Uganda was different. If German engineers gained control of Lake Victoria, who could say what they might do at Egypt's expense? The British were now wide awake, determined that Uganda must not fall under German rule.

Emin Pasha

The Englishman General Gordon had been killed by the Mahdi's men in 1885, but one of his colleagues in the Egyptian army was still alive. This was a German officer, Dr Schnitzer, who had become a Muslim and taken a Muslim name. Emin Pasha, as he was now called, was governor of the southernmost province of the Sudan. He and his troops could not make their way back northward, because the Khalifa controlled the whole of the Sudan; and Emin was being pressed so hard by the Khalifa's troops that it was even doubtful whether he would be able to escape southward into Uganda. There was much anxiety over him in Britain. The government had been much blamed for not rescuing Gordon from the Mahdi; surely, people said, it would rescue Gordon's friend Emin from the Khalifa? Germany too was anxious, the more so as Emin himself was a German.

Salisbury would not send a military expedition, but he saw no reason why the British East Africa Association should not rescue him if it could. In September 1888 he granted the Association a royal charter. The Association was renamed the Imperial British East Africa Company, and became the agent of the British government, with responsibility for opening up and developing as much of East Africa as it could. But this responsibility was granted under severe restrictions. The Company received no financial help from the government; it was expected to raise its funds from private investors and to pay them a dividend on their investment. The Company had no monopoly of trade, and had to refer all political and administrative problems to the government in London.

The Company was in no hurry to send a special expedition to look for Emin, for a large expedition, financed by public subscriptions in Britain and America and led by the explorer Stanley, was advancing up the Congo to rescue him. Expeditions into the interior of Africa were slow and costly. They had to go on foot, carrying with them not only their provisions and the trade goods they hoped to sell, but large quantities of goods which they would have to distribute in presents (almost like customs duties) to one African chief after another in return for permission to travel through his territory. Once they had vanished from sight of the coast, nothing more might be heard of them for months. The Company could not afford many distant expeditions, and it already had one expedition in the interior, led by F. J. Jackson. Jackson left Mombasa early in 1889 to make treaties with the chiefs and see what prospects there were of trade. He was ordered not to enter Uganda, which was regarded as too far off and too unsettled for profitable trade. So in November, when he arrived at Mumia's in Kavirondo, Jackson turned northward to explore the country towards Lake Rudolf, meaning to return to Mumia's before beginning the homeward march to Mombasa.

Again the Germans moved more quickly than the British. Peters announced that he would lead an expedition from Pangani in German East Africa, and would travel through Karagwe to Uganda, and so up to Emin's headquarters in the Sudan. But just as his party was leaving Germany, Peters announced that he had changed his plan, and would march through the British sphere of influence. The IBEA Company protested; but the only help that the Foreign Office in London gave them was to get the German government to promise that it would not support Peters if he marched through British territory.

Peters landed near Witu in June 1889, and a month later set off on his march up the Tana river. The British company had already established trading stations for 250 miles up the river. Peters looted the stores, tore down the British flag and hoisted the German, and made his violent way up the river, shooting anyone who opposed him. In March 1890 he reached Mumia's, and learned that Jackson had been there before him, and that Stanley's expedition had already rescued Emin. But Peters was not the man to turn back merely because the object of his expedition had already been achieved by someone else. He decided to go to Uganda and see what he could do for Germany's interests there.

The situation in Uganda

Uganda was in an unhappy state. Kabaka Mutesa died in 1884, and was succeeded by his son Mwanga, then eighteen years old. By this time, Christianity had made great progress among the Baganda, and Islam too, which had been introduced by the Arab traders, had become strong, both among the Baganda and the Banyoro. Mwanga was not a strong ruler. When he found that his people were split into hostile parties, his first idea was that Christianity was a bad thing for the country, and should be stopped. He was encouraged in this by the Muslims, who warned him that Christian missionaries were only the advance scouts of the European powers; presently they would be followed by troops and treaties, and Buganda, like the Congo and part of East Africa, would fall under foreign rule. Mwanga decided to put down Christianity in his country. In January 1885 he had three CMS converts killed. In October he heard that the CMS were sending out a bishop, named Hannington, and on Mwanga's orders one of the Busoga chiefs blocked the road and killed the bishop. In May 1886 Mwanga demanded that all the officers of his court should give up Christianity. More than thirty of them, both Protestants and Catholics, refused to do so and were put to death, many of them being burnt alive. Others were beaten and imprisoned. But the Protestants and Catholics of Buganda remained faithful to their religion. The example of the Christian martyrs encouraged the Church still more, and nothing that the Kabaka could do stopped Christianity from spreading.

In 1888, Mwanga went further. Still trying to get back to the old days when the Kabaka commanded the absolute loyalty of all his people, he decided to suppress the other foreign religion, Islam, as well as Christianity. The Christian and Muslim Baganda rose up together in revolt and drove out the Kabaka. He fled to Karagwe; the rebel chiefs made his brother Kiwewa Kabaka in his place, and Catholic, Protestant and Muslim chiefs shared the positions of power. This uneasy situation did not last long. The Muslims hoped to make themselves supreme, and they invited Kiwewa to declare himself a Muslim and put down the Christians. Kiwewa refused, whereupon the Muslims deposed him after a reign of only one month, and put up another brother, Kalema, to succeed him. Civil war followed between Kiwewa and Kalema; Kiwewa was killed, and many Christian Baganda abandoned their country and took refuge in Ankole.

Buganda had been in this state of persecution and civil war for five years, so it is not surprising that the IBEA Company saw no prospect of successful trade there, and ordered Jackson not to take his expedition into Uganda.

Peters and Jackson in Uganda
When Jackson reached Mumia's in November 1889, he received a letter from Mwanga, written for him in June by Father Lourdel, the senior Catholic missionary. Mwanga wrote from his place of refuge in Karagwe; he urged Jackson to come and save Uganda, so that 'we Christians may join together'. The letter placed Jackson in a difficulty. It was five months old, he had strict orders not to go into Uganda, and he heard rumours that since the letter had been written, Mwanga had in fact returned to Kampala and no longer needed saving. He sent messengers to find out the latest position, and learned that Mwanga had indeed defeated Kalema in October 1889 and was once more Kabaka; Kalema and his people had fled to seek help from Kabarega of Bunyoro. In view of his orders, Jackson decided that he need not go into Uganda;

he sent the Kabaka one of his Company's flags, and went off on his trip to Lake Rudolf.

Before Jackson returned to Mumia's, Karl Peters in his turn arrived there, and while at Mumia's he was given a mailbag addressed to Jackson. He read the letters, and found another urgent appeal for help from Mwanga, written (like the earlier letter) by Father Lourdel. Kalema had obtained from Bunyoro the help he asked for, and at the end of November he and the Muslims had again driven Mwanga and the Christians away to Ankole and Karagwe. Father Lourdel added a message of his own to Jackson: the Catholic missionaries, he said, would welcome British help in restoring peace and order to Buganda.

To Peters, this seemed a great opportunity. Jackson was safely out of the way; why should not he go to Kampala as the saviour whom Mwanga and the French missionaries were longing for, and bring Buganda peace and German rule? He arrived in Kampala on February 25, 1890, and made a treaty with the Kabaka. Father Lourdel wisely advised the Kabaka not to grant exclusive rights of trade to any company, nor to place his country under the protection of any European power. Mwanga followed this advice, and agreed to sign a treaty of friendship with Germany: of friendship, but no more. To Peters, this seemed enough. In those days, a treaty of friendship would surely be sufficient ground for Bismarck to claim Uganda as a German sphere of influence. Jackson might have had a similar treaty if he had chosen, but he had lost his chance; Peters and Germany were first in the field.

Peters got his treaty on March 3. He must now do as he had done six years before: hurry back to Germany and get his treaty published and supported by his government. But meanwhile Jackson had returned from Lake Rudolf to Mumia's, and had heard what had happened to his mail. He sent a runner to Kampala with a message to Peters: Emin Pasha had been found and was safe; Peters had no right to fight and make treaties in a British sphere of influence; and Peters' own government had disowned him. This message reached Peters in Kampala on March 22. He tried to get his Somali porters to stay and fight Jackson's men, but they refused; so he hastily left the country and escaped through Karagwe into German East Africa before Jackson arrived.

Jackson decided that he was now justified in entering Buganda in spite of his orders. He arrived at Kampala in April, and invited the Kabaka to sign a fresh treaty. But the Kabaka, having just signed one treaty with Peters, was not inclined to sign another, even if it was only a treaty of friendship and not of protection. It was plain to Mwanga's adviser, Father Lourdel, that the fate of Uganda did not depend on Peters or Jackson; it would be settled by the British and German

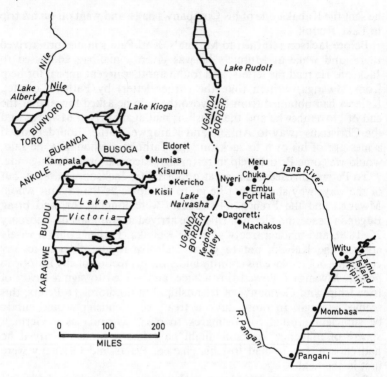

EAST AFRICA
in the days of Lugard
and Karl Peters

governments. There was nothing Jackson could do, so he left Kampala and started back to the coast.

The Anglo–German agreement of 1890
Before he reached Mombasa, the British and German governments had sensibly come to a full agreement, which settled all their differences in Africa. Bismarck saw that Salisbury's Britain, awake and determined to remain in Egypt, could not be treated like Gladstone's Britain, which was anxious only to keep out of trouble and responsibility.

Under the agreement, Germany made great concessions. (1) Uganda was recognized as a British sphere of influence. (2) Germany gave up

Witu. (These two concessions threw away all the results of Peters' latest expedition.) (3) Germany agreed that Britain should assume a protectorate over Zanzibar. Other clauses of the agreement settled, on the usual give-and-take principle, the frontiers of the German territories of Togo, the Cameroons, and South West Africa.

Britain for her part made two concessions in Africa and one outside. (1) Germany was allowed to buy outright the Sultan's ten-mile strip south of the Umba river, whereas north of the river the British continued to fly the Sultan's flag in the coastal strip and make him an annual payment for it.[4] (2) The frontier between modern Zambia and Tanzania was adjusted slightly in Germany's favour.

As far as Africa was concerned, Britain had much the better of the bargain. But to Germany, all this was amply compensated by the one concession which Britain made in Europe. Since 1815 the little island of Heligoland at the mouth of the German river Elbe had belonged to Britain. Germany had just decided to build a strong navy; and the island, strongly fortified and in German hands, would make a valuable protection for the German naval bases. Britain offered Heligoland to Germany, and the German government jumped at the offer. A small rocky island near home seemed much more valuable than vast areas of forest, swamp and mountain far away.

The British protectorate over Zanzibar

In November 1890, Britain declared a protectorate over Zanzibar in accordance with the Anglo–German agreement. Twenty years earlier, Sultan Barghash had wished for a British protectorate. But the protectorate of 1890 was by no means the sort of thing that Barghash had desired. He had hoped that the British would help him to open up and administer his mainland territories, holding off the other European powers and working in partnership with him. The 1890 protectorate was declared after nearly all the Sultan's mainland territories had been lost. The British were not the Sultan's partners, they were his masters.

Next year, the partition of East Africa was completed by the Anglo–Italian agreement, which formally confirmed the understanding of 1889. Frontiers were agreed, and while Italy promised not to interfere with the water level in the Atbara or the Blue Nile, Britain recognized Ethiopia as an Italian sphere of influence. Italy already had a treaty with Ethiopia, signed in 1889, the treaty of Wichale. (The Italians spell the name Ucciali.) Italy regarded this treaty as giving her a protectorate over Ethiopia, but Ethiopia did not accept this interpretation. The

---

[4] The payment was calculated as equal to the whole of the annual revenue which the coastal strip brought the Sultan in 1886, plus half of any subsequent increase.

dispute led to war; in 1896 an Italian army set out from Eritrea to conquer Ethiopia, but was completely defeated at the battle of Adowa; and that was the end of Italy's dream for forty years.

The partition of East Africa does not make a pleasant story. Perhaps Sir John Kirk is the man who comes out of it with most credit. He was sincere in wishing to uphold the power of the Sultan of Zanzibar, with no thought of furthering British interests in any way. Others, like Johnston and Lugard, who worked to bring Africa under colonial rule, were at the same time passionately devoted to the work of putting down the slave trade and of bringing European medicine and education to the African people. But on the whole, the European powers partitioned Africa in their own interests. Tribes were cut in half, one section becoming British while the other became Belgian or German; and these mistakes made in ignorance were not corrected when the colonial governments learned the true facts. We might perhaps wish that the Europeans could have left Africa alone to build up its own civilization. But any hope of this had already been destroyed by the Arab slave trade. If the Europeans had not colonized East Africa, it would probably have been organized into a chain of kingdoms ruled by such men as Mirambo and Tippoo Tib, owing some vague sort of allegiance to Zanzibar. In such conditions, progress would have been slow. Any trading expedition to Africa had to spend a large proportion of its goods in paying one African chief after another for permission to pass through his territory. As long as this was so, no European businessman would risk much money in African trade. Once Europe had overcome its fear of Africa and had learned instead to look on Africa as a profitable field for business, the colonial partition was probably inevitable. In those days there was no United Nations and no international programme of technical assistance. European political control, with all its disadvantages, was the only way by which Africa could become part of the modern world.

This does not alter the fact that in carrying out the partition the European powers were thinking mainly of their own interests. Livingstone or Lugard might think of the slave trade as the cause of intolerable human suffering, but most governments thought of it much more as a hindrance to ordinary commerce: they thought it a pity that the land and the people wasted in the slave trade could not be put to better use, in producing minerals and tropical crops and in buying European manufactures. Whether Africans liked it or not, the European governments meant to make them conform with European ideas. Africa was indeed to become part of the modern world, but the modern world was to be dominated by European interests.

Chapter 3

THE BEGINNINGS OF COLONIAL RULE

The agreements which Britain made with Germany in 1890 and with Italy in 1891 fixed the colonial frontiers in East Africa. The British government's only direct responsibility for the time being was its newly declared protectorate over Zanzibar. The countries now called Kenya and Uganda were British spheres of influence, and the Imperial British East Africa Company was at work exploring their commercial possibilities. Neither was yet a British protectorate, and the British government was not yet ready to assume any direct responsibility for them.

Even the protectorate over Zanzibar at first cost the British government very little trouble. Sultan Barghash, a broken and disappointed man, died in 1888, and he was succeeded by his brother Khalifa, who had spent the last six years in prison because Barghash suspected him of plotting to make himself Sultan. Khalifa died only two years later, and in 1890 was succeeded by yet another brother, Ali, the youngest son of the great Seyyid Said. Ali's short reign of three years is notable chiefly for the new anti-slavery decree which he signed. All sale, exchange and purchase of slaves was forbidden. Slaves were entitled to buy their freedom at reasonable prices; and if a slave-owner died childless, his death was to set his slaves free, so that they could not be inherited by a stranger.

GERMAN EAST AFRICA TO 1914

The energetic Germans lost no time in setting up a colonial administration in their sphere south of the Umba river. Like the British, they entrusted their colonial responsibilities to a commercial company. In 1888, the German consul in Zanzibar made an agreement with Sultan Khalifa that the German company should be free to regulate commerce, develop communications, dig for minerals, and collect customs dues in the mainland territory which the Sultan had formerly regarded as his own. In August, the company's agent began to act on this agreement: he hoisted the company's flag in several towns along the coast, and began to administer the country as a colony. Karl Peters was appointed chairman of the committee of administration, and he tried to extend German authority by violence and brutal discipline.

Peters and his committee soon ran into trouble. A number of Arab chiefs hated the new way of life, and in August 1888 they revolted. They found a good leader, Bushiri the half-Arab chief of Pangani. Bushiri took command of the Arab forces; he made his headquarters at Bagamoyo, and was joined by an African chief, Bwana Heri. Peters and his German forces were outnumbered and could not cope with the revolt. The company appealed for help to the German government, which sent an experienced officer, Captain Hermann Wissmann. Karl Peters handed over his command to Wissmann and went off on his expedition up the Tana to Uganda.

Wissmann gathered about a thousand men: about 600 Sudanese and 350 Zulus, with a valuable nucleus of fifty trained and disciplined Somali who had served in the Egyptian army and had seen fighting against the Mahdi. Sultan Khalifa ordered his people in Zanzibar not to supply Bushiri with arms, and British and German warships set up a blockade of the coast to make sure that the Sultan's order was effective. The German warships lent Captain Wissmann their marines, and, with these well-trained German troops and his African force, Wissmann advanced from Dar-es-Salaam to Bagamoyo, Bushiri retiring before him. In May 1889 the German force was assembled in Bagamoyo, and Wissmann methodically set about conquering the coastal strip. He advanced inland as far as Mpwapwa, where he built a fort. Short of weapons, and faced by disciplined German troops, Bushiri and Bwana Heri had no hope of victory. Bushiri was betrayed to the Germans in December 1889 and was hanged. Fresh German troops came ashore at Kilwa and seized Kilwa and Lindi; Bwana Heri gave up hope and made his peace with the Germans; early in 1891 Wissmann was able to report that the country was quiet.

The German government had learnt its lesson. It decided to take direct control in East Africa, and to restrict the company to commercial matters. The change took effect in November 1890. Karl Peters and some others of the company's staff became officials of the German government in East Africa.

The German conquest

The land so far occupied by Germany was only a small part of the future Tanganyika. Many expeditions had still to be made to hoist the German flag and to explain the fact of German rule to peoples who knew nothing of it. Emin Pasha was appointed a commissioner, and in 1890 he led a German expedition to Tabora. Mirambo had died in 1884, and his son Siki had succeeded him. Siki continued his father's policy of resisting the Arabs of Tabora, and he was giving them a great deal of trouble by harassing their trading caravans. The Arabs there had learnt their lesson by the defeat of Bushiri. They welcomed Emin and allied themselves with him, hoping that the German forces would put an end to the difficulties they were having with Siki. Towards the end of 1892, Emin attacked Siki and defeated him; and then Emin went on and established German forts at Bukoba and Mwanza. His orders were to return from Mwanza to the coast, but he disobeyed them; he formed the plan of going westward through the Congo and coming out on the Atlantic coast in the new German colony of the Cameroons. Perhaps he thought that having such long experience of Africa and being himself a Muslim, he could get on well with Arabs. But he was mistaken; he was now a German officer leading a German expedition, and the Arabs in the Congo attacked and killed him.

Siki's people, the Nyamwezi, were not the only African nation to resist the Germans. In June 1891, only a few months after the end of Bwana Heri's revolt, a German officer named Zelewski left Bagamoyo with three companies of African troops to march against the Hehe, whose chief Mkwawa refused to accept German rule. In August his little army was caught in an ambush; Zelewski himself and nine other German officers were killed, with 300 men, and very few struggled back through the bush to safety. A year later, in June 1892, another expedition was sent against the Chagga people of Kilimanjaro, but the Chagga, under their chief Meli, repelled the Germans near Moshi, and the Germans retreated with the loss of two officers.

The German government now decided that it was useless to send small expeditions under junior officers against these experienced African war-chiefs. Much stronger forces must be sent, and each African nation must be so thoroughly beaten that it would give up hope of further resistance. More troops were sent out, and a senior officer, Colonel von Schele, was appointed to command them. Colonel von Schele marched his men methodically round the country dealing with the African leaders in turn. After being defeated by Emin, Siki and the Nyamwezi had become active again; in January 1893 they were defeated, and Siki killed himself. In August of that year, Meli and his Chagga were defeated; in the spring of 1894 Bwana Heri and in October even Mkwawa and the Hehe were beaten by the formidable new German commander. Mkwawa, though defeated in October 1894, kept up the war; with small forces he kept attacking the Germans and slipping away again into the bush before they could rally. In August 1896 the Germans built a fort at Iringa to try and control the Hehe, but Mkwawa kept up his guerrilla warfare throughout 1897 and 1898. But as time went on, the German hold on his country became tighter and tighter; in the end his people were exhausted, and Mkwawa himself committed suicide to avoid being captured. In 1899 the German government was at last able to pause, feeling that on the whole the country was now quiet. Even then there remained the province of Urundi, which was able to keep its independence until 1903.

2   A SMALL FORTIFIED POST
Built by the Germans during the Maji-Maji rising

The German administration

By 1903 German East Africa was divided into administrative districts, each under its commissioner. Each village had its headman, called a *jumbe*, and several villages were grouped under an Arab or half-Arab sub-commissioner called an *akida*, who was responsible to the German commissioner. Much power was left to the jumbe and the akida; in particular, they were responsible for collecting taxes and paying them in at district headquarters. The German commissioner was supposed to stay in his *boma* (headquarters) most of the time; he had to ask permission before spending a night away from it. He had no chance of getting to know his people; he depended on the akida for his information. This was quite different from the British colonial system, which laid stress on the commissioner's going on tour round his district and getting to know his people, either in a formal *baraza* or in informal chatting.

The Germans did not use the akida system all over the country. Where there were strong chiefs, who had great authority among their people, the Germans were sensible enough not to introduce foreign akidas; they were content to recognize the chiefs and govern their people through the chiefs in a sort of indirect rule.

Economic development

In another respect, German administration was different from British. The British were always unwilling to spend any public money on their colonies. They expected a colony to pay its way, and would make a grant from the British Treasury only if the colony was so poor as to be unable to afford even the essentials of government. The Germans were ready to spend money from the German Treasury in the hope of stimulating economic progress. Money spent on communications, health, education and research, they thought, would bring in revenue later on. Between 1894 and 1906 the German government invested well over four million pounds in East Africa,[1] and German private firms too invested large sums.

Railway building in German East Africa began in 1893. The line from Tanga reached Mombo in 1895 and was extended to Moshi in 1912. In 1905 the government began building the central line from Dar-es-Salaam along the old trade route, the line which the Frenchman Rabaud had wished to build twenty-five years earlier. The line reached Morogoro in 1907, Tabora in 1912, and Kigoma in March 1914. (The Mwanza branch was built, much later, by the British.)

The Germans spent much energy in developing agriculture. In 1902 they began the agricultural research station at Amani. Cotton and sisal were the two main export crops. Sisal was introduced as early as 1892, and it throve; in 1906 the country exported nearly £70,000 worth of sisal, and during the next six years the annual export was multiplied nearly five times.[2] Rubber too was exported; in those days, the motor-car industry was just beginning, and the demand for rubber tyres was growing fast. German East Africa exported nearly £130,000 worth of rubber in 1906 and more than three times as much in 1912. But then the new rubber plantations in Malaya and Indonesia came into pro-

---

[1] Worth eight or ten times as much at 1971 prices.
[2] The figure of £70,000 should also be multiplied by eight or ten to get present-day values.

duction. The Western world had more rubber than it needed, and the price fell; East African rubber could not compete with rubber from the Far East, and the East African rubber industry collapsed. Coffee-growing began in a small way in Bukoba and in the Kilimanjaro district.

Cotton, however, was the export crop which the Germans pushed hardest. They distributed cotton seed free, and they compelled people to grow cotton whether they wished to or not. They helped the farmers in their cultivation, and set up ginneries and a marketing organization. They produced leaflets on cotton-growing, printed in several African languages. In 1910 they encouraged the African growers by fixing a guaranteed minimum price, but this was too successful: it produced such floods of cotton that the government had to abolish the minimum price two years later. In 1902 the country exported half a ton of cotton; in 1912 it exported over 1,800 tons.

Not all the cotton was grown on African farms. The German government encouraged European settlers. In 1895 all the land in German East Africa was declared Crown land, but the decree said that all existing rights in land were to be recognized and preserved; this of course included tribal rights. A commission was appointed to survey the land and see how much would be available for European settlers. After studying the African system of shifting agriculture, the commission recommended that to make sure that African farmers had enough land, each tribe should be allotted four times as much land as it was actually cultivating at the moment. On the whole, this recommendation was followed; but in a few regions which were the most attractive to German settlers, too many settlers were allowed in, so that the African tribes were more closely pinched, and there was some land hunger.

Education

Like the British, the Germans left education mainly to the missionary societies. The Church Missionary Society and the Universities Mission to Central Africa, the White Fathers and the Holy Ghost Fathers were the main educational missions. But quite early on, unlike the British, the Germans began to provide some government schools also: primary schools, trade schools, and secondary schools. The government schools aimed at training craftsmen and clerks; they were not ambitious, but like everything the Germans did, they were very thorough. In 1914 there were 14 German officials in the education department. There were 99 government schools; ten of them (with 2,400 pupils) were primary and the rest of a lower grade. There were also over 1,800 mission schools with over 108,000 children. There was the beginning of secondary education at Tanga and elsewhere. Twenty new government schools were planned for 1914. When the British took over Tanganyika they were impressed with the results of German education. They found that every akida and village headman was able to read and write Swahili, and the German officers were accustomed to sending written instructions, which the British could not do in their territories because no one could read them. The Germans had had much success in educating people to work with their government, and they had deliberately encouraged the spread of the Swahili language so as to unify the country and make administration easier. Education, like other things in German colonies, benefited because Germany was prepared to spend money from the German Treasury on providing schools.

Anti-slavery measures

After a conference held in Brussels in 1890 concerning the suppression of the slave trade, all countries (including Britain and Germany) who signed the Brussels agreement were required to do all they could to put down slavery and the slave trade in their colonies. The construction of railways was suggested as one method: railways would make it easier to bring police or troops into the interior to deal with slave raiders.

The German government made a decree in 1895 declaring it to be a punishable offence to carry out a slave raid, or to buy and sell slaves. It considered abolishing slavery altogether, but thought this would raise too big a storm among the Arabs of the coastal strip. It decided to go cautiously. In 1901 it decreed that household slaves must be able to buy their freedom at reasonable rates, and six years later it decreed that all children born after 1906 were born free. But the German government did not succeed in formally abolishing the institution of slavery; that final step was taken by the British, who took over German East Africa after the 1914 war.

The Maji-Maji rising

German East Africa owed much to Count Adolf von Götzen, who was governor from 1901 to 1906. When he arrived, he was shocked at the brutal and violent way in which many of the Germans behaved towards the Africans, and he set himself to stamp out the flogging and shooting. He developed agriculture and education, pushed ahead with building railways, and did his best to understand African ways and cooperate with the African chiefs and people. By 1905 he must have felt that he had set the colony on its feet. He received an unpleasant shock when the Maji-Maji rising broke out in July 1905.

The African people were far from being contented under colonial rule. The people of German East Africa were the first to experience it, but it came before long to Kenya and Uganda as well. When European administrators saw Africans practising subsistence agriculture on land which might be profitably used to produce a heavy crop of cotton, their first idea was that Africans used the land in this way only because they knew no better. But when the Africans, having had the matter carefully explained to them, still preferred to use their land for subsistence farming, the Europeans could not understand it, for they regarded it as almost a man's duty to obtain as much profit as he could from his profession or his land. If the Africans did not wish to make the most profitable use of their land, they must be compelled to. This deep-seated conflict between the outlook and the customs of the two races (maybe due to differences of climate) was one of the main causes of trouble in the colonial period. The Africans could work hard enough when it was necessary, but they hated the strictly disciplined European way of life; they wanted to be free to come and go, to work and rest as they chose. The Europeans seldom tried to understand the African point of view. It was enough for them that they were the masters, and therefore the Africans must adopt European ways.

Again, the Europeans did not realize that Africans were deeply humiliated by the loss of their independence. They thought that by bringing in Western commerce, medicine, education and skills of all kinds, they were conferring a benefit on Africa; they were 'civilizing' it. They thought that Africans ought to be willing to give up their independence in order to secure the benefits of European civilization. But the Africans did not see it this way. It seemed to them that these homeless ones, the *wazungu*, in spite of their almost magical power, had no right to settle in Africa and make themselves masters of the country and the people. The Africans were fighting men. When they were ordered to leave off fighting and become cotton-growers, they felt they were losing their manhood. It was better to make a great effort and throw off this European rule before it was too late.

There were other causes of the rising. The system of forced labour was one. Another was probably the akida system; the akida often oppressed the village people and stood between them and the German officer who ought to protect them. It was noticeable that the area of the Maji-Maji rising largely coincided with the area governed on the akida system. The big tribes whom the Germans ruled through their own chiefs took little or no part in the rising.

The Swahili word *maji* means 'water', and the rising gets its name from the magic 'water' which the medicine-men gave the African fighters to bathe in; German bullets were expected to turn to water as they struck African flesh that had been bathed in the magic liquid. The Maji-Maji rising was different from the Arab rising under Bushiri, and from the fighting carried out by the chiefs like Siki and Mkwawa and Meli. Bushiri had been willing to allow the Germans to trade and to control the customs posts, as long as they did not interfere with the Arabs in their trading activities. The Chagga, the Hehe and the Nyamwezi did not mind the Germans occupying the coastal strip; they fought in order that German rule should not be extended from the coastal strip over their tribal territory. But the Maji-Maji rising was carefully planned about a year in advance by the leaders of several tribes that had so far given little trouble, and its object was nothing less than to drive the Germans out of East Africa altogether. It caught the colonial government ment completely by surprise; it burst out in several places almost at once, and rapidly spread till it covered all the southern part of the colony from Songea and Lindi to Kilosa and Dar-es-Salaam. German officials, traders and missionaries were killed, and until more troops arrived from Germany there was very little that the colonial government could do.

The first fighting broke out at Kilwa in July 1905, and pushing out-wards from Kilwa, the rebels seized the villages of Kibata and Liwale. Small parties of German troops were attacked, and the rebels planned an advance on Dar-es-Salaam from different directions. Lieutenant von Hassel with sixty men was besieged at Mahenge, but Captain Nigmann advanced from the fort at Iringa and relieved him. A German detachment attacked Kibata in vain, and another detachment advancing against Liwale was wiped out. A second attack on Kibata, led by Major Johannes, succeeded in taking the village and holding it. Dar-es-Salaam was now fairly safe on that side; meanwhile another rebel force from the west took Kilosa town (though it could not capture the boma) and advanced eastwards, but was defeated at Morogoro. The governor's fear was that the great fighting nations, the Hehe, the Chagga and the Nyamwezi, who had already given the Germans so much trouble, might join the rising; the Nyamwezi alone were supposed to have 30,000 fighting men armed with guns of some kind. But these nations remained quiet, so that Captain Nigmann, as we have seen, could afford to leave Iringa and advance to Mahenge. This was a great relief to the governor; it meant that the greatest danger was over, and all he had to do was to sit quiet and await help from Germany.

In October, three months after the rising began, the first troops arrived from Germany, and the reconquest of the south began. The troops came ashore at several places, and by the end of 1905 they had occupied all the coastline and held a line 250 miles long covering Morogoro and Dar-es-Salaam and resting on the river Rovuma. Then they began a slow but steady advance. They taught the Maji-Maji men a terrible lesson. To avoid fighting and to economize German lives they

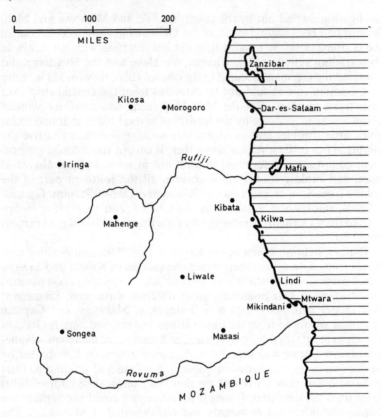

SOUTHERN TANGANYIKA
The Maji-Maji rising

burned the villages and the crops and drove the fighting men into the bush. Thousands of people died of hunger, and many of the leaders of the rising were caught and executed. But in spite of it all, some of the Ngoni kept up the war until January 1907, eighteen long months.

The reforms after the rising

The Maji-Maji rising came as a terrible shock to Germany. The government set up an inquiry into the causes of the rising, and the German public and parliament were shocked to hear of flogging and other cruelties carried out both by settlers and by officials. The government took matters in hand. It set up a separate Colonial Office, with a minister at its head. The first minister, Dr Dernburg, came out to East Africa to see conditions there for himself. He decided that the strictness of the German system must be relaxed; the government must cooperate more with the Arab and African people instead of compelling them to live in the German way. Limits must be set to the spread of European plantations and the use of forced labour. Africans must be encouraged to grow cotton and other cash crops by the hope of reward instead of by the fear of punishment. (As we have seen, this new kind of encouragement proved too successful, and was abandoned.) Africans working on European farms must be protected by labour legislation. Above all, the district commissioners must not rely so much on the akidas, but must get out of their bomas and learn to know the chiefs and people in their district. The government must work much more through traditional chiefs than through foreign akidas.

The new governor, Baron von Rechenberg, put this new policy into effect. The measures he took to protect African labour naturally brought him into conflict with the European settlers, who thought, like settlers in other countries, that the government's first duty should be to provide them with ample supplies of cheap labour. There were not many of them: fewer than 200 at the outbreak of the Maji-Maji rising, and fewer than 900 at the outbreak of war in 1914. The colonial government did nothing to give the European settlers a voice in politics. The governor had an advisory council, but the settlers were not represented on it. Their newspapers were kept under strict control. The emphasis of Governor von Rechenberg's administration was on preserving African ways of life but encouraging Africans to grow cash crops on their own farms.

Though Dr Schnee, who succeeded Baron von Rechenberg as governor in 1912, was slightly more favourable to the European settlers, this period from 1906 to 1914 was a time of great reform in German East Africa. But in 1914 the country was involved in the first world war, and the fruits of this reforming energy were lost.

The German administration was always strict, and before 1906 many cruel things were done by German officials, traders and settlers. During the next eight years Germany made strenuous efforts to reform her colonial administration, on lines which were in many ways a copy of the best in British methods. In spite of this, the peace treaty of 1919 deprived Germany of all her colonies in Africa and elsewhere; they were placed under the supervision of the League of Nations and entrusted by the League under mandate to Britain, France and other powers. The greater part of German East Africa was entrusted to Britain; Ruanda and Urundi were entrusted to Belgium.

THE BRITISH IN UGANDA

The Anglo–German agreement of July 1890 declared that Uganda was to be a British sphere of influence. But the people of Uganda had not been consulted in the matter. Nothing had been done to define the frontiers. Uganda was some 600 miles from the coast, and all goods had to be carried on porters' heads at a cost of from £250 to £300 a ton from Mombasa. The British government, still determined to take no direct responsibility for Uganda, expected the IBEA Company to establish British authority there and make it a paying concern. It was a hopeless situation.

Nevertheless George Mackenzie, the IBEA Company's administrator, had to do what he could, and in August he sent out a caravan from Mombasa under the command of Captain F. D. Lugard, to try and make an agreement with Mwanga the Kabaka and to impose British authority.

Lugard already had experience in Africa. As a captain in the British army of India, he had spent part of his long leave from India commanding the troops of the African Lakes Company against the Arab slave raiders in Malawi. He had seen the slave trade, and hated it; he was immensely fair and patient; and he believed in seeing to all the details of a job himself and not relying on other people to do his work for him. His present job was likely to be a difficult one. He had 50 Somali and Sudanese soldiers and about 270 porters. The Company had to be economical, so he was allowed only a small supply of ammunition. But he had one old machine-gun, which had already been backwards and forwards through Africa with one of Stanley's expeditions. It was in bad order, but the Company hoped it might be useful in an emergency. However, everyone hoped that there would be no fighting. If Lugard was to succeed in his difficult mission, it must be by diplomacy.

Meanwhile Sir William Mackinnon was protesting to the government in London at being expected to take on this heavy responsibility. The IBEA Company was a commercial company and would prefer to spend its time in developing commerce nearer the coast, in what is now Kenya. If the government wished it to undertake these expensive operations so far away, he said, it should pay for them. The very least it should do was to guarantee the interest on the capital cost of building a railway to make communication easy. How could the Company hope to develop Uganda when it took four months to get from Mombasa to Kampala?

The Conservative prime minister, Lord Salisbury, was sympathetic. But there was such a strong body of opinion in parliament hostile to the idea of spending public money in opening up Africa, that Salisbury dared not ask parliament for such an expenditure. What he did ask for was £25,000 for the cost of a railway survey, £5,000 of which was to be refunded by the Company. Even that was refused him; so he asked the Company to pay the whole cost of the survey for the time being, in the hope that he might persuade parliament later on. Mackinnon reluctantly agreed to this, and towards the end of 1891 the survey began. But these unhappy negotiations discouraged private investors in England from lending their money to the IBEA Company. No wonder it had to count its stores and ammunition carefully when sending Lugard on his long journey.

Lugard in Uganda

It was the custom for all travellers going to Uganda to wait on the east bank of the Nile until the Kabaka gave them permission to cross and enter his country. But when Lugard arrived at the river bank in December, he had no intention of following the custom. He knew that Buganda was again on the point of civil war, and that a British trader called Stokes was on his way there with a large supply of firearms and ammunition; unless Lugard could get there before Stokes, he would be too late. The Kabaka had ordered that all the canoes should be taken over to the west bank of the river, but one tiny canoe had been overlooked, and Lugard found it. He went backwards and forwards in this one canoe himself, taking over a few of his men at a time. The local chief could easily have had Lugard killed, as he had had Bishop Hannington killed five years before; but he saw that times were changing, and he was afraid. On December 18, Lugard and his men arrived at the capital[3] and made their camp on Kampala hill; to Lugard's great relief, Stokes had not yet arrived.

The Kabaka himself was a Catholic, a Fransa; his senior chiefs were divided almost equally between Fransa and Ingleza, but the Fransa were the stronger party among the people. There had already been civil war in Buganda, and the Muslims had more than once driven the Kabaka and all the Christians out of Kampala. At the moment, the Kabaka was back in power, and the Muslims had been driven away to the Bunyoro border. There they lay, with Kabarega of Bunyoro supporting them, awaiting a chance to attack once more. It was only a few months since the Kabaka had signed his treaty with Peters and refused to sign another with Jackson. Two Baganda delegates, a Fransa and an Ingleza, had gone back with Jackson to Mombasa

[3] The capital of Uganda is built on several hills. The Kabaka lived on Mengo hill. The Fransa headquarters was on Rubaga, the Ingleza headquarters on Namirembe. Kampala hill was unoccupied, and that is why Lugard chose it. For convenience, we shall call the city by its modern name of Kampala.

to make inquiries there and find out the truth about the Anglo–German agreement.

Lugard's position was difficult. He wanted to bring peace to Uganda and to make both Fransa and Ingleza accept British authority. He had nothing to do with their quarrels and wished to remain neutral. But the Fransa would not accept him as neutral; they expected him to take the Ingleza side. The Ingleza too expected that, as an Englishman, Lugard would be bound to help them against the Fransa in their struggle for power and influence. The Kabaka was frightened of Lugard, for he thought that Lugard had come to punish him for the murder of Bishop Hannington.

After a week of discussion with Fransa and Ingleza chiefs and with the French and British missionaries, Lugard offered the Kabaka a treaty. The Kabaka, it said, would place Buganda under the protection of the IBEA Company, and accept the Company's authority. There must be freedom of religion, and freedom of trade. The slave trade must be stopped, and the trade in arms controlled by the Company; no liquor would be sold. A British Resident would be stationed in Kampala to advise the Kabaka and to look after any Europeans who might be stationed there. The Company would do all it could to improve communications with the coast, and to develop trade.

The Kabaka of course wished to sign no more treaties. The Ingleza chiefs naturally pressed him to sign. Luckily for Lugard, the Fransa chiefs also advised him to sign. Some of them had come to like and trust Lugard; all of them agreed that if Uganda was to become British, they had better make the best terms they could. The Kabaka could always accept the treaty with the proviso that it would be invalid if he found out afterwards that the Anglo–German agreement was not a fact, and that Germany was still interested in Uganda. On this understanding, the Kabaka reluctantly signed.

At the end of January 1891 Lugard received reinforcements: Captain Williams arrived from the coast with 75 more troops, and soon after the two envoys returned to confirm the news of the Anglo–German agreement. But Lugard's position was still weak. In spite of all he could do to win them over, the French missionaries and some of the Fransa chiefs persisted in regarding him as the ally of their enemies the Ingleza. Civil war was still possible, and the Muslim army was still on the Bunyoro frontier awaiting its opportunity.

In this difficulty, Lugard did what many kings and commanders have done: he called on the Fransa and Ingleza to forget their quarrels and unite against a common enemy, the Muslims and the Banyoro. A large army was gathered, with the Ingleza *katikiro* (chief minister) Apolo Kagwa in command. In May 1891, Lugard's troops and the Buganda army defeated the Muslims; but the katikiro's army then returned home in triumph, without dealing with the Banyoro. Lugard then took another risk, and went on to deal with the Banyoro himself. He felt sure there would be more trouble as long as Kabarega of Bunyoro remained undefeated; but how could he defeat him without the help of the Baganda? There was one chance. Somewhere up near Lake Albert there was a force of Sudanese troops under a Sudanese officer, Selim Bey. They had been part of Emin Pasha's army, and when Emin returned to Germany, they had stayed where they were. If Lugard could persuade Selim and his men to enter the Company's service, his position would be far stronger. But he must hurry; for Emin Pasha was now back in German service; he was anxious to find his old troops, and was supposed to be marching northward from Bukoba.

Lugard sent Williams back to hold the fort at Kampala and keep the flag flying there, while he himself with part of the troops went off to explore the west and find Selim Bey. He went to Buddu, Ankole and Toro. At Toro he found that the young chief Kasagama had been driven off his throne by Kabarega, and Lugard restored him. Both in Toro and Ankole he made agreements by which they accepted the Company's protection. Lugard marched on to Bunyoro and defeated Kabarega; on the shore of Lake Albert he found Selim Bey and invited him to enter the British service.

Lugard formed a great admiration for Selim Bey. For ten years, he and his men had been quite cut off from their homes in the Sudan by the Mahdi, and they had received neither news nor pay. Yet they had kept their military discipline; and when Selim heard Lugard's invitation, he replied that he was an officer in the service of the Khedive of Egypt, and he could not leave the Khedive's service and enter the British service unless the Khedive gave him permission. He was willing to march south with Lugard provided Lugard obtained this permission, and this Lugard promised to do. Selim had about 600 troops and about 9,000 camp-followers, women and children and non-combatants. Lugard brought them all down into Uganda, building a chain of forts and leaving some of the men to garrison them. At the end of 1891 he arrived back in Kampala. He had occupied all the west of Uganda up to the watershed between the Congo and the Nile; he had cleared the Banyoro troops out of Toro; he had built and garrisoned seven forts and had added Selim Bey's troops to the Company's forces. All this he had done almost without cost to the Company, for he had used very little of his precious ammunition, and had brought down enough ivory to pay the whole cost of his 700-mile march.

In Kampala he received bad news. Williams reported that the Fransa and Ingleza were quarrelling again. Worse than that: there were letters for Lugard from the Company, saying that it could spend no more money on Uganda affairs. He was to leave Uganda and return to the coast, leaving an officer behind him to represent the Company. The Company would reoccupy Uganda when it could afford to do so.

Lugard was in despair. If he left Uganda now, all his work would be thrown away. Everyone would think that he had given up his task. Fighting would break out again, Kabarega would reoccupy Toro, all the agreements would be abandoned, and the Belgians and the Germans might move in from the south and west. If the Company ever did decide to reoccupy Uganda, it would find the task much harder than before. Luckily, fresh orders reached him on January 7, 1892: the Company had raised enough money to enable it to stay in Uganda one year more, so his orders to return to the coast were cancelled.

Towards the end of January the expected civil war between the Fransa and the Ingleza broke out, and the Fransa were soon winning. Lugard had hoped to remain neutral, but this was now impossible. If the Fransa won, they would drive the Ingleza out to the frontiers like the Muslims, and they and the Kabaka would then turn on Lugard and tell him to go. But Lugard's orders were to stay and impose British authority. So he helped the weaker party, the Ingleza, and with his help they were victorious. All that Lugard could then do was to soften the peace terms. He persuaded the victorious Ingleza not to drive out the Fransa altogether, but to allow them to occupy the rich province of Buddu, while the Ingleza took the remaining five-sevenths of Buganda. The Kabaka had fled into German territory, but Lugard persuaded him to return to Kampala. As his final stroke, Lugard was able to arrange for the Muslim Baganda to leave their threatening position on the Bunyoro border and to settle in three districts of Buganda. This settlement was confirmed by a fresh treaty or agreement in April 1892.

No one knew better than Lugard how insecure these arrangements were. Everything depended on his personality and on the few hundred troops he commanded. Everywhere there was uncertainty, which could be finally removed only if the British government declared a protectorate over the country. In June 1892 Lugard left Uganda and went to England to urge the government to declare a protectorate. He found himself again in trouble. The French missionaries had sent home bitter complaints about his behaviour, and especially about his supporting the Ingleza in the civil war. Some of the British missionaries too complained, because Lugard should, they thought, have been their ally from the beginning; they could not understand why he tried so long to be neutral. Lugard had to defend himself against these attacks. He had also to persuade the British people and the government that they must not leave Uganda to an indefinite continuance of civil war, but must make it British and must enforce peace. Lugard's efforts in this direction were helped from a surprising source. The Kabaka himself wrote, both to the Company and to Queen Victoria, saying that after all that had happened the best thing for Uganda was that the British government should make it a British protectorate, and should send Lugard back to become its governor; and this was what he and his chiefs wished.

The British protectorate

Even this did not convince the British government. As an intermediate step, it decided to finance the Company's occupation of Uganda for a few weeks more, and meanwhile to send out an officer to study the position and make an independent report.

It sent the consul-general in Zanzibar, Sir Gerald Portal. He arrived at Kampala in March 1893, and on April 1 he hoisted the British flag to replace that of the IBEA Company. Thus, for the moment at least, all the eastern part of Uganda became British: Buganda, Ankole, Toro, Busoga and everything east of Busoga. The eastern boundary of Uganda in those days was the Kedong river near Naivasha in what is now Kenya. Portal was in favour of keeping Uganda, and of building the railway which Mackinnon had so long been asking for. But he recommended that Uganda should be administered by a commissioner responsible to the consul-general at Zanzibar, an arrangement which would hardly be workable.

Portal did some useful work while he was in Uganda: he made a new agreement which gave the defeated Fransa some additional territory, and which gave the British government some control over Buganda's finances.

Lugard never returned to Uganda. When Portal left, he was replaced as British commissioner by Colonel Colvile. Colvile decided to show the British flag in the west of the country to make sure that there was no danger of a Belgian or German occupation there. His Baganda advisers told him that he could hope for no cooperation from Kabarega, and this confirmed what he had heard about Kabarega in Britain as a result of Baker's reports. Colvile decided to make an end of Kabarega and the Muslim danger, and in December 1893 an army of Baganda and Sudanese occupied Hoima. Kabarega himself escaped, but the Baganda overran his country, and much of eastern and south-eastern Bunyoro was annexed and became part of Buganda. This area included Mubende, the burial-place of the kings of Bunyoro. The Banyoro could never agree to give up this sacred soil, and always looked for the day when they might be able to recover it. But their defeat was decisive, and a British officer was left in charge of Bunyoro, though Kabarega kept up guerrilla warfare until November 1894, when he was at last driven across the Nile.

While Colvile was busy in Bunyoro, the government in London made up its mind to accept Portal's advice. On August 27, 1894 Colvile proclaimed a British protectorate over Buganda, though over Buganda alone. It was left to the succeeding government under Lord Salisbury to extend the protectorate over Bunyoro, Toro, Ankole and Busoga; this was done in July 1896.

The end of the IBEA Company

The IBEA Company had never wanted to interfere in Uganda. It had gone there only because the government asked—almost ordered—it to do so. It had spent large sums of money on its Uganda expeditions and had received very little financial help, or even thanks. By 1893 the Company was ruined. Its capital had never been sufficient for its enormous responsibilities, and by refusing to sell liquor and firearms it had denied itself revenue. If it had been allowed to leave Uganda alone and to develop trade in what is now Kenya, the Company might in time have paid its way. But the expense of administering Uganda broke it; and it only remained to ask the government what compensation it would pay the Company for surrendering its charter and handing over its work. The government was ungenerous. It paid the Company £250,000, but only one-fifth of the sum came from the pocket of the British taxpayer. The remaining £200,000 was money belonging to the Sultan of Zanzibar, which was lying in a British bank, and which the government persuaded him to invest at three per cent. The shareholders in the Company, who had received no dividend on their investment, lost half their capital; they were repaid at ten shillings in the pound.

The Uganda railway

Now that Uganda was under British administration, the railway had to be built, and built quickly. Africans would not come in large numbers to work for long periods, so thousands of Indian labourers were brought over under contract, and then skilled railway staff from India came to get the line working. The Indian government supervised the contracts, and insisted that at the end of his contract a man should have the choice of being sent home all the way to his village at the British government's expense, or of being allowed to stay and make his home in Africa. Most of them went home, but the news spread in India of a land of good opportunity in East Africa. Indian traders were already well established on the coast; many of them were rich, and for many years they had provided the capital to finance Arab expeditions into the interior.

Others came from India to join them; as soon as the line of communications was open, they moved inland and settled, and they played a great part in developing trade in Kenya and Uganda.

Construction began in 1895. The workers suffered great hardship. There was much malaria and smallpox, and 2,500 Indian workers died. They worked barefoot, and suffered much from jiggers. Some of the work already done was washed away by the torrential rain; after the rain came drought, and the engineers had difficulty in obtaining food for their workmen. Near Tsavo the work was held up by man-eating lions; when the line reached Nandi country it was again held up by the Nandi warriors, who hated having the strangers in their country and often raided the line, killing the workers and carrying off telephone wire and other supplies. There were great engineering difficulties in building the line over the steep slopes of the Rift Valley and the Mau summit. In 1896 the line reached Voi, and in June 1899 it reached a stream which was well known to the Masai as a good drinking-place for their cattle; they called it Cold-Water, Nairobi. Here the engineers began the most difficult part of their work, and here they collected large quantities of stores, so that Nairobi came to be a convenient place for the railway offices and administrative headquarters, and quickly grew into a little town of corrugated-iron sheds and offices and houses. In 1902 the line was opened to Kisumu, and there for many years it ended; from Kisumu to near Kampala the journey was made by ship. The cost of the line was paid by the British government. As so often happens, the final cost was much bigger than the original estimate; it totalled nearly eight million pounds, a very large sum in those days. Not only had the line been expensive to build, it was still expensive to run, for there was very little paying traffic. For many years the British government hoped that the governments in East Africa would be able to repay the cost of the line out of their profits, but in the end it gave up this hope.

British administration

In 1895, Ernest Berkeley was appointed commissioner for Uganda, and George Wilson sub-commissioner for the kingdom of Buganda. Buganda was still in the condition which had resulted from the Ingleza victory over the Fransa. The Ingleza held most of the important chiefships, and their leader Apolo Kagwa (who had commanded the army against Bunyoro in 1891) held the traditional place of katikiro or chief minister. But under Portal's agreement, the Fransa too held many chiefships, so many that a second post of katikiro was created for their leader Stanislas Mugwanya. One important chief was a Muslim. All three parties had fully accepted the Portal settlement.

The general lines of the British administration in Buganda were laid down by George Wilson. The Kabaka had always held councils of his chiefs. Wilson organized these somewhat informal meetings into a regular council or Lukiko, which had a fixed membership and met at fixed times with Wilson in attendance. He also helped the Kabaka to organize the administration of justice into a regular system of higher and lower courts. Wilson and his successors advised the Kabaka and his chiefs on what they felt to be the general principles of wise government, but left them free in matters of detail. In those days the system worked well, because the British officers and the chiefs knew one another so well and because the work of government was so simple. There were no problems of education, agriculture, European settlers, housing, or employment; these were matters which did not yet concern the government of the Protectorate.

Indirect rule

This method of governing a country through its traditional chiefs and their councils (the native authorities, as the British called them) is the British system of indirect rule. It was strongly advocated by Lugard, who found it useful when he had conquered Northern Nigeria and had to administer the country with only a handful of British district officers. The system had the great advantage that it was cheap. The native authority could administer a district more cheaply than the British officer could, and if much of the routine of administration could be left to the native authorities, the government could run the country with fewer district officers.

But Lugard advocated indirect rule on other grounds. He said that people would rather take orders from their traditional rulers than from foreign administrative officers, and so the British ought never to give direct orders if they could help it. If a new road were needed in a German colony, the German district officer would summon the akida and give the necessary orders, and in due course the jumbe would make the villagers do the work. But a British district officer, on the Lugard principle, would call on the chief and his elders and try to persuade them that the road would be useful; and unless he succeeded in persuading them, the road would not be built.

There was seldom any difficulty over roads; anyone could see that roads brought trade, and trade brought money. In other matters the native authorities were not so easily persuaded; in Kenya for example there was the supply of labour for European farms, in West Africa the setting aside of land for forest reserves. This brings us to the other side of indirect rule. Not only, said Lugard, must the British work through the native authorities, but they must educate the native authorities in new ideas, so that they could take on greater responsibilities. The

British hoped to see the native authorities collecting their own taxes and running their own schools, hospitals, power stations, water supplies, and so on; and they hoped in time to see the native authorities coming together in regional councils, and perhaps in a national parliament.

In Lugard's eyes, both these aspects of indirect rule were important. But such rule would work well only if there existed strong native authorities accustomed to giving orders to their people, and if those authorities were ready to learn new ideas and take on greater responsibilities. In many places, there were no strong native authorities, but only groups of clan elders; and nearly everywhere, the young educated men who could understand the new ideas came to work for the colonial government instead of working for the native authority. Consequently, indirect rule on the whole did not work out as Lugard hoped.

The Uganda–Usoga agreement

When the British protectorate was extended to Bunyoro, Ankole, Toro and Busoga in 1896, the Kabaka of Buganda promptly claimed that all these four countries were subject to him. Wilson investigated the Kabaka's claim. Bunyoro in early days had indeed been the dominant power and had held parts of modern Buganda, Ankole, and Toro; but in the nineteenth century Buganda had reversed this position. She was certainly at that time the dominant power; she had greatly expanded her territory, and was in the habit of raiding Ankole and Toro and parts of Busoga. Perhaps if the Arabs and the Europeans had not arrived, Buganda might have conquered these kingdoms; but she had not yet done so. Wilson decided that Busoga had sometimes paid tribute to Buganda, but Ankole and Toro had never done so, much less Buganda's powerful rival Bunyoro. Busoga consisted of about fifteen independent chiefdoms, but the British officer in Busoga persuaded the Busoga chiefs to settle their quarrels. In December 1895, Berkeley brought about an agreement (the Uganda–Usoga agreement) between himself, the Kabaka, and the Busoga chiefs. By this agreement the Kabaka handed over to the British all the authority he had claimed over Busoga, and the Busoga chiefs agreed to pay the Kabaka a regular tribute.

The crisis of 1897

Berkeley would have liked to simplify his administrative pattern by incorporating all Bunyoro, Ankole and Toro in Buganda, making their three rulers into provincial governors subject to the Kabaka. But the scheme had to be abandoned because of a dangerous crisis which arose in 1897. In any case, it would probably have led to serious trouble.

In July, Kabaka Mwanga suddenly rose up against British rule. He fled again to Buddu; his own people, Fransa, Ingleza and Muslim, all rose against him and defeated him; he escaped into German territory, and the Baganda chose his infant son Daudi Chwa to be Kabaka in his place. A regency was set up, consisting of the two katikiros Kagwa and Mugwanya, and a third chief named Kisingiri. This was hardly the moment to run the risk of making the three other kingdoms into provinces of Buganda.

In September, some of the Sudanese troops mutinied and killed three of their British officers. The danger was great, and the British commissioner called on the Baganda for help. A Baganda force defeated the mutineers, and Apolo Kagwa saw his chance of demanding a price. He had noticed that British officials were tending to treat Buganda as a subject state. It was now plain that the British needed Buganda just as much as Buganda needed the British; and Kagwa began to insist that the Kabaka's government should be treated with deference as an ally. He might not be able to claim, as Mwanga had done, that Buganda was supreme over the other kingdoms, but at least he could claim that she was more important than they. Here we see the beginning of Buganda's special position in the protectorate.

Next year, Mwanga left German territory and took refuge with his old enemy Kabarega of Bunyoro. The two of them raised some men and caused trouble by raiding in the protectorate. But in April 1899 both were captured and deported, first to the coast, and later to the Seychelles.

All these military affairs were costly. The grant which the protectorate government received from the British Treasury was £50,000 a year until 1897; by 1899 it had jumped to nearly eight times that sum. The Treasury was horrified, the British Press was very critical; something had to be done. The government in London decided to send out a special commissioner to reform the administration of Uganda and make the protectorate able to pay its way. The man it chose was Sir Harry Johnston.

Semei Kakunguru and the north-east

Before we consider Johnston's work, we must turn aside for a moment to look at what was happening north and east of Buganda. The successful Muganda general Semei Kakunguru had distinguished himself in the campaign against Bunyoro in 1893, and again in 1898. He had been given one of the districts of Bunyoro as his share of the spoil, and he settled down to organize it in his own way. Then he advanced north of Lake Kioga into Teso country and turned east into Bugisu and Bukedi. Like Lugard, he built forts as he advanced, and garrisoned them with

Baganda troops; he linked his forts by a system of roads. In three years he conquered ten thousand square miles, and he appointed his Baganda officers as chiefs, responsible to him for the administration of their districts. For some years the British left him alone; they were busy elsewhere, and he was doing their work for them at no cost to the Treasury. But in the end, an unfortunate misunderstanding arose: Kakunguru regarded himself as an independent ruler; the British

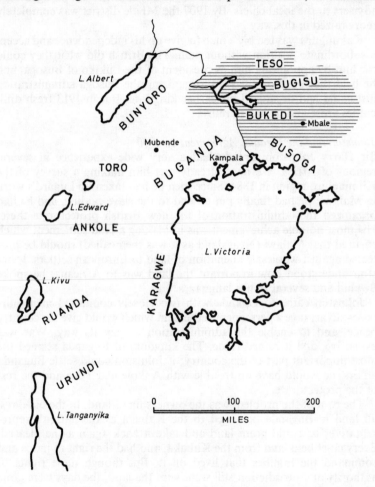

BUGANDA AND HER NEIGHBOURS

Area shaded was organized by Semei Kakunguru

regarded him as merely their agent. In 1903 the British occupied his headquarters at Mbale, and they took over his administration almost intact. They made one modification. They did not like having Baganda chiefs ruling over Teso or Bagisu subjects; they thought it would be better for the Teso or the Bagisu to develop chiefs of their own. They encouraged this development, and gradually brought Kakunguru's Baganda officers to look on themselves not as chiefs but as 'agents' or advisers to the local chiefs. By 1907 the Mbale district was completely reorganized in this way.

Kakunguru was too big a man to give up his independence and accept a subordinate position without pain. The British did what they could for him by appointing him as president of the Lukiko of Busoga, and he held that position till 1913, organizing the Busoga administration just as he had organized his earlier kingdom. But in 1913 fresh difficulties arose and he had to retire.

Johnston and the Uganda Agreement of 1900

Sir Harry Johnston already had a very wide experience in several regions of Africa. We have already met him making a survey of the Kilimanjaro region in 1884. Since then he had taken up Lugard's work in Malawi; he had finally put an end to the slave raiding, and he had organized the administration of the new British protectorate there. His most notable achievement was in making a land settlement which ensured that Malawi (Nyasaland as it was then called) should be protected against wholesale alienation of land to European settlers. Johnston understood how important the land was to Africans; he spoke Swahili and several Bantu languages.

Johnston came to Uganda with two closely connected main purposes: to arrange a permanent settlement which would give the country peace, and to enable the administration to pay its way. War was expensive, and it ruined trade. The kingdom of Buganda seemed the most important part of the country; if Johnston could settle Buganda affairs, he would have no trouble with Ankole and Toro and the rest of the protectorate.

The root of the problem was the ownership of land. In the old days, all land in Buganda belonged to the Kabaka as the nation's representative; he could grant land and take it back again as he pleased. Every chief held land from the Kabaka, and had the right to judge and command the families that lived on it. But though these rights of authority and jurisdiction still went with the land, the days were gone when the Kabaka could grant land at his pleasure. The bitter rivalry between the Fransa and Ingleza had come to mean that if the chief of this county was a Fransa, then to keep the balance, the chief of that county must be an Ingleza. The long civil wars had led to great confusion. The Fransa, the Ingleza and the Muslims had all in turn been defeated, driven from their lands, and later resettled. There were now Fransa districts, Ingleza districts, and Muslim districts. The country was full of jealousy; there would be no real peace in Buganda until the land question had been fairly settled.

Luckily, Uganda was not thickly peopled, and there was plenty of unoccupied land. Johnston's first idea was to give every occupier a freehold tenure: that is, to make the land his personal property which he could sell or lease at his pleasure. The chiefs objected to this because they feared it would deprive them of their rights of jurisdiction. Then Johnston proposed to limit freehold tenure to the senior chiefs, and to make all other occupiers hold their land as tenants of a Buganda government board of trustees. This too was unwelcome. Then Johnston suggested a compromise, which was accepted by everybody. The Kabaka, his ministers, the members of the royal family and the senior chiefs were given fixed estates in freehold. In addition to this, 8,000 square miles of land were set aside to be allotted to other chiefs and landowners in freehold, and Johnston left it to the Lukiko to make the allotment. These freehold estates together took up rather less than half the country. The rest, some 10,500 square miles, was declared Crown land and was placed under the control of the protectorate government. Crown land which was unoccupied would be available for granting to African farmers as the population grew. (It would also be available for granting to European settlers, though Johnston had no such idea at the time, and no one was yet thinking of European settlement in Uganda.) The blocks of freehold land were measured in square miles, and the Baganda took the English world *mile* into their language in the form *mailo*, so that this freehold land became known as mailo land.

This land settlement was an important part of the agreement which Johnston made, on behalf of the British government, with the government of Buganda: that is, with the three regents and the Lukiko. All owners of mailo land were sure to want the agreement to be maintained, for their estates depended on it. In a few years, mailo land had been so much bought and sold that it would have been impossible to change the system without causing widespread hardship.

Johnston then turned to the question of the organization of the kingdom of Buganda. The agreement declared that Buganda was to be one province of the protectorate; that is to say, the British were not to split it up for their own administrative convenience. (This article was to cause difficulty later on, when Buganda was afraid of being outvoted in the legislative council by other provinces.) His Highness the Kabaka (this was to be his official title) was to continue to govern Buganda directly. He would be assisted by three ministers (the katikiro, the chief justice, and the treasurer) and by the Lukiko. The composition of the Lukiko was fixed at 89 members, all appointed by the Kabaka: the county chief and three members from each of the twenty *sazas* or counties, six picked from Buganda as a whole, plus the three ministers. The Kabaka was not bound to follow the Lukiko's advice, but he was bound to follow any advice given him by the protectorate government. One article of the agreement declared that the Kabaka and his chiefs and people would cooperate with the protectorate government and obey its laws. Another article declared that if the Buganda government went against the policy of the protectorate government, the agreement would become void. These two articles became important in political discussions more than fifty years later.

There was no difficulty in reaching agreement over finance. The Buganda government agreed to collect taxes on houses and guns and pay the proceeds to the protectorate government. No fresh taxation was to be imposed on Buganda without the consent of the Buganda government. The Kabaka and his ministers and senior chiefs were to be paid salaries at rates fixed by the agreement.

One article, which was much more important than Johnston and the British government perhaps realized, fixed the frontiers of Buganda. Mubende and the six counties which had been taken from Bunyoro in 1894 were declared to be part of Buganda, and the Bunyoro grievance thus became perpetual.

Having thus made a settlement of the affairs of Buganda, Johnston moved on to make agreements with Toro and Ankole: Toro in June 1900 and Ankole in August 1901. These agreements were similar to the Buganda agreement, but with one great difference: there was no large distribution of mailo land. Johnston had no love for freehold land in principle. He introduced it in Buganda only because the traditional system of land-holding had been so broken up by long years of civil war. In Toro and Ankole the traditional system had been very little disturbed, and Johnston was content to leave it alone.

From 1900 onwards, this agreement which Johnston made with Buganda—the British always called it the Uganda Agreement—controlled the affairs of the protectorate. The agreement gave Buganda what Apolo Kagwa had desired. Buganda was very largely self-governing in internal affairs, and the British treated Buganda as very much the senior of the four kingdoms. This was merely a recognition of the facts of 1900: Buganda, though terribly torn by civil war, was nevertheless the strongest and most developed province of the protectorate. There might some day be trouble if other provinces drew level with

Buganda and began to question her privileged position. But if Johnston had foreseen this and tried to deny Buganda this position, he would never have secured his agreement.

On the other hand, the agreement did not restore the Kabaka to his old standing. He was no longer supreme. He was bound to receive, even if he did not follow, the advice of his ministers and the Lukiko, and he had altogether lost his control over land. The fact that for many years to come the Kabaka was a child, and the power was in the hands of the regents, still further strengthened his ministers and senior chiefs at his expense.

The agreement had one weakness which in 1900 was inevitable, and showed itself only long afterwards. It concentrated political power in the hands of the senior chiefs and did not contemplate strengthening the government by bringing in young educated men. Such an idea was unheard-of in 1900, especially as secondary education was only just beginning.

The three agreements have caused much difficulty in recent years; but at the time they were a great achievement. They were genuine agreements, reached after long discussion and generally accepted; now at last the protectorate could settle down to peaceful development. Still, the agreements did not cover the whole country. Bunyoro had no agreement, and did not want one. Semei Kakunguru's work had brought Busoga, Bugisu and Bukedi into line with the Buganda type of administration; but the north was still untouched. It was only very gradually, from about 1909 onwards, that British administration was introduced there. It was a matter of building roads, stopping the fighting and cattle-raiding, and helping the clan heads or other natural rulers to take on new responsibilities. Much of this work was carried on by Baganda 'agents', whom the British appointed, as Kakunguru had done, to introduce and explain modern ways. The British always looked forward to the time when the 'agent' would no longer be needed and local government in the north could be carried on through councils of chiefs. But this process was still very far from complete in 1914.

Frontier changes

One step which the British took in 1902 merely as a matter of administrative convenience turned out to be very important. The eastern frontier of Uganda then was at the Kedong river near Naivasha. By 1902 the railway had reached Kisumu, and for the moment there was no talk of taking it further. The British thought it would be convenient to have the whole length of the railway in one territory, so that its accounts and business affairs could be handled by one government instead of two. So they detached the eastern part of Uganda and took it into what is now Kenya. This took from Uganda all the high ground from Nakuru westwards, including such places as Kericho and Eldoret, the land which afterwards formed part of Kenya's 'White Highlands'. After this change, nearly the whole of Uganda was below the 4,500-foot level, and European settlers much preferred the Highlands of Kenya. This is why Kenya's European problem was always much more serious than Uganda's.

Other frontier adjustments were made later. In 1911 and 1912 Britain and Belgium exchanged some territory. Belgium ceded to Britain the land which is now the West Nile province of Uganda; in exchange, Britain ceded to Belgium some land in the Sudan and also some land

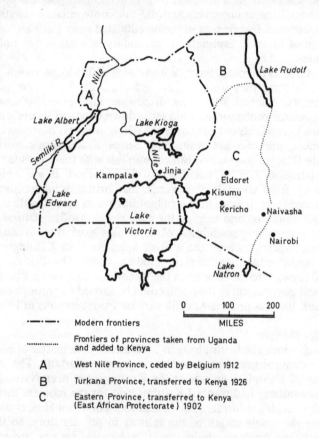

- - - · - - · Modern frontiers

··············· Frontiers of provinces taken from Uganda and added to Kenya

A   West Nile Province, ceded by Belgium 1912

B   Turkana Province, transferred to Kenya 1926

C   Eastern Province, transferred to Kenya (East African Protectorate) 1902

THE FRONTIERS OF UGANDA

on the western borders of Toro and Ankole. In 1926, the Turkana region near Lake Rudolf was transferred to Kenya.

The British at first governed Uganda through a commissioner, who was responsible to the Foreign Office, the department of the British government which deals with independent foreign countries. In 1907 the control of Uganda was transferred to the Colonial Office, which was the department of the government dealing with the affairs of British colonies and protectorates. Up to 1907, the British government was thinking of Uganda as a foreign country which had made a treaty with Britain; after 1907 it thought of it as a country no longer independent, but under British control. When the Colonial Office took over the administration of the country, the commissioner became a governor. This transfer of control from the Foreign Office to the Colonial Office was called in question by the Kabaka some fifty years later.

We shall discuss the early economic development of Uganda in Chapter 7.

THE BRITISH BEGINNINGS IN KENYA

Britain was slow to assume responsibility even for Uganda, which was an attractive country for many reasons: it was a centre of British missionary work, it produced a good deal of ivory, and above all, it controlled the source of the Nile. Britain was slower still to take control of Kenya, which had none of these attractions. Kenya was thinly peopled, it contained no powerful and well-organized states like Buganda, and there was much desert and tsetse-fly country. Except for the coastal strip, Kenya was a country which the IBEA Company did not want, but it had to hold Kenya because it was the approach route to Uganda, for which the government had made the Company responsible.

Even the coastal strip had its problems. Sultan Simba at Witu was now under British authority, but he was a difficult man and the Company would have preferred to leave him alone. However, there was some trouble at Witu in which some German traders were killed, and Germany called on Britain to punish Simba. The navy attacked Simba, burned his town and deposed him; and Witu was handed over to the Company's administration. It was an unwelcome gift, because the place was full of undesirables, men who had found themselves in trouble with the Sultan of Zanzibar and had taken refuge with Simba. In 1893 the Company even begged the British government to let it abandon Witu, but of course the request was refused. At some other places too the Company had difficulty in establishing its authority.

The Company did good work in the coastal strip in developing a rubber industry, and was very successful in freeing slaves and then helping them to establish themselves. But the Company's commercial prospects were severely damaged in 1892 when the British government included all British East Africa in the free trade zone established by the Berlin Act of 1885. With all its heavy expenses in administering Uganda, the Company now had to compete for its trade against other firms, both British and foreign, who had no administrative expenses whatever.

Opening up the interior
Its work inland brought the Company heavy expense and no corresponding reward. It began the building of a chain of fortified trading stations to protect the route to Uganda. This work was begun by Lugard, who built forts at Machakos in 1889 and at Dagoretti in 1890. Another was built after Lugard's day at Mumia's in 1894. When Lugard left Dagoreti to go to Uganda, his colleague George Wilson took command of the fort with a garrison of thirty riflemen. Both Lugard and Wilson were impressed with their Kikuyu neighbours, and for a time relations between the Kikuyu and the garrison were most friendly. But this did not last long. Wilson was unable to stop passing caravans from raiding the Kikuyu crops for their food supplies, and the local Kikuyu naturally resented this. In the end, things became so bad that they turned on the fort, and Wilson and his men were besieged; they cut their way out and retreated to Machakos, while the Kikuyu destroyed the empty fort. It was rebuilt in 1891, but in 1893 the Kikuyu again attacked it. This time it was relieved by John Ainsworth, who commanded the Company's fort at Machakos.

After the end of the IBEA Company, other forts were built: Fort Hall in 1900, Nyeri in 1902, and Embu, Meru and others from 1906 onwards. But until 1914, much of modern Kenya was still almost beyond the reach of the British administration.

Ainsworth was one of the Company's most successful officers. He got on well with the Kamba around Machakos, and organized a successful system of buying provisions for passing caravans, so that they had no need to make themselves a nuisance as they did at Dagoreti. He reported that his district would be suitable for many subtropical crops; all it needed was skilled men to grow them and a railway to carry them.

While it was so empty of people, East Africa could not produce much trade. The immediate result of setting the slaves free in the coastal strip was the same as in other countries: the freed slaves were no longer willing to grow export crops on their masters' estates, but preferred to make their own farms and live by subsistence agriculture. Thus the export of tropical crops went down. The Company's first idea was to invite Indians to settle in the coastal strip and grow cotton, rubber, sugar and other crops. But very few accepted the invitation. In 1894 the Company first allowed land in the highlands to be leased, but even then it was thinking mainly of Indians. No Europeans came to settle in East Africa until the railway line was built.

Thus, except for the coastal strip, Kenya was a land without interest for the Company, but a land which had to be crossed in order to reach Uganda. It would have been awkward if Germany or Italy had chosen to creep in behind Mombasa and annex part of the country on the plea that there was no proper administration there. When Uganda had become a British protectorate, the British government clearly had to take over the country to protect the line of communication with Uganda. The British protectorate was proclaimed on July 1, 1895; the country was named the East Africa Protectorate. The capital was moved from Mombasa to Nairobi in 1907.

The peoples of the protectorate did not want European protection, or European rule. They knew the Europeans as missionaries, explorers and traders; they did not realize that the Europeans were now to become their masters. Some of them made up their minds that it was better to be for the British than against them; others refused to accept British rule and brought out their spears.

Much depended on the Masai. All the early European travellers were impressed with the power of the Masai warriors. The Kamba in their hills and the Kikuyu in their forests were able to hold their ground against the Masai, but out on the open grassy plains the Masai were supreme. In 1890 the Masai *laibon* Mbatian died, and his sons Sendeyo and Lenana fought each other for the succession; for some years this civil war weakened the Masai nation. During the 1890s, the Kamba and the Kikuyu were weakened by smallpox, and both they and the Masai lost large numbers of their cattle from disease. This weakening of the three peoples made the Nandi and the Kipsigis stronger, just when the British were beginning to use the route to Uganda much more. The British knew how strong the Masai were and took care not to provoke them; they went to Uganda through the Kamba and Kikuyu country instead of going through the Masai plains. From 1893 onwards, some Masai sub-tribes who had lost cattle and were in great hardship were helped by the British, so the Masai were friendly. In 1895 there was a battle between the Masai and the Kikuyu, which the Masai won. But there were three Europeans there, a Scot named Andrew Dick and two Frenchmen. They decided to help the Kikuyu, and they took their rifles and attacked the Masai. All three were killed, but they killed 100 Masai warriors before being speared. The British held an inquiry into this incident, and came to the conclusion that the Kikuyu had been to blame for the fight. The new laibon, Lenana, was greatly impressed by this: impressed both by the white men's military power, and also by the British justice. From then on Lenana and his Masai were friendly to the British, who left them alone to live in their old ways.

The Kamba on the whole cooperated with the British; so did some of the Kikuyu. But other Kikuyu clans resisted, and made war against their fellow-Kikuyu who accepted the British. To control the Embu and these hostile Kikuyu clans, forts were built at Embu in 1906, Meru in 1908 and at Chuka in 1913, after three British expeditions had been sent against them.

One great ally of the British was chief Nabongo Mumia, who ruled over one section of the Luyia. In 1894 a post was established at his capital of Elureko, and the British came to call this place Mumia's. From 1894 to 1900 a British officer, C. W. Hobley, gradually extended British authority from Mumia's round the Kavirondo gulf. Mumia helped; his spearmen were always ready to help the British riflemen. There was a good deal of fighting against some sections of the Luo and the Luyia peoples, but it was over by 1900.

The Nandi people did not approve of the Luo and Luyia country coming under British rule, for they were in the habit of raiding it. In 1895 they carried out a raid and killed a British trader. The government sent a force against them, but the Nandi retreated into their hills with some losses, and the expedition was inconclusive. By 1900 the railway construction work was approaching the gulf, and the Nandi frequently raided the working parties; this brought on more British expeditions, without much success. It was not till September 1905 that the British gathered a large force and determined to follow the Nandi wherever they went. This time a senior *orkoiyot*[4] of the Nandi was killed, and the Nandi lost heart; they withdrew into country north of the railway line and gave no more trouble.

There was more fighting in 1908: the most northerly of the Luyia peoples, the Bugusu, were defeated, and when the Gusii killed the British officer who had been stationed at Kisii, they too were punished. But even as late as 1913 and 1914 there were minor incidents in the African resistance to British rule.

This sort of fighting was new to the Africans. Not only were the British rifles and machine-guns all-powerful against the African spears, but the British behaviour was something they had never experienced. There was plenty of fighting and raiding in African life: a strong tribe like the Nandi or the Masai would raid a weaker tribe, and then retire with its booty until it felt the impulse to raid again. The booty consisted mainly of sheep and cattle, so there was no point in raiding the same

---

[4] The Nandi *orkoiyot*, like the Masai *laibon*, was a hereditary prophet.

3   AFRICAN WARRIORS, OLD AND NEW STYLES

Shortly before Kenyan independence, a team of men from the King's
African Rifles visited Britain. They are seen being interviewed by a
broadcaster before leaving Africa. Four of the soldiers are wearing
tribal dress. From left to right they are a Luo, a Samburu, a Kamba,
and a Nandi

people too often; but when their herds had increased again, they must
expect to be raided once more. But when the British had made a
successful expedition and had captured the Nandi cattle, they did not
retire and leave the Nandi alone; they stayed, they built a fort, and
established peace. The British deprived the strong fighting men of their
pleasure, but made things easier for the weak. There was no need now
to surround villages with a strong mud wall, or leave a wide stretch of
ground uncultivated as a no-man's-land. The Kikuyu had left a broad
belt of forest between themselves and the Masai; now the forest was no
longer needed, and they began to cut it down and make their farms there.

The Kenya tribes did not organize a large-scale rising like the Maji-
Maji. They fought for their independence one by one as the British came
to deal with them. But the British found this long-drawn process of
breaking African resistance troublesome and expensive. What were
they to do with this vast empty country, with its long line of railway: a

country which was costing them so much money and trouble, and seemed to have nothing to offer? What hope had the British Treasury of ever receiving any interest on its eight million pounds, much less any repayment of the capital sum?

But there was empty land, which must surely be capable of producing something. There were African tribesmen, who would no longer spend their time in warfare, and could surely be taught to become useful agricultural workers. Why should not the East African Protectorate become as prosperous as Cape Colony in South Africa? Could not European settlers be brought out to see what they could get out of the country? We do not know who first thought of this idea of European settlement. Both Lugard and Johnston thought that parts of East Africa had possibilities as a 'white man's country'. By 1901 the idea was well rooted in the minds of the Foreign Office in London. And so the Kenya land problem arose.

Chapter 4

THE FIRST WORLD WAR

The war of 1914–18 began in Europe, but it is called a world war because, before it was over, most countries in the world were taking part in it. Only twelve countries in the end remained neutral: three in America, two in Asia, two in Africa, and five in Europe. Africa and most of Asia were involved in the war simply because they were ruled by European colonial powers, and their men fought for their colonial rulers.

Before 1914 it was possible to think of East Africa as being only loosely linked with Europe and the outside world. Ever since 1914 it has been plain that life for everyone in East Africa is intimately affected by events outside. For good or ill the whole world is now one, and East Africa is part of it.

In the nineteenth century the six strongest countries of Europe, commonly called the Great Powers, were Britain, France, Germany, Austria-Hungary, Italy and Russia. By 1914 they had grouped themselves into two hostile alliances: Germany, Austria-Hungary and Italy against the other three. In such a tense situation, any small international incident was dangerous. There were such incidents, each bringing a threat of war, in 1905, 1908, and 1911; in 1914 there was a fourth incident, and this time war broke out. Italy, which was bound by treaty to help Germany and Austria-Hungary, did not do so; after hesitating for some months, she joined the war as an ally of Britain and France.

THE WAR IN EAST AFRICA

The causes of the war lay in Europe; and it seemed to many Europeans then, as it seems to us all now, that it would be wrong to expect Africans to fight in a European quarrel. Except in the turbulent south-eastern peninsula of Europe, the Balkans, there had been no fighting in Europe since 1871, and people in Europe were beginning to hope that the days of warfare were ended. During this long period of peace the great spurt had taken place in European travel and missionary work in East Africa. Missionaries and travellers were horrified to see so much fighting there: the fighting brought about by the slave trade, and the constant raiding between villages. The desire to bring peace to Africa had been one of the motives in the partition. British, French, Belgians and Germans felt that they had the same tasks in Africa. Having preached to the Africans that tribal warfare was wrong, how could they possibly call on them to fight in a much bigger war? True, they said, the war would not last long: only a few weeks or a few months. If the war was to be short, all the more reason for leaving Africa in peace. On this, most British and Germans in East Africa were agreed.

But one very important German in East Africa thought differently. This was General von Lettow-Vorbeck, the commander of the German troops in Tanganyika. He knew that the war would be won and lost on the Western Front in Europe, where the French and British armies were facing superior numbers of German troops. He knew also that the British navy would quickly cut off the German colonies from all contact with Germany, so that he could not count on getting any more supplies from home. He argued from this that it would be in Britain's interest to keep East Africa out of the war; if so, as many British men as wished would be able to go home, join the army, and increase the forces fighting against Germany on the Western Front. If, then, it was in Britain's interest to keep the war out of Africa, it must be in Germany's interest to bring the war into Africa. In that case, no men would go from Kenya and Uganda to fight in Europe, and perhaps British troops might even have to be sent from Europe to fight in East Africa. He could not hope with his small forces to conquer Kenya and Uganda, but at all events he could keep the British there very busy.

That was von Lettow-Vorbeck's argument; but he was not the governor. The governor was Dr Schnee, and he believed East Africa should remain at peace. The general tried to convince his governor; and suddenly something happened which brought the governor round to his view. The captains of two British warships cruising in the Indian Ocean had the idea that if the radio stations at Dar-es-Salaam and Tanga were destroyed, communications between the Germans in Tanganyika and their home country would be weakened. On August 8, 1914 they put the radio station at Dar-es-Salaam out of action; on August 17, one of them did the same thing at Tanga. Dr Schnee was furious, and told his general to carry out the proposed scheme.

Lettow-Vorbeck's idea was to make himself as much of a nuisance as he could. He crossed the Kenya border and occupied Taveta, from where he sent out parties of men to damage the railway and cut communications between Mombasa and Nairobi. Now that the war had come, both British and German civilians rushed to join their armies, and both sides called up thousands of Africans to carry supplies for the armies. Both British and German governments had regiments of African troops with European officers; these were thrown at once into the fighting.

The German scheme quickly began to produce the results that Lettow-Vorbeck had wanted. A force of Indian troops, which would otherwise have gone to join the fighting in Europe, was diverted to East Africa. Two attacks were made on the German base at Tanga, the first by sea and the second by land from Mombasa. Both failed, and after the second failure in January 1915 there was little more serious fighting for a year. The Germans were strongly posted in the Kilimanjaro foothills, and unless fresh forces arrived it seemed possible that both sides might spend the rest of the war where they were.

But fresh forces did arrive. In 1916 the South African General Smuts brought a South African army with him to East Africa, and other troops came from Britain and elsewhere. The Germans too received some slight help. In spite of the British navy, one or two ships did get through to the Tanganyika coast with cargoes of arms. And in July 1915 a German warship, the *Königsberg*, was chased by the British into East African waters and was destroyed in the Rufiji delta. This brought the German general a few hundred fresh German fighting men; and the German sailors took out some of their ships' heavy guns and brought them into action on land.

In March 1916 Smuts was ready, and the fighting flared up again. Smuts now had much stronger forces than the German commander, and he set out to drive the Germans out of the Kilimanjaro region and trap them in more open and level country. Again and again Smuts and Lettow-Vorbeck manoeuvred round each other, but the German always managed to slip out of the net. But Smuts's superior numbers gave him the advantage, and after six months' fighting the German army was driven south of Tanganyika's main railway line into the dry tsetse-infested scrub of the south-east. Meanwhile, Belgian troops from the Congo occupied the north-west corner of Tanganyika, the provinces of Ruanda and Urundi; and a small British army from Rhodesia and Nyasaland moved north. This fresh double attack had the effect of closing the whole of western Tanganyika to the German army and shutting it in between Lake Nyasa and the sea.

4   THE WAR IN EAST AFRICA
   British troops are wading through a river in pursuit of General von Lettow-Vorbeck

The German general, however, was not to be caught. He simply moved south into fresh country in Mozambique; this was quite allow-able, because Portugal had joined in the war against Germany, and Portuguese troops were fighting in France. All through the early months of 1918 he was in Mozambique, with the British still hunting him. Then he turned sharply back north along the eastern shore of Lake Nyasa, and slipped into Northern Rhodesia (the modern Zambia); and he and his tiny army were still free and unbeaten on British soil when the end of the war came.

From the general's point of view, he had fought a brilliant and successful war, as the British themselves were ready to admit. He had kept tens of thousands of British, Indian, Belgian and South African

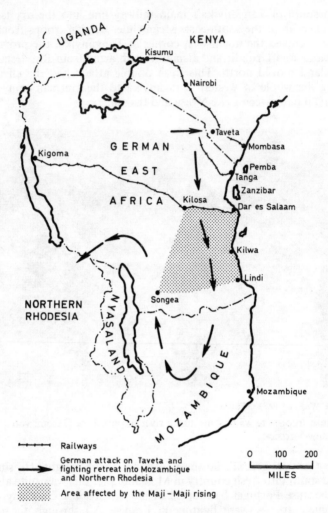

Railways

German attack on Taveta and
fighting retreat into Mozambique
and Northern Rhodesia

Area affected by the Maji–Maji rising

0   100   200

MILES

GERMAN EAST AFRICA – The Maji–Maji rising and the War of 1914–1919

troops hard at work in East Africa at a time when they could otherwise have been in France.

But he had wrecked Tanganyika. Farms and plantations had been left to go back to bush. Railways, roads and buildings had been destroyed. Above all, vast numbers of Africans had been called up to serve either as soldiers or carriers, and many thousands had died in battle or from disease. There was great suffering in the villages; for four years there had been no strong men to work on the farms, and there was famine. In the British territories too things were bad enough. From Kenya alone, 163,000 Africans had served in the war. Here too serving men had died; food production had gone down; village life had suffered. But, except for the damage to the railway at the start of the war, Kenya had not suffered like Tanganyika from being fought over for four years; its roads and railways and buildings were intact. The fighting had not touched Uganda at all, though many men from Uganda had served in the war.

THE RESULTS OF THE WAR

Nobody in Europe had expected the war to last over four years. The loss of life and the economic damage had been far greater than anyone had ever imagined possible. All the wealth that would normally have been circulating in trade and in economic development—such as the building of roads, railways, schools, hospitals, and the development of mining and agriculture—had been used solely for purposes of destruction. When the fighting ceased, the cry in every country was, 'Let us get our men out of uniform and back into civilian life, so that we can begin to repair the damage and get trade moving again.'

The first result of the war for East Africa was that Europe, parts of which had been near famine, set to work to buy African food and raw materials. The prices of coffee, cotton, sisal and everything else shot up, and people in East Africa thought that a time of prosperity was coming. They were wrong; after a few months Europe had satisfied its immediate needs, and prices fell again. East Africa was not alone in this experience; these abrupt price changes were felt all over the world. At the same time, all European manufactured goods were scarce, and so their prices rose and went on rising.

In any case, many producers in East Africa were unable to take advantage of the high prices of 1920. Many European-owned farms had been neglected while their owners and many of the African workers were away in the fighting. When the owners returned, they found that their farms had gone back to bush, and that they had fewer African workers than before. The workers said that they could not live on the wages they had received before the war, for the cost of living had risen so much. The employers said that they could not afford to pay higher wages, for until the farm was again producing crops, they would get no money from sales. This led to a crisis in labour relations, which we discuss in Chapter 5.

The second result of the war was that Germany lost all her colonies. They were not simply added to the colonial empires of the victorious allies. The newly established League of Nations (the forerunner of today's United Nations) thought they should be helped to gain their independence as soon as possible. For this purpose it set up a Mandates Commission (something like the United Nations Trusteeship Council) and entrusted the former German colonies in Africa to Britain, France and Belgium on a mandate. This meant that the administering powers were to report annually to the League on the progress of their work, and the League was empowered to supervise and criticize them. As for Tanganyika, the two provinces of Ruanda and Urundi were placed under Belgian administration, the rest of the country under British.

Tanganyika (except for Ruanda and Urundi) thus became a British mandated territory, and Britain had the responsibility of repairing the war damage and of developing the country towards independence. The British replaced the German system of direct rule by their own system of indirect rule, working through whatever chiefs they were able to discover.

The third result was that East Africa, like many other parts of the world, suffered a monetary crisis, sometimes called a currency crisis. The war had completely upset the world's financial system. Many new states had come into existence and established their own currencies; many took the easy but dangerous way of printing more and more paper money to meet the difficulties of rising prices. The value of money, like that of cotton or coffee, depends on how much of it there is. For international trade, it is essential that states should be able to buy and sell one another's currency. But it may easily happen that a state so mismanages its currency that no other country wants to buy it. It may be a poor country, producing little and finding it hard to import what it needs; and it makes the mistake of printing more paper money to pay for its imports. Or perhaps its workers succeed in their demands for higher wages, but they do not increase their production of goods to correspond with their higher wages. In either case, foreign countries are unwilling to buy that currency, and the country suffers a monetary crisis.

Before 1914, East African currency was the Indian rupee, fifteen rupees being worth a pound. For various reasons unconnected with East Africa, the value of the Indian rupee rose during the war, and by 1918 Indians could buy a British pound with only seven rupees.

If a country's currency rises in value, that country finds it easier to buy goods from abroad; but on the other hand, its own goods become so expensive that people elsewhere find it difficult to buy them. Thus, the country imports more than it exports; in normal times this process goes on until the value of the currency gradually adjusts itself to the old level. But at the end of the war, times were very far from normal. The rise in the value of the rupee had both good results and bad, but for East Africa the bad results far outweighed the good. The good result was that East African produce sold in Britain brought a much bigger return measured in pounds. If a Kenya coffee-grower exported 1,500 rupees worth of coffee to England in 1914, he received £100 for it; if he exported the same 1,500 rupees worth in 1918, he would receive more than £200. This was one reason for the sudden rise in the value of East African exports immediately after the war. Kenya was not in great need of goods from England; what Kenya needed was money. The bad results all followed from this. Most European settlers had borrowed money from the banks to build their houses and stock their farms. They had borrowed the money in rupees, they had to repay it in rupees; and these were becoming dearer. New settlers were coming out from Britain, many of them ex-servicemen who were hoping to establish themselves in East Africa with the money they brought from home. But their English pounds were now worth less than half what they had been; when they changed their English money they received only seven rupees for a pound instead of fifteen. Coffee and cotton and sisal were fetching high prices in Britain; but the trouble was that the East African farms were not yet in working order again, and so were not producing much. The European farmers had to pay their African workers four or five rupees a month; if the men did not get their money, they simply left the farm and went back to their villages. By the time that the farms were getting back into working order, the prices of East African produce were falling again. Coffee fetched £150 a ton early in 1920, but only £60 a ton a year later; sisal fell from £96 a ton to £12.50; flax fell from £500 a ton to £100. In 1922 the coffee crop was ruined by drought, so that many farmers went bankrupt. East Africa derived very little benefit from the high prices that its produce could fetch for a time on the British market.

If the value of the rupee had remained high, things would not have been so bad. There would have been some hardship, but bankers and farmers and businessmen would have adjusted to the new value. The hardship is much more serious when the currency changes its value rapidly. All trade suffers, because no one can quote a fixed price. Those who have goods to sell wish to sell quickly before the price goes down; and if prices are going up, they prefer to wait in the hope of getting a higher price. Similarly, buyers prefer to wait when prices are falling, but they all rush to buy if prices rise. Both in India and East Africa the businessmen, European and Asian, wanted their governments to do something to keep the value of the rupee steady. Unfortunately the governments were far from understanding the reasons why the rupee fluctuated in value, and the remedy they proposed was almost as bad as the disease.

The normal value of the rupee was sixteen pence (240 pence making a pound), and the value rose to 34. The Europeans in East Africa all depended, directly or indirectly, on agriculture for their living. To be able to import goods cheaply from Britain seemed to them less important than to have plenty of rupees in their pockets for local trade and for paying their men's wages. They wanted to get back to the good old days when fifteen rupees went to the pound, and they clamoured for the government to fix the rupee at its pre-war value of sixteen pence. The governor of Kenya went to London to discuss the matter, but he was told there that it was impossible to fix the value of the rupee at sixteen pence when it was standing at 34. The Indian government's financial advisers thought that the value was likely to fall again, but not as low as sixteen pence; they thought it would fall to 24. The Indian government accordingly fixed the value of the rupee at 24 pence, and in April 1920 the Kenya government did likewise. The Europeans in Kenya passed a resolution thanking the governor for trying to get the rupee fixed at sixteen pence, and accepting 24 pence as a reasonable compromise.

The Indian government's financial advisers were wrong; the rupee did not stick at 24 pence; its value on the free market fell right back to the pre-war rate of sixteen. This meant that all debts incurred when the rupee was worth 24 pence were now increased by one-half; for creditors insisted that a rupee was a rupee, and they wanted their money repaid rupee for rupee, whatever the rupee's value might be. East Africa was starved of rupees. In July 1920 the East African governments prohibited the import of Indian rupee notes and coins; but in spite of the prohibition, both Asian and European businessmen continued to smuggle them into the country.

The European settlers in East Africa decided that the only solution was to cut away altogether from the Indian rupee and adopt a new currency based on the pound sterling. The governments in Nairobi and London agreed to this. As a first step, the Kenya government took drastic action. On February 7, 1921 it declared that although rupee coins would still be valid in Kenya, Indian rupee paper notes were no longer legal tender. The government gave no previous warning, and offered no facilities for people to exchange their notes for coin. This was the more scandalous because thousands of Africans who had served in the Tanganyika campaign had been paid in rupee notes. They had been reluctant to accept these pieces of paper, and had been assured that the notes could later be exchanged for coin. These men's earnings were now suddenly declared to be worthless. Only a few days before the decree, government officials had been paying their government labourers in rupee notes. Some of these European officials protested, and said that they could never face their men again if they cheated them in this way. The government agreed to make an exception for these government labourers, and to allow them to exchange their rupee notes for coin. But it would do nothing to help the ex-servicemen and others. In 1922 the government provided a new currency of shillings, based on the pound sterling.

This is a sad story. No doubt some change was necessary, but the change was carried out so clumsily as to cause much suffering. Similar mistakes were made in other countries. The truth is that no governments had previously attempted to fix the value of currency, or had had any experience of dealing with currencies which were jumping unsteadily up and down. It seemed to the financiers that steadiness in the currency was the thing that mattered most. 'Let us fix a figure and stick to it,' they thought; 'whatever figure we choose, there will be some hardship, but there will be less hardship if we can hold the figure steady than if it continues to jump about like this.' Again, we must admit that the European farmers were in terrible difficulty. Their farms were overgrown, they were loaded with debts which they could not repay, and their only hope of surviving was to get their farms producing again. This they could not do without their African labourers, and month after month they had to pay the labourers while the crops were growing and no money was coming in. It is understandable that many of them were almost frantic in their desire to cut their labour costs.

Having said this, we must also say that the government's action in calling in the rupee notes, without offering to exchange them for coin, was quite inexcusable: it amounted to repudiating part of its debt. Inexcusable also was the behaviour of a group of Europeans who openly acted on the assumption that African wage-earners had no right to fair treatment, that only European interests mattered. There were many Europeans who treated their people decently and disapproved of much of what their leaders said and did.

All this misery and uncertainty over prices had a great effect in bringing about the Kikuyu political movement which Harry Thuku led in 1921 and 1922.[1]

These were the three immediate results of the war for East Africa: the transference of Tanganyika from German to British rule; the short-lived boom in prices followed by a sudden fall; and the monetary crisis.

[1] See Chapter 6.

Further results of the war

The war went on producing results for East Africa and the rest of the world long after 1922. When the fighting ceased in 1918, people in Europe hoped that after a year or two they would be able to restore the prosperity which their continent had known before the war. But the war had left behind it so much fear and hatred and selfishness that they failed. There was a handful of wise men who knew, and said clearly, what should be done; but their advice was not heeded.

The victors felt, rightly or wrongly, that Germany had been mainly responsible for the war. France in particular felt that Germany had been responsible for two wars, in 1870 and in 1914, and would start a third war if she were able. France concluded that Germany must be prevented from recovering enough power to make a third war possible. In the first place Germany must be made to repay the cost of the frightful damage she had caused. In the second place she must be kept militarily weak, and in particular must be forbidden to station troops between the river Rhine and the French frontier. Britain at first agreed with France that it would be just to make Germany pay reparations for the damage she had caused. But as time went on, Britain found herself more and more coming to feel that it was impossible to crush a great industrial nation like Germany without destroying the whole system of international trade. French and British policies thus began to diverge.

Britain and France might very well have lost the war without the help of the United States, which was then just emerging as a first-class financial and industrial power. Not only had they bought guns and ships and all kinds of war materials from the United States on credit, but they had also borrowed money. They were faced now with the question of how to repay these huge war debts. Britain and France disagreed over the whole question. Britain said that for the sake of restoring international trade (which was much more important to Britain than to France) the best thing to do would be to forget altogether about war debts and German reparations. But France and the United States would not agree to this; the United States pressed Britain and the other countries to repay the large debts they owed her, and France clung to the hope of somehow making Germany pay for everything.

In the end, what happened was just what Britain feared. The attempt to make these large transfers of wealth finally broke down the system of international trade and finance. Britain and France and other countries were unable to repay their debts to the United States. In October 1929, public confidence in the United States broke. Everyone rushed to sell shares, share prices fell, companies were ruined, banks closed their doors, wealthy men found themselves reduced to poverty. This happened in the richest and strongest country in the world. Two years later, in 1931, there was a crash of confidence in Germany exactly like the one in America. The German currency collapsed in hopeless ruin, and the collapse of Germany brought down Britain and the rest of the world.

For rich manufacturing countries, this meant widespread unemployment; for regions like East Africa, which lived by exporting raw materials, it meant another big drop in prices. People in Europe and America still wanted coffee and cotton and sisal, but they no longer had the money to pay for them. By 1932, prices were even lower than before the war. The East African governments drew most of their revenue from duties on exports and imports, and when trade stopped they lost this revenue. They could not extend education or other social services; they had to cut the salaries of their officials, and even dismiss some of the European officials altogether because they could not pay them.

This terrible time lasted for about four years, from 1931 to about 1935. Then a slight improvement began, but it was not much felt in East Africa. In the United States, President Roosevelt began the new economic policy which he called his New Deal. Italy and Germany had submitted to the rule of dictators, Mussolini and Hitler. Japan began to attack China. Germany, Italy and Japan began to increase their armaments, and so there arose a new demand for manganese, copper, aluminium, rubber and other products needed by the armaments industry. This demand helped countries like the Gold Coast (Ghana), which produced manganese and aluminium, and Northern Rhodesia (Zambia), which produced copper. But the East African countries at that time produced none of these things. The League of Nations tried in vain to halt the slide towards another war; and in 1939 the second world war came.

Between 1929 and 1934 the value of world trade fell to about one third of what it had been. For the entire period between the two world wars, East Africa, like the rest of the world, was struggling to repair the economic damage caused by the 1914 war, and was struggling in vain.

All men wish to be richer, and the economists can give nations useful advice on the policy to follow in order to become richer. The world would be a simpler place to understand if nations followed this advice and concentrated on their economic interests. But very often their fear or hatred of some other nation is stronger than their desire for prosperity, and to gain power or take revenge, they will do things which the economists tell them are unwise. The economic damage of the 1914 war could have been more quickly repaired if the nations had concentrated on getting international trade running smoothly again. But most of them preferred to go for their own political aims, thinking that they could make sure of these first, and then could turn and cooperate with others to secure greater prosperity.

THE ITALIANS IN ETHIOPIA

One of these nations was Italy. In 1914, Italy was a member of the triple alliance of Germany, Austria and Italy, but in 1915 she forsook her allies and entered the war on the side of France and Britain. She did so as the result of a secret treaty, by which France and Britain promised that she should be given all (and in fact, more than all) the Austrian territory still inhabited by Italian-speaking people. This promise was duly fulfilled. But there was another promise in the treaty. If France and Britain were to add to their colonial empires as a result of the war, they would give Italy 'equitable compensation'. Italy took this to mean that she would be given a respectable slice of African territory. But she received nothing except two small strips which Britain gave her.

In 1923, Italy's new leader, Mussolini, decided to make his country feared as a first-class fighting power. During the scramble for Africa, Italy had succeeded in occupying the Ethiopian province of Eritrea and a strip of the Somali coast; but she had hoped to do more, and turn the whole of Ethiopia into an Italian protectorate. This hope vanished when her army was defeated by the Ethiopian army at Adowa in 1896; and it was small consolation to Italy that in 1911 (without any excuse) she had seized the Turkish province of Tripoli between Egypt and Tunisia.

Mussolini built up a large army, navy and air force, and he was determined to wipe out the defeat of Adowa and annex Ethiopia—not because Ethiopia had done Italy any harm, but simply because if Italy was to show the world that she was a first-class power, she needed an African conquest.

As early as 1932, Mussolini had made his decision. Between that date and the outbreak of the fighting in 1935, Italy gave, at various times, the following reasons for her attack on Ethiopia: (a) Italy was a poor country with a large population; Italians could no longer emigrate in large numbers to America because the American government was now restricting immigration; the conquest of Ethiopia would provide land for Italian settlers. (b) Italy had been asking her allies (Britain and France) to give her some colonial territory ever since 1920, but they had given her none.[2] (c) Ethiopia was backward and uncivilized; in particular, the status of slavery still existed there, and the Emperor had very little control over his powerful chiefs. (d) Italy feared that Ethiopia meant to attack her East African colonies.

Nobody really believed that the Emperor Haile Selassie meant to attack Italian East Africa. He had far too much work to do at home to think of making war. Against the other Italian arguments, it was urged that colonial wars of conquest were out of date. But it is understandable that Mussolini was not prepared to listen to Britain and France when they said this. The British had many colonies, and Mussolini did not see why if it was right for the British to colonise Africa yesterday, it was wrong for him today. It was a fair reply; for it was only just over thirty years since Lugard had conquered Northern Nigeria, and much less than that since the Nandi had been conquered in Kenya. If it was right for Britain to send settlers to Kenya or Rhodesia, would it not be right for Italy to send settlers to Ethiopia? However true it was that colonial wars were out of date, the argument did not come well from Britain or France.

There were stronger arguments against the Italian case. The Emperor Haile Selassie had been on his throne only five years. In that time he had made a good deal of progress in modernizing his country, and it was only reasonable that he should be given time to continue his work. Further, in 1906 Italy had signed a treaty with France and Britain, by which all three countries agreed not to encroach in any way upon Ethiopia's independence. Lastly, Ethiopia, like Italy, was a member of the League of Nations, to which she had been admitted in September 1923 with Italy's support. Every member of the League was bound not to make war on a fellow-member.

The Emperor's attitude was correctness itself. He admitted that from time to time there were quarrels between his people and those of the neighbouring Italian colonies over grazing rights and the use of water-holes. The frontiers had not been properly surveyed, and it was not always easy to say whether cattle were on Ethiopian territory or Italian. But if Italy had a grievance, he was prepared to have the case settled by the League.

Mussolini did not want a legal decision, he wanted a war and a conquest. In December 1934 there was a quarrel over a water-hole, and next month, Ethiopia asked the League to settle the matter. The League

[2] Except for two gifts from Britain. In 1920, Britain gave a strip of Kenya known as Jubaland to be added to Italian Somaliland. The frontier was moved back from the river Juba to a new line about 100 miles west. Italy thus gained the port of Kismayu. Britain similarly adjusted the frontiers of Egypt and the Sudan, so that the Italian colony of Libya gained some desert territory and the oasis of Kufra.

declined; it asked Italy and Ethiopia to settle their quarrel together. Mussolini began pouring troops into his Italian colonies, and in March, April, and again in May 1935 the Emperor begged the League to intervene. In May, the Council of the League appointed a committee of six to investigate the affair, and it resolved that if the committee could not settle it by the end of August, the Council itself would take it up.

This decision did at last produce some action. In June, Britain put forward a plan by which Ethiopia should make some concessions to Italy, and in return, Britain would give Ethiopia the port of Zeila in British Somaliland and a corridor down to the sea. The offer was not a good one from Ethiopia's point of view, but Italy refused it; nothing but conquest would satisfy Mussolini. In July, the Emperor again appealed, not only to the League but also to the United States, which was not a member of the League. As a result of this appeal, the League forbade the supply of arms to either side; but since Italy was already well armed and Ethiopia was not, this did nothing to discourage Mussolini. In August, the committee of six reported to the League that it had no success. According to the Council's resolution in May, the Council itself should then have taken action. It did not do so; instead, it asked Britain and France to discuss the matter with Italy and try to reach a settlement. By this time, Italy had nearly a million men under arms and was ready to begin the attack as soon as the rainy season was over. Britain and France could do nothing with her.

The Council of the League met on September 4, 1935 and began to discuss the Ethiopian affair. It was still discussing on October 2, when the Italian troops invaded Ethiopia. A few days later the League's committee of six formally reported to the Council that Italy had gone to war, and thus had broken the Covenant of the League.[3] The Council adopted the report by 50 votes against four, and at once took action. It lifted the ban on the export of arms to Ethiopia, but forbade all member states to export arms to Italy. It forbade them to give Italy any financial help, or to export to her any raw materials, such as rubber or nickel, which might be useful in the war. But in this list it did not include oil, which was necessary for the Italian lorries, tanks and aircraft. Mussolini announced that he would regard it as an act of war if any country interfered with his supplies of oil. Britain and France were afraid to risk it, and consequently the League did nothing more.

Fighting began in October 1935. The Ethiopians had no aircraft or motor vehicles, no anti-aircraft guns, and very few doctors. By May

---

[3] The Covenant of the League of Nations corresponded to the Charter of the United Nations of today.

1936 the Italians had occupied Addis Ababa; the Emperor fled to Britain; and Ethiopia became an Italian colony.

This is a sad story, and no one comes out of it with credit except the Emperor Haile Selassie. It was a great shock to African opinion in East Africa and elsewhere. The Ghanaian leader Kwame Nkrumah said that for him the news of the Italian conquest of Ethiopia was the turning-point; it was then he decided that he must overthrow the colonial system and make his country independent of Britain. It seemed as if the League of Nations, faced with a dispute between a European power and a weak African state, had deliberately stood aside and allowed the European power to make a colonial conquest. What then was the value of European promises or treaties, or of the Covenant of the League? Could Africa ever hope to obtain justice until African countries became independent and were able to sit and vote in the Council of the League?

Why was the League so ineffective? It was a much smaller body than the United Nations; it had only 57 member states, 29 of which were in Europe. The United States was never a member. The European members, who dominated the League, had other matters to think about. Hitler had become leader of Germany in 1933, and all Europe was watching him anxiously. In March 1935 he announced that he had broken two clauses of the peace treaty: those which limited the strength of the German army and forbade Germany to possess an air force. France feared that Hitler would go on to break other clauses of the treaty, notably that which forbade Germany to station troops in the Rhineland. France made an agreement with Italy, by which Italy promised to help France if Germany did this; and in return, France promised not to interfere with Italy's plans in Ethiopia.

Britain on the whole wished to support Ethiopia and the League. But she feared that the Italian air force would bomb Malta and the British fleet in the Mediterranean. Moreover, Britain was anxious that Italy should join her in preventing Hitler from annexing Austria. There were so many matters threatening the peace of Europe that the European members of the League had no time to listen to Ethiopia. When at length they did listen, it was too late: Mussolini was ready for his war in Ethiopia, and told them bluntly that if they interfered with him, it meant war in Europe. Through their fears and weakness, the members of the League (notably Britain and France) allowed Hitler and Mussolini to feel sure that whatever they did, the League would talk and pass resolutions, but would not act. If the League had stood by its Covenant and given firm support to Ethiopia, it is even possible that the war of 1939 might have been prevented.

But the trouble really goes back to the secret treaty of 1915, by which

Britain and France promised Italy 'equitable compensation' if they obtained the German colonies at the end of the war. All they gave her was Jubaland and a strip of Libya, and these could not be regarded as sufficient compensation for Togoland, Cameroon, Tanganyika and South West Africa. And so the war of 1914 led on to the Italian conquest of Ethiopia and the second world war.

EDUCATIONAL DEVELOPMENT

There was another result of the 1914 war which was more satisfactory. This was a change for the better in the way in which Britain came to regard her colonies. Before the war, the British government felt that it had done its duty if it stopped the slave trade and tribal warfare, provided a system of justice, and built roads and railways to open up the country and encourage commerce. The task of providing education and other social services over the vast areas of tropical Africa was beyond the government's power. If missionary societies chose to provide schools and hospitals, that was admirable, and the colonial governments would give them what help they could; but it must be understood that government help would be limited. There could be no question of financing social services in Africa from the British Treasury in London.

The war brought about a change in this outlook. The British were impressed by the way in which such large numbers of Africans had fought with such gallantry in a quarrel which was not theirs. In 1922, Lugard published his book, *The Dual Mandate in British Tropical Africa*, in which he argued that the government had a duty not only to develop the agricultural and mineral wealth of Africa but also to 'promote the moral and educational progress' of the African people. Lugard's book had a great influence on thinking in Britain. In 1920 and 1924, the Phelps Stokes Fund of America sent two missions round the British territories in Africa to study the state of education there. The missions reported that the missionary societies were doing a great deal of good work in education, but that the colonial governments ought to be giving them much more help. These Phelps Stokes reports also had much effect.

Besides all this, the end of the war brought about a wave of idealism in Europe. People felt that they would make a fresh start and build a new world, free from the evils of the old world which had been destroyed in the war. The word *trusteeship* came into fashion; Britain regarded herself as trustee for the African peoples until the time came for them to take control of their own affairs, though most people in Britain thought that that time would be distant.

The government in London took some practical steps to carry out its new responsibilities in education. It set up a committee to study the problems of education in the colonies and to advise the colonial governments how to deal with them. It began to send out a series of educational memoranda. It urged colonial governments to cooperate in education with the missionary societies and the Churches. At Achimota in the Gold Coast (Ghana) and at Makerere in Uganda, it arranged for the establishment of government secondary schools, which it hoped might one day develop into university colleges. As a result of all these measures, there gradually developed an educational policy for the

5 EDUCATIONAL DEVELOPMENT
A blind Kikuyu boy is being taught arithmetic

colonies. No such policy had existed before 1920, for each colony had been left to decide its own policy, and education had been regarded as primarily a matter for the Churches, not for the governments.

This was an important result of the war. The colonial governments began to provide more schools of their own to supplement the work of the Church schools; they paid bigger grants to the Churches for their educational work; they laid down stricter minimum conditions of efficiency; they began to consult with the Churches and missionaries and make long-term plans instead of living from year to year. Progress began slowly, but its speed increased. The difficulty was always money, for colonial revenues were uncertain, and the government in London had not yet come to recognize that it had a duty to finance social services in Africa from the British Treasury. But at least the war had taught the colonial governments that they had a duty to provide as much education as their funds would allow.

Chapter 5

LAND AND LABOUR IN KENYA TO 1945

The story of the Kenya land question is a tale of honest misunderstandings, of well-meaning men trying to be fair but not fully understanding the problem, and of hard-headed men determined to get their own way no matter who else suffered. This chapter deals fully with those problems of land and labour, as they are at the heart of many of Kenya's troubles.

The Imperial British East Africa Company made in all ninety-seven treaties with Kenya chiefs, but none of them gave the Company any rights over the land. In 1894 the Foreign Office in London took over the responsibility for the protectorate from the Company. The territory produced no revenue whatever, and the administration was maintained by a grant from the British Treasury. The Treasury was anxious to reduce the grant, and under the Treasury stimulus the Foreign Office decided that something must be done to develop local revenue. The method it proposed was to invite British settlers to go out to East Africa and to produce whatever they found the country capable of producing.

Before inviting settlers, the Foreign Office had to satisfy itself that it had a right to make grants of land. In 1896 it consulted the Colonial Office, which replied that the IBEA treaties gave the Queen no rights over land in East Africa. But, said the Colonial Office, the object which the Foreign Office had in view might be attained in another way. If land had no owners and was vacant, no one had any power to make a treaty about it. In such a case, the British authorities might allow a person to take possession of the land, on suitable conditions, and would recognize him as the rightful occupier. He would not strictly be the owner, but he would be able to act as if he were the owner; the courts would protect him against anyone who wanted to turn him off the land.

The Foreign Office accepted this advice, and in 1897 it issued a set of land regulations. The Commissioner of the protectorate was authorized to issue land certificates, valid for 21 years in the first place, and renewable for another 21 years. In 1898 the 21-year term was extended to 99 years.

When the construction of the railway began in 1896, it became a matter of importance that the government should be able to acquire land which was needed for the railway. There was in India a Land Acquisition Act for this purpose; it enabled the government of India to acquire land for its railways, but not to resell land if it found it had taken more than it needed. In 1897 an Order in Council applied this Act to the East Africa Protectorate, and next year a further Order authorized the East African government to do what the Indian government was not authorized to do: to resell superfluous land.

This was all very well; but if European settlers were to develop the country, they must somehow be enabled to acquire blocks of land at some distance from the railway line. In 1899 the Foreign Office again asked for advice. It was now plain, it said, that the Crown had the right to acquire, and to resell, a strip of land along the railway track. But had the Crown also the right to acquire land away from the railway track? The Foreign Office pointed out that African custom did not recognize the possibility of any ownership of land. Africans recognized that if a man was growing his crops or grazing his cattle on a piece of land, he was entitled to the crops and the grass, but not to the land itself. He had a right to use the land, but the land did not belong to him, just as he had a right to fill his water-pot from the river, but the river did not belong to him. But, said the Foreign Office, it was now agreed that if the railway surveyors wanted a piece of land for the railway track, the Crown was entitled to take it; and even if someone was living there, the Crown was still entitled to take it, provided it paid him compensation. If then the Crown had a right to take land which was in use, surely it must have a right to take land which was empty? To this query, the law officers of the Crown replied, Yes. 'In such regions,' they said, 'the right of dealing with waste and unoccupied land accrues to Her Majesty by virtue of her right to the Protectorate. . . . Her Majesty might if she pleased declare them to be Crown lands, or make grants of them to individuals in fee simple or for any term.'

All this solemn legal argument merely amounts to saying, 'For our own convenience in governing Uganda, we need a railway line through Kenya, and European settlers to enable Kenya to pay its way. We will take whatever land we require for these settlers, provided that, as far as we can see, no one else is using it.' The British government was using the word 'right' in a somewhat doubtful sense. Strictly speaking, there can be no right without a system of law; we can speak of rights only if there is a court of law to protect them and to enforce its judgments. Those who proclaim that every human being has certain rights do so because they assume the existence of a divine law or a law of nature; and to establish those rights, the United Nations urges its member states to subscribe to a sort of legal document which recognizes its authority to protect them. But in 1900 there was no United Nations, and there was no system of law to regulate the relations between the British government and the peoples of East Africa.

Having received this legal advice, the Foreign Office took action, and another Order in Council was issued, the East Africa (Lands) Order in Council of 1901. This Order defined Crown land as being

'all public lands within the East Africa Protectorate which for the time being are subject to the control of His[1] Majesty by virtue of any treaty, convention or agreement, or of His Majesty's Protectorate, and all lands which have been or may hereafter be acquired by His Majesty under the Lands Acquisition Act 1894, or otherwise howsoever.'

The Order thus defined Crown lands by referring to public lands, which must be opposed to private lands. The Order did not attempt to say which land was public and which was private. This difficult decision it left to the officials in East Africa. But common sense would suggest that land actually occupied by African villages should be regarded as private land; and for many years the government did so regard it.

The Crown Lands Ordinance of 1902
In 1901 a new Commissioner, Sir Charles Eliot, arrived to administer the East Africa Protectorate, a large country, with hardly any revenue,

---

[1] Queen Victoria died in January 1901 and was succeeded by King Edward VII.

and dependent on the British Treasury grant of £250,000 a year. There were very few Europeans in the country, but there were already many Asians, who had followed the railway line as it was pushed inland from Mombasa and had set up their shops and trading posts all the way from sea to lake. Most of the Indian labourers who had helped to build the line had taken their pay and gone home; many of these traders were newcomers, enterprising and hardworking men who saw a great chance opening out before them in an undeveloped country.

Eliot thought it wrong that good land should be left empty and idle when it might be producing valuable crops. He thought it wrong too that men should be idle instead of doing useful work; and if tribal warfare were stopped, the fighting men among the Kenya peoples would be deprived of their traditional occupation and would slip, he thought, into idleness. They must learn to work and must learn new skills; and who could teach them new skills except the Europeans? For both these reasons, Eliot was anxious to attract European settlers; and the settlers would create trade, they would grow crops to load into railway trucks and increase the railway revenue.

We cannot look ahead fifty years and foresee the results of our actions. Like Livingstone, Eliot looked forward to a time when European and African farmers and businessmen would be developing Kenya together, the Africans having quickly picked up European skills. He did not foresee that Europeans would want to keep Africans down in subordinate positions; that Africans would be so reluctant to give up their traditional ways of farming and cattle-keeping; that Kenya political life would be spoiled by bitter jealousy and rivalry between the three races.

On April 1, 1902, the Foreign Office transferred the Eastern Province of Uganda to the East African Protectorate. It did so because the railway had reached its terminus at Kisumu and there was no thought of extending it; it would be convenient to have the whole of the line administered by one government. The transfer was thought of in London as quite an unimportant matter, but it had important results. It brought into Kenya the high ground between the Rift Valley and the lake, the country of the Nandi and others, much of it uninhabited; it greatly increased the amount of Kenya land which was attractive to European settlers.

In that same month of April 1902, Eliot took his first step: he announced that his government would make empty land available for European settlement. The land would be sold at two rupees an acre, or leased at an annual rent of fifteen rupees for 100 acres. Very shortly afterwards, he issued the Crown Lands Ordinance, which had been drafted in the Foreign Office. Under the Ordinance, Crown land could be sold, leased, or occupied under a temporary licence. Not more than 1,000 acres were to be sold in one lot without special permission from London, and if the purchaser did not occupy the land and develop it, the Commissioner might declare the land forfeited. No one was to lease land for more than ninety-nine years. He must undertake to pay his rent and taxes, to use the land and develop it with all reasonable speed, to keep buildings in repair, and to provide land for roads; he was forbidden to interfere with African villages or houses which he found on his land, and forbidden also to transfer his lease without the government's permission.

So much for sales and leases. Temporary licences to occupy Crown land might be issued to Africans and Asians for not more than one year and for not more than five acres. It looked as if the government were thinking of selling or leasing land to Europeans only. This alarmed the Indians, some of whom were anxious to settle on Crown land and farm it. Eliot's deputy commissioner, Jackson, assured them that they would be treated in just the same way as Europeans, but both he and Eliot thought it would be unwise to mix Indian farmers with European farmers. Indians, they thought, would be better growing cotton or sugar in hotter parts of the country.

This Crown Lands Ordinance was designed to attract settlers who were prepared to work hard on their land and develop it. The danger which the officials sought to guard against was that Europeans would come to East Africa not to settle and work but to buy or lease land cheaply and sell it or sub-let it at a profit. The government wanted farmers; it did not want land speculators.

There were at that time only about a dozen European settlers, all of them farming land near the Kikuyu country. But the news of the cheap land in the wide open spaces of East Africa was beginning to spread, and more settlers were beginning to arrive; by April 1903 there were nearly 100 of them.

Lord Delamere

Among them was Lord Delamere. Delamere was a very rich Englishman, who first came to Kenya in 1897 as a big-game hunter. He fell in love with the country and resolved to make his home there; from 1903 he was permanently living in Kenya. Delamere was a complex character. He was an obstinate and hot-tempered man, determined to get his own way. He was capable of crazy actions, such as riding down the Nairobi streets shooting at the street lamps, and locking up a Nairobi hotel manager in his own meat-safe. Delamere was the leader of the European settlers, who disliked the Crown Lands Ordinance and were scornful of the government officials whose careful routine prevented them from taking large blocks of land wherever they fancied. On the other hand, he was a friend of the Masai; he lived in Masai country and spoke their language, and he was always ready to defend his Masai friends when they were in trouble.

Delamere and the other settlers wanted to get large blocks of land and to be free to sell or sub-let them as they chose. Eliot saw that if he wanted settlers to come in large numbers he must modify his strict rules. He began making free grants of land in less popular districts to Europeans who would be willing to make their homes there; and in July 1903 he announced that he would allow land which was good for cattle, but not for crops, to be leased in blocks of from 1,000 to 100,000 acres.

This was much more the sort of thing that Delamere and his friends wanted. Delamere himself took 100,000 acres in the Masai country, and stocked the land with European sheep. But this was land which the Masai had never used, and Delamere's sheep died in hundreds. No one at the time knew why; it was afterwards found that the soil was deficient in certain essential minerals. Delamere was paying nearly £200 a year in rent, and it did not seem as if he had made a good bargain; no one else accepted the government's offer of free land in that area. Having failed with sheep, Delamere tried again with cattle, but his European cattle died from tropical diseases, notably East Coast fever, to which the Masai cattle were more or less immune. A new government farm was established, and began making experiments to see how imported European livestock could be enabled to acclimatize themselves to African conditions. Meanwhile, Delamere himself went over to the growing of wheat. But his wheat was killed by a rust fungus, and Delamere was half ruined. However, he swore that Africa should not beat him; he went home, raised every penny that he could on his English estates, and came back to Kenya, to live for eleven years in comparative poverty while the scientists that he employed found out how to breed wheat that would resist the East African rust, and sheep and cattle that could stand up to the hard life of East Africa.

Agriculture in Kenya owes Delamere so much that it is not surprising that the Europeans came to look on him as their leader. In 1904, hundreds more settlers arrived, mostly from South Africa. These men were accustomed to large farms and, like Delamere, they were impatient with the slow legal formalities of the Kenya Land Department. They wanted plenty of land, and they wanted it quickly. The government did its best to speed things up. It made a special survey of the land which lay to the south of the land then occupied by the Kikuyu. And this brought trouble. The Kikuyu had lost many of their people through an epidemic of smallpox, and land which they had formerly occupied was now lying empty. The officer making the survey was instructed to work quickly, and was not given enough time to make the thorough inquiry that he should have made. Through trying to work quickly, he included a good deal of this apparently empty land in the area available for settlement, and it was quickly parcelled out among the European newcomers. A few years later, when the Kikuyu again increased in numbers and wanted to reoccupy their land, they found Europeans living on it. This mistake was the start of much of the bitterness between Africans and Europeans over the land question.

Delamere and his friends were still dissatisfied over the working of Crown Lands Ordinance. Sir Charles Eliot left Kenya in 1904, and his successor, Sir Donald Stewart, was sufficiently impressed with the settlers' complaints to appoint a committee to examine the position. In spite of its official majority, the committee was soon dominated by Lord Delamere. It reported that although land speculation was not to be encouraged, it was important to give an impetus to genuine business and to attract capital to the country. This could not be done unless settlers were given security of title to their land and freedom to transfer it. Put into plain English, the report means, 'If you want to make Kenya a rich country, you must attract rich men to it. Rich men go wherever they find the best opportunities of using their money and becoming still richer. If they are not able to buy and sell land freely in large amounts—or even to speculate in it—they will not come to Kenya.' Sir Charles Eliot's dream of a Kenya peopled by European and African farmers on farms of moderate size was vanishing. Delamere was dreaming of something very different: a Kenya divided into large European estates, freely bought and sold.

On April 1, 1905, British East Africa passed from Foreign Office to Colonial Office control. The Secretary of State for the Colonies, Lord Elgin, was opposed to the idea of large European estates and was anxious to protect African rights over land. This report of Sir Donald Stewart's committee presented Elgin with a complicated problem. Not only did the committee recommend more freedom in land transfers, but it recommended that the Highlands should be reserved for European settlers, and that Indians should not be allowed to farm there. It said,

'There is of course no objection to the general proposition that Indians should hold land in the Protectorate, but considering that only a comparatively small area of the Protectorate is suitable for European settlement and colonization, it is desirable that land within that area should be reserved for the support and maintenance of a white population. . . . Some witnesses suggested that if an area in the High-lands should be reserved for Europeans, other areas equally suitable for agriculture should be reserved for Asiatics. . . . There is however no doubt that while in practice it might be possible to exclude Asiatics from the areas reserved for Europeans, it would not be possible, nor would it be politic, to restrain the energies and capital of European planters within limited bounds, and not to permit them to be used for the development of the country outside those bounds. . . .'

This was plain speaking. The Europeans were to be protected in the Highlands against Indian competition, but the Indians were not to be protected in the low country against competition from Europeans. The Indians saw their danger, and they laid their case before the Commis-sioner, before the government of India, and before the Secretary of State in London.

Sir Donald Stewart died in October 1905, and his successor, Sir James Hayes Sadler, was believed to be in favour of treating Indians and Europeans equally. But it was with the Secretary of State, Lord Elgin, that the decision lay. No British government could possibly adopt a deliberate policy of giving one race preferential treatment. The question for Elgin was twofold. Would it be better to have Indian and European farmers living side by side in the Highlands, or to adopt a White High-lands policy? And if the government did adopt a White Highlands policy, would the Indians be justified in complaining that they were not receiving equal treatment?

Elgin's land policy
In 1906 Lord Elgin gave his decision on the recommendations of the land committee. He said he could not agree to any scheme which allowed large areas of land to be held for speculative purposes. He proposed to replace the Ordinance of 1902 by a new ordinance. The maximum lease should be reduced from 99 to 21 years; transfers of land should be restricted; measures should be taken to stop 'dummying'—that is, a trick to increase a family's holding of land beyond the legal maximum by making application in the names of a man's wife and children. Lord Elgin was opposed to the Delamere recommendations; he was getting back to the old idea of safeguarding African interests. Sir James Hayes Sadler protested, and Elgin made one concession: he allowed the 99-year lease to stand, on condition that rents should be increased after 33 and 66 years, and that there should be a graduated land tax. Such an ordinance as this would have been fought tooth and nail by Delamere and his friends; three successive governors (Hayes Sadler, Girouard, and Belfield) all refused to force any such measure through the legislative

council by using their official majority. There seemed to be a deadlock, which lasted until 1912.

On the question of Indians in the Highlands, Lord Elgin was more willing to accept the settlers' point of view. He wrote,

'It would not be in accordance with the policy of His Majesty's Government to exclude any class of His subjects from holding land in any part of a British Protectorate, but in view of the comparatively limited area in the Protectorate suitable for European colonists, a reasonable discretion will be exercised in dealing with applications for land on the part of natives of India and other non-Europeans. . . . I approve of your adhering to the principle acted on by your predecessors, viz. that land outside municipal limits, roughly lying between Kiu and Fort Ternan, should be granted only to European settlers.'

The British government had thus accepted the White Highlands policy, and the settlers were delighted. They called this despatch 'The Elgin Pledge'. The Indians were correspondingly indignant, and there was a good deal of bitter feeling between Indians and Europeans in East Africa.

Outside East Africa, the White Highlands policy did not go unchallenged. Even Elgin's own Under-Secretary, Winston Churchill, disapproved of it, and had the temerity to say so both in London and in East Africa. But Elgin maintained his decision. In March 1908 he repeated,

'It is not consonant with the views of His Majesty's Government to impose legal restrictions on any particular section of the community, but as a matter of administrative convenience, grants in the upland areas should not be made to Indians.'

The White Highlands policy was now established, and a great part of Kenya's political life for many years centred on it: the Europeans defending it, the Indians, and much later the Africans also, attacking it. The African attacks became fiercer in later years as African land-hunger increased, and large parts of the Highlands were still lying empty, reserved by the government for European settlers who had not yet arrived. Settlers did not flock into the country in large numbers. There were nearly 100 European land-holders in 1903, about 1,200 in 1913, about 1,700 in 1924, and over 2,000 in 1929.

The White Highlands

The government was thus faced with a growing body of European settlers, who had clear and decided views about what sort of a country

Kenya should become. They had come from Britain or South Africa in the hope of obtaining big farms, which they would develop with the help of African labour until they were able to live comfortably and well as masters of their land. They were not afraid of hard work, but they expected their work to be rewarded; if a man took a thousand acres of African grass-land and turned it into a productive farm, he thought it unreasonable that the government, which had done little or nothing to help him, should increase his rent or put difficulties in his way if he wished to sell his farm or divide it. These men were not interested in Sir Charles Eliot's dream of a Kenya in which farmers of all three races should be working, if not side by side, at all events on more or less equal terms. They had been told that the Highlands of Kenya had a climate in which white men could work and bring up their children; it could be a white man's country, and they were determined to make it so.

Further, these European settlers were accustomed to politics: to speaking, voting, and electing. They saw no reason why they should submit to whatever the governor or the Colonial Office proposed. They quickly organized themselves. In 1903 they founded the Farmers' and Planters' Association. Originally merely a marketing association, it speedily became a political body, and renamed itself the Colonists' Association. As early as 1905, the Colonists' Association was asking to be given a voice in the government; and in 1907 the governor, Hayes Sadler, opened the first meeting of Kenya's legislative council. The council consisted of five official members and three nominated unofficial members, one of whom was Lord Delamere. Within a year or two, the Colonists' Association split into several small local bodies; but these small associations were held together by a coordinating committee, and in 1911 this coordinating committee developed into a formidable body called the Convention of Associations, nicknamed by the settlers themselves 'The Settlers' Parliament'.

These early European political associations had four main aims. The first was to keep the whole of the Highlands as a reserve for European farmers: the so-called White Highlands policy. The second aim was to secure a satisfactory supply of African labour for the farms. The third was to secure a satisfactory system of land tenure; this aim was blocked by Elgin, but was reasonably well achieved by the Crown Lands Ordinance of 1915, which we shall shortly discuss. The fourth aim was more advanced, and was put forward somewhat later: it was to secure elected European representation in the legislative council. Delamere and his colleagues were nominated by the governor; from 1913 onwards, the settlers were pressing to be allowed to elect their own representatives.

The Crown Lands Ordinance of 1915

Elgin's land policy, as we have seen, was satisfactory to the European settlers in the matter of the White Highlands. But he could not accept their views on land tenure. In this matter, there was a deadlock between the settlers and the government. The deadlock was at last broken in 1912, when a new Secretary of State, Lewis Harcourt, gave way to the settlers almost completely: he dropped the ideas of land tax and anti-dummying measures, and accepted rent increases much smaller than those proposed by Lord Elgin.

A new Crown Lands Ordinance was passed in 1915. It introduced a new definition of Crown land, which was now held to include 'all lands occupied by the native tribes of the Protectorate and all lands reserved for the use of any members of any native tribe'. Hitherto, the government had acted as though land in African occupation was private, not public land; and private land could not be Crown land. But by the new definition all land in African occupation was now included in Crown land. This was an important change; and its full meaning was shown six years later, when a court decision by the Chief Justice of Kenya held that 'the natives in occupation of Crown land become tenants at will of the Crown of the land actually occupied'. This interpretation of the law meant that the Crown—that is, the government of Kenya—had the legal right to turn anyone out of his village and give the village and its land to European settlers. If this was the law, the Africans henceforth had no security whatever.

Under the new ordinance, land in towns could be leased for 99 years and agricultural land for 999 years. No provision was made for freehold land (though a 999-year lease is almost as good as freehold) but with the Secretary of State's approval, the governor might grant land on any terms he chose, so that there was nothing to stop him granting land in freehold. The rent of leasehold land was to be slightly increased every thirty years. The lessee must carry out at least a minimum programme of development, and he must not transfer, divide, or sub-let his estate without the permission of the governor in council. A land registration scheme was introduced to provide settlers with written documents of title.

The settlers naturally disliked the provision for rent increases, however small, but on the whole they were delighted with the 1915 Ordinance, and they were prepared to submit to this disadvantage rather than risk having the whole question reopened. The Ordinance lasted until 1945 without serious modification.

The Masai agreements

Early European travellers in East Africa found much of the land empty.

As late as 1903, Sir Charles Eliot wrote:

'One remarkable feature of the Rift Valley and the Mau is the paucity
—and in large areas the absence—of native population. . . . At times
one may make a journey from Naivasha to Fort Ternan without
seeing a single human being or a hut, except the railway servants and
their houses.'

One reason for this emptiness was the Masai and their herds. They
moved with their cattle up and down an immense area of East Africa,
roughly 400 miles long and 100 or more miles wide, using only a little
of the area themselves but denying the whole of it to other peoples.

The railway cut across the Masai country and brought the European
settlers. The railway strip was not at first a serious inconvenience to the
Masai, for they still had plenty of land on either side of the line. In
1904, with no difficulty, an agreement was made between Sir Donald
Stewart and the Masai laibon, Lenana.[2] Two reserves were marked out,
one north of the railway and one south; they were to be linked by a
track half a mile wide so that the Masai and their cattle could move
from one to the other. The Masai of course would have preferred to be
left alone; but they accepted this arrangement, and the agreement said
that it was to remain in force 'so long as the Masai as a race shall exist'.

But the agreement was not properly carried out. Some of the Masai
would not go to either reserve, but continued to wander as they chose.
Those who went to the northern reserve in Laikipia did not stay within
it, but spread outside its boundaries. This was not altogether their
fault, for Laikipia was fresh land, and on its rich pastures their cattle
multiplied greatly. The half-mile cattle road was not a success. It soon
became trodden and fouled and full of ticks; the European farmers on
either side of it objected strongly to having their cattle infected by the
tick-borne diseases; and in 1908, contrary to the agreement, the
government closed the road and prohibited the movement of cattle
from one reserve to the other.

Although the Laikipia reserve had twice been enlarged to suit the
needs of the Masai living there, the 1904 agreement was becoming
unworkable. As Sir Donald Stewart had foreseen, European settlers
were coveting the Laikipia land. Lenana himself lived in the south, and
found it difficult to control the northern Masai, who had a laibon of
their own, Legalishu. One possible solution was to close the Laikipia

[2] The Europeans regarded Lenana as the paramount chief of the Masai. The *laibon*
was a hereditary prophet rather than a chief; but he undoubtedly had great political
influence over his people.

reserve and bring the Masai there down to the south, extending the southern reserve to provide room for them. From the European point of view, this would have the advantage of opening the Laikipia country to European settlements; from Lenana's point of view, it would have the advantage of bringing the whole nation together again. Lenana was strongly in favour of the scheme. Two government officers inspected the proposed southern extension of the reserve and reported that it would be suitable for the Masai cattle; Masai elders inspected it on behalf of Lenana and Legalishu and agreed. Legalishu made it plain that he would rather stay in Laikipia; but in February 1909 he formally accepted the scheme on behalf of his people, and during the next few weeks the move began.

At this point the matter was complicated by the intervention of the Secretary of State, who declared that the 1904 agreement must not be set aside unless it was replaced by a new agreement. The northern Masai and their herds had already begun their journey, and it was not easy to make them stop and turn back to Laikipia. When invited to make a new agreement, Legalishu had second thoughts; perhaps it might be better for his people to stay where they were. However, eventually a new agreement was made in February 1911. Lenana died, and on his death-bed urged his people from the north to come south. After more hesitation, Legalishu, who succeeded him as laibon, said that he and his people were ready to move, and in 1912 the move was completed.

Again there was trouble. The government had no idea how large the Laikipia herds had become, and quite inadequate arrangements were made for feeding and watering them on the long journey. The Masai from the north numbered 10,000 people, with 200,000 cattle and half a million sheep; many beasts perished on the march. Moreover, a few European settlers had already made their homes on the land set aside for the extension of the southern reserve. These people had to move, and the governor, Girouard, promised them that they should be compensated with new land in Laikipia. For some reason, the Secretary of State, Lewis Harcourt, refused to allow these Europeans from the south to be granted land in Laikipia. Evidently he did not realize that they had already received a promise; and when this was explained to him, he accused the governor of exceeding his powers, whereupon the governor resigned.

It was a sad story of muddle and hesitation. The 1911 agreement was not in itself a bad one. As a result of it, said the government,

'An area of 4,500 square miles on Laikipia, of which not more than 1,200 was well watered, was to be exchanged for 6,500 square miles in the south, of which some 1,500 was described as some of the best

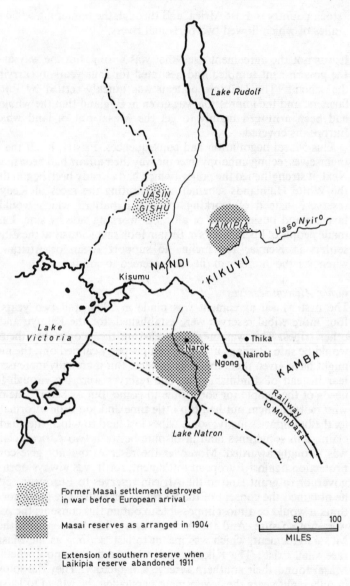

Lake Rudolf

UASIN GISHU

LAIKIPIA

Uaso Nyiro

NANDI

'KIKUYU'

Kisumu

Lake Victoria

Thika

Narok

Nairobi

Ngong

KAMBA

Railway to Mombasa

Lake Natron

▓ Former Masai settlement destroyed
in war before European arrival

▓ Masai reserves as arranged in 1904

⋮ Extension of southern reserve when
Laikipia reserve abandoned 1911

0   50   100
MILES

THE MASAI AGREEMENTS

stock country in East Africa, and through the remaining 5,000 square miles of which flowed two perennial rivers.'

It was not the agreement itself that was wrong, but the way in which the government fumbled and hesitated for four years in carrying out the scheme. The Laikipia plateau was quickly settled by European farmers, and the impression was given in England that the whole affair had been arranged mainly to get the Masai out of land which the Europeans coveted.

This Masai negotiation had consequences. Firstly, it left the Masai themselves feeling unhappy over the way their affairs had been muddled. Next, it strengthened the policy (which had already been begun through the White Highlands scheme) of separating the races of Kenya into reserves, instead of working towards a pattern which would have farmers and businessmen of all races working side by side. Lastly, it made people of liberal views in Britain look suspiciously at the European settlers in Kenya, and incline to support Asian or African views whenever the interests of the races seemed to conflict.

Other African reserves
The first Masai agreement was made in 1904, and two years later, four more tribal reserves were established, for the Kikuyu and three other tribes. This was meant to reassure the people that their lands would be safe. Perhaps if it had been properly carried out, the measure might have given them that reassurance. But it actually increased their fear instead of diminishing it. The reserves were big enough for the needs of the people for some time to come. But as before, the officers who marked them out had too little time and too little information to fix the boundaries justly: some tribes lost land to which they had a just claim, and sometimes land in dispute between two African claimants was wrongly awarded. Moreover the reserves did not give complete protection against European settlement, for it was always open to the governor to grant land in the African reserves to European settlers if he obtained the consent of the Secretary of State. The governor might think it would be almost impossible to obtain this consent; the Africans were not so sure. And the Africans saw what happened to the 1904 Masai agreement, which was meant to last 'so long as the Masai as a race shall exist'. The Kikuyu and others did not know whether the Masai found their southern reserve satisfactory. They did know that in only eight years the government persuaded the Masai to leave their northern reserve and, the moment they had gone, the land was settled by Europeans.

So Kenya became a country of reserves: Masai reserve, Kikuyu reserve, European reserve and so forth. For the moment perhaps the reserves were large enough. Would they remain so as more European and Asian settlers arrived, and as the Africans and their cattle increased in numbers?

THE PROBLEM OF FINDING LABOUR

The European settlers had obtained the Elgin Pledge; and the 1915 Crown Lands Ordinance, though not ideal, seemed to most of them fairly satisfactory. But what was the use of having land in Kenya unless they could obtain African labour to help them to work it? The Europeans did not want small farms, which they could work with the help of their families and one or two African assistants; they wanted large farms after the South African manner, which needed African workers in great numbers. The Land Committee put the European point of view very forcibly in its 1905 report:

'There is no doubt that the future success or failure of the country depends entirely on the methods that will be employed in dealing with native labour. The country must look for its development to the labour of the natives, and if proper steps are not taken, with due care and forethought, to render the natives contented and their labour easily available, and if the laws dealing with the natives are not framed in a wise and liberal spirit and enforced with a firm hand, the future prospects of the country may be irretrievably damaged.'

The difficulty was that if the reserves were really adequate, there would never be enough labour to satisfy the settlers. No one would wish to leave the reserves to work for long on European land. A man might come and work for a few months to earn enough to pay his tax and buy something he wanted—a blanket, a coat and hat, a bicycle— but then he would go back to the reserve to rest and enjoy himself. But that would not suit the European settler. He did not want men who came to him for a few months, knowing nothing when they arrived and needing to be taught, and then leaving his farm just when they were becoming useful. He wanted men who would work for him year after year.

The government was willing to give the settlers what help it could: but within limits. It would allow its district officers to talk to chiefs and elders and try to persuade them to encourage their young men to go and work on European farms. But it refused to compel the young men to work, and nothing short of compulsion would satisfy the settlers.

The Masters and Servants Ordinance of 1906

In 1906 the government passed a Masters and Servants Ordinance, based on a similar law in the Transvaal. The Ordinance was intended to protect the employer against workers who broke their agreement to work for a given time. Many employers complained that a man came and agreed to work for three or six months; they gave him a blanket, and at the end of his first month they gave him his month's pay; and the man then walked off the farm and went home. Here was another misunderstanding. The African came to work only because he wanted a blanket. Now he had it, and what was a blanket to a white man, who was rich enough to give away a thousand blankets? The employer on the other hand felt far from rich. He had brought a few hundred pounds from England, and would have no more money until his farm began to produce saleable crops. How could he hope to start producing unless he had enough men who understood what he wanted them to do? And if a man agreed to work for six months, he should work for six months, not for six weeks.

The Ordinance gave the employers two kinds of help. They were allowed to pay their men partly in kind: the blankets and food they gave them were to be reckoned as part of their wages. If a man broke his agreement by leaving the farm before his time was up, he could be imprisoned by the government. The Ordinance thus increased the hold that the employer had over his workers once he had got them.

But it did nothing to help him to get men; in fact, men would be even less willing to go to work on the settler's farm if they knew that they might then be compelled to stay. The government still refused to compel Africans to work; so there sprang up a new profession, that of labour recruiter. This was a man who undertook to collect men from the reserves to work on the farms, and received a fee from the employer for every man he brought. How he found the men was his affair: no doubt he made all sorts of promises and maybe some threats as well. The government soon began to receive complaints that men recruited in this way were not receiving the sort of treatment they had been promised. In 1907 it appointed an official, the Secretary for Native Affairs, to look after African interests and to look specially into this matter of labour supply. The first Secretary, Claud Hollis, quickly found a great deal that was wrong; he drew up and published a set of labour regulations, he sent round a circular to say that there was to be no compulsory labour on European farms, and he told all district officers to explain carefully to the chiefs and elders in their district that no one was bound to leave home and work for the white man if he did not wish to.

As was to be expected, Hollis was soon in trouble. In March 1908 a public meeting was held to protest against these new regulations.

Many of the Europeans there said that though they knew it was illegal to flog their workers, they often did so; and the meeting demanded that flogging should be made lawful, that pass laws on the South African model[3] should be introduced, and (of course) that Mr Hollis's new labour regulations should be withdrawn. Although the governor, Sir James Hayes Sadler, had addressed the meeting and stayed to listen to the speeches, the meeting was extremely outspoken, and the settlers apparently expected him to announce there and then that he would agree to what they proposed. But he would not; he said that the labour regulations were justified and that his duty was to help both Europeans and Africans. That afternoon, Delamere and a group who had been at the meeting went up to Government House to put pressure on the governor, and Hayes Sadler thought that Delamere and the other unofficial member of the legislative council behaved so badly that he suspended them from membership of the council.

A Labour Commission, which Hayes Sadler had appointed to inquire into the problem, in due course made its report. No commission in those days could very well be formed without Delamere, and any commission on which he sat was likely to express his views. This commission now recommended that recruiting by professional agents should be abolished, and that district officers should be directed 'in unequivocal language' to encourage Africans to come and work on the farms. The hut tax should not be increased, but there should be a system of identification papers for Africans. The government should start technical and agricultural education for Africans, and should help the missions in the work they were doing in primary education.

Very little came of this report. The governor introduced an African poll-tax to supplement the hut tax; he thought this might cause young unmarried men to come and work. But whatever the governor might have thought, the Secretary of State forbade district officers to recruit labour for the settlers. In 1912 the Secretary of State repeated this and added that the taxation system was to raise money for government expenses, not to secure a supply of labour for European farms. The two objects were quite distinct, and must be kept so. He did on the other hand approve of the idea of identification papers for Africans, and in 1915 they were provided for by a Native Registration Ordinance. But the ordinance was not enforced; it was not until 1920 that such papers were introduced.

[3] In South Africa, Africans were compelled by law to carry a set of papers, or passes, which must be shown to the police on demand: papers to identify them, to explain what reason they had to be in a European area, to certify that they had paid their taxes, and so on.

The Masters and Servants Ordinance of 1910

The Masters and Servants Ordinance of 1906 was made in the interests of the employers. In 1910 it was supplemented by another ordinance with the same title; this one was made in the interests of the workers. It laid down minimum conditions of food, blankets, housing, and medical care which employers were bound to provide for their men. Shortly afterwards, government labour inspectors were appointed to enforce these conditions. Many of the better European employers were already treating their men well and needed no compulsion. Such laws are made for the bad minority who do only what they are compelled to do.

Another Native Labour Commission reported in 1912; but no amount of commissions or reports could overcome the fact that the interests of the Africans and of the Europeans were opposed. Africans had no wish to leave their own land, except to earn money to pay their tax and buy the European goods they wanted. They disliked working on European farms and would get back to their own land as soon as they could. The Europeans were always demanding that African taxes should be increased, African reserves cut down, and government officers instructed to use compulsion to provide a supply of labour. The district officers hated this idea, and they were supported by the Secretary of State. The African chiefs were not unwilling to send their men to work. Sometimes they were paid by labour recruiters for the men they provided; always they (like all other Africans at that time) found it difficult to distinguish between official and unofficial Europeans. To them, all white men were the government, and so had to be obeyed.

The Resident Natives Ordinance of 1918

By the time war broke out in 1914, large numbers of Africans, especially Kikuyu, had come to live on European land, and this eased the labour problem somewhat. Most of these 'squatters' (as they were called) were paying for their farming and grazing rights by working for the European farmer, the number of days in the year being fixed by agreement. Some, however, instead of working were paying a rent in crops or livestock; and a few (though an increasing number) were paying rent in money. Such a system is not in itself bad. It is, or has been, found in many parts of the world. The system may develop in different ways. After existing for many hundreds of years in England, it developed into a system by which some of the villagers lost all their land and worked all the year for pay, while others owned their land or leased it, and employed paid labour. In France, it developed into a system whereby large estates were broken up into small individual farms. It might have developed in some such way in Kenya also.

But most of the European settlers disliked any arrangement by which Africans living on European land paid rent either in kind or in money. They did not want the Africans' money or cattle; they wanted their labour. In 1918 the government passed the Resident Natives Ordinance to meet their view. It provided that no European should accept rent in money or in kind from Africans living on his land; all rent must be paid in labour. No African was to live on a European farm unless he worked for the farmer 180 days in the year; if he was unwilling to do this, he must go back to the reserve. This Ordinance fixed the land system and prevented any development; it condemned the Africans to remain as wage-earners on European farms.

At the end of the war in 1918, the demand for African labour increased still more. Not only had the European farms, abandoned during the fighting, to be brought back into cultivation, but more settlers were arriving from England. Large numbers of ex-servicemen were encouraged to go out to Kenya with the promise of farms free or at cheap rates. Under one such scheme, 257 farms of 160 acres each were offered free, and over a thousand larger farms were offered for sale. The government found the land by taking a hundred square miles out of the Nandi reserve. The Nandi villagers living there were told to go, and were paid five rupees compensation for every hut they left. The total paid in compensation was nearly £2,500, so that about 3,500 huts were abandoned.[4] The scheme was a failure; 1,246 farms were taken up, but after five years only 545 of them were still held by the original settlers. The unfortunate ex-servicemen did not know what they were coming to; most of them knew nothing about farming and lost all their money in the scheme. It is the Kenya government that must be blamed for thus ignoring wise advice that had been given it by the Land Committee in 1906: 'Once the government has given its word to the native in fixing a reserve, the reserve so fixed should be absolutely inviolable.'

The Native Registration Ordinance of 1920

In the difficult days after the war, the government at last put into force the recommendation (made as long ago as 1907) that all African workers should be registered. The Native Registration Ordinance of 1920 repealed the ordinance of 1915 (which had never been put into force) and provided that every African man over the age of sixteen must be registered and must carry with him a registration certificate — the so-called *kipande*. The main (but not the only) purpose of the ordinance was to protect the European employer. A government labour

[4] Counting seven rupees to the pound.

inspector, whose sympathy on the whole was with the African workers, had admitted to the Labour Commission of 1912,

'Any wrongs of the employees can be remedied by complaint to any government post, and the whole force of the administration lies behind the complainant. Wrongs of the employer however (desertion, bad work, insolence, neglect &c) are very seldom capable of redress, because the other party to the contract has left the jurisdiction and cannot be found.'

The worker knew his employer; but once the worker had left the farm and gone back to his village, the employer could never get hold of him again. The ordinance would change this. The kipande was useful to the government in other ways; it served as a convenient place to record that the bearer had paid his tax, and it helped the police in tracing criminals.

But the ordinance was not entirely for the benefit of the employers. It was intended also to protect the workers against one injustice. It often happened that when a man returned to his village after working for some months on a European farm, his chief would send him out again at once to meet the needs of a labour recruiter. The poor man would have no means of proving to the recruiter, or to the district officer, that he had only just finished a term of work and was entitled to a rest. The kipande which the ordinance made him carry would show this; and if he took it to the district officer, he would be sent back home. Still, this benefit which the ordinance gave to the worker was small compared with the benefit which it gave to the European employer and the government.

For the moment, the needs of the European settlers were given preference. Very little was done to improve conditions in the reserves, and on the whole the European settlers disapproved of anything being done to make life there happier and more prosperous, for the all-sufficient reason that the more comfortable the Africans were in the reserves, the harder it would be to get them out to work. The Kenya coffee industry grew fairly quickly between 1907 and 1913, and in 1918 the government passed an ordinance requiring every coffee-grower to take out an annual licence. No one could object to this; but as in the matter of the White Highlands, the government went further, and 'as a matter of administrative convenience' it instructed its district officers not to issue licences to African applicants. Meanwhile, coffee was being grown by Africans both in Uganda and in Tanganyika, and in 1925 there was a proposal that Africans should begin growing it in Kenya too. But the Europeans succeeded in stopping it. The reserves were not meant for growing profitable cash crops; they were for subsistence agriculture only.

The Labour Circular of 1919

Sir Edward Northey, who arrived as governor of Kenya in February 1919, was convinced that the needs of the Europeans must be given preference. In a circular issued soon after his arrival, he made this plain to the Indians of Kenya. 'His Excellency believes,' said the document, 'that although Indian interests should not be lost sight of, European interests must be paramount throughout the Protectorate.' The main interest of the Europeans at that time, even more important than the right to elect their representatives to the legislative council, was to obtain a regular supply of African labour. In October 1919 the governor set out to provide it.

The Chief Native Commissioner was John Ainsworth, a very experienced official who had been one of the Company's men in the 1890s. He had the difficult job of trying to persuade Africans to offer themselves for work on European farms, and at the same time protecting them from the demands of settlers who always needed more labour than they could get. There would have been still fewer men coming out of the reserves to work if the Africans had not known and trusted John Ainsworth. This did not save him from being severely criticized by European farmers for being too kindly and gentle towards Africans.

Ainsworth now found his difficulties increased. The new governor ordered him to draft a circular to all government officials, urging them to increase the number of African labourers. He produced his draft, but the governor found it too mild; the governor amended it to stiffen the wording, and in October 1919 it was issued.

This important document marked the highest point of the government's endeavour to meet the European settlers' desires in the matter of the labour supply:

'. . . His Excellency trusts that those officers who are in charge of what are termed labour-supplying districts are doing what they can to induce the augmentation of the supply of labour for the various farms and plantations in the Protectorate, and he feels assured that all officers will agree with him that the larger and more continuous the flow of labour is from the reserves, the more satisfactory will be the relations between the native people and the settlers and between the settlers and the government. . . .

His Excellency desires to reiterate certain of his wishes and to add further instructions as follows:

1. All government officials in charge of native areas must exercise every possible lawful influence to induce able-bodied male natives to go into the labour field. . . .

2. Native chiefs and elders must at all times render all possible lawful assistance on the foregoing lines. . . .

3. District commissioners will keep a record of the names of those chiefs and headmen who are helpful and of those who are not helpful, and will make reports to me from time to time for the information of His Excellency. . . .

4. District commissioners will, as often as occasion requires, hold public meetings at convenient centres, to be attended by the native authorities. At these meetings, labour requirements, places, nature of work and rates of pay must be explained. . . .

5. Employers or their agents requiring labour will be invited and encouraged to enter freely any native reserve and get in touch with chiefs, headmen, and natives. . . .'

There was more of it. Where the journey from their homes to the European farm was not too great, women and children also were to be encouraged to go and work. If sufficient labour could not be obtained in Kenya, the government would try and recruit it in Tanganyika; and the district officers should point out to their people how unfortunate it would be if good money, which they themselves might have earned, should be earned instead by people from the other side of the border.

It is to be noticed that the circular says nothing about compulsion. No one was to be compelled to work on a European farm; men could be induced, persuaded, and encouraged, but not compelled. But the whole tone of the circular made it difficult both for the district officers and for the African chiefs to distinguish between persuasion and compulsion. Chiefs who are helpful and chiefs who are unhelpful are to have their names reported to the governor; it is plainly implied that the helpful will be in favour and the unhelpful in disfavour. It is to be noticed again that the circular makes no new demands. District officers had always been told to do what they could to persuade Africans to work on European farms. The difference is that Northey left his officers no discretion; he gave them strict orders.

The circular aroused great attention, both in Kenya and in England: not only for what it said, but for the assumptions that lay behind it. In a letter to the European organization, the Convention of Associations, the governor made it plain that he regarded Africans as lazy, and thought it would be bad for them to be allowed to stay idle in the reserves.

Opposition quickly came from the European missionaries. The

Bishops of Mombasa and Uganda, and the senior missionary of the Church of Scotland, Dr J. W. Arthur, told the governor that he was wrong:

'. . . In the present memorandum, technically no "compulsion" is to be exercised; but "it is the wish of the government that natives should come out into the labour field". To the native mind, a hint and an order on the part of the government are indistinguishable, particularly when the governor himself calls upon the administrative officials, provincial commissioners and district commissioners, to exercise "an insistent advocacy of the government's wishes in this connection". No district commissioner can mistake the significance of these terms. . . .'

On the question of African idleness, they say:

'The memorandum apparently assumes that the choice lies between useful work done for the European and idleness in the reserves. No one will deny that there are days or months of practical idleness; but no one who has lived in a reserve and had the opportunity of closely watching native life but will realise that the native also has his months of strenuous work: cultivating and planting, harvesting, building, &c. The native has also his home, his crops, and his plans for development. The demands on his time may not be constant, but they are insistent. To leave his own plantation, perhaps at a critical time, for the benefit of someone else's plantation; to leave his house unthatched, his crops unreaped, his wife unguarded perhaps for months at a time, in return for cash which he does not want, on the "advice" of his chief—which he dare not disregard—is not a proposal calculated to inspire loyalty to the government from which the advice emanates. . . .'

The missionaries did not disapprove of all compulsory labour, but they laid down strict conditions. No women or children should ever be compelled to work. Compulsory labour should be used only for necessary government work such as road-building: never for private employers. The government should guarantee and enforce the conditions, so that each man knew just how much he had to do, and the work was shared fairly. Above all, there should be a government labour bureau to make all the arrangements; district officers should no longer be expected to have anything to do with supplying labour.

Still stronger opposition came from Frank Weston, the Bishop of Zanzibar. 'I wish to make it clear', he wrote, 'that those of us who are missionaries will not agree to any such policy. We regard forced labour, apart from war, as in itself immoral; and we hold that forcing Africans to work in the interests of European civilization is a betrayal of the weaker to the financial interests of the stronger race.'

This missionary opposition could not be ignored; for the missionaries had their societies at home in England, who could, and did, bring pressure on the Secretary of State. The matter was much discussed in the British Press, and public opinion on the whole was with the missionaries and against the governor. The Secretary of State, Lord Milner, had long experience in South Africa. He was inclined to side with the governor, especially when some of the more extreme liberals in England wanted to forbid even the small amounts of compulsory labour for communal needs which had always been customary in African life. But he could not altogether resist the public outcry. In July 1920, on his instructions, an amending circular was issued in Nairobi. Women and children were to be allowed to go home every night; care was to be taken that chiefs should not use favouritism or oppression when selecting men for work; men were not to be sent to work when their labour was needed on their own farms in the reserve. But the government maintained its view that the chiefs should 'advise and encourage' their men to go and work on European farms. As for work on government projects, an ordinance was passed which empowered the government to call men up for sixty days work in the year for the government— but never for private employers.

Next year, 1921, Lord Milner was succeeded as Secretary of State by Winston Churchill. Churchill knew East Africa, and had no sympathy with Northey's idea that European interests must be paramount there. He had already protested against the Elgin Pledge; he supported the Indians' claim to membership of the legislative council: now he reversed Milner's policy over labour. He told the governor that compulsory labour was not to be used at all unless it could not be avoided; and he made the Kenya government pass an amending ordinance, which required the governor to obtain the Secretary of State's permission before using its power to call up compulsory labour. This permission was only once given. In 1925, the government was permitted to call up 4,000 men for railway construction, and it actually called up only 2,800. There was no more compulsory labour in Kenya after 1925.

LAND IN KENYA FROM 1920 TO 1945

By the early 1920s, the Kikuyu in particular were beginning to realize that the Europeans had come to stay, and that the White Highlands were in danger of being for ever lost to the African people. Until then,

Africans had hardly realized how serious their position was becoming. They had always been ready to allow other people to live for a time on their land until they needed it for themselves. They had not at first realized that Europeans had very different ideas, and that once they had settled on land would never leave it. Moreover, many of the early European settlements had been made at a time when the population had been reduced by disease, and land had been left empty; so that the European farmers had not at first been a nuisance to the Africans.

But now the African population was increasing again. The Kikuyu were pressing southward once more into the districts near Nairobi. Nairobi was no longer merely a watering-place for the Masai cattle, no longer even a collection of railway offices and workshops; it was the capital of Kenya and was a bustling city of European and Asian businessmen. It drew the young Kikuyu to gaze at its marvels and to seek for work in it; and it brought home to the African people that the strangers were here to stay.

The Africans' anxiety over their land could not be ignored, and the Kenya government recognized that something must be done to set African minds at rest. A commission was appointed from England in 1924 to see what could be done to improve the social conditions of the Africans and their relationships with Asians and Europeans. The commission recommended that the boundaries of the African reserves should be fixed, so that no further land could be taken from them and alienated to Europeans. This was done in 1926. In 1930 a new ordinance (the Native Lands Trust Ordinance) was passed; it declared that the African reserves were to be set aside for ever for the benefit of the African peoples.

Unluckily, in 1932 gold was discovered at Kakamega in the Kavirondo reserve. Great pressure was at once put on the government to make this land available for European mining. The Secretary of State, Cunliffe-Lister (later Lord Swinton), agreed to an amendment of the Native Lands Trust Ordinance, and the gold-bearing land was taken out of the reserve and alienated. The Kavirondo who lost their land received compensation in money, but not in land. Africans could not have any confidence that the Kenya government would ever be able to make an effective stand in defence of their interests against pressure from European farmers, miners, and businessmen.

The Carter commission

All these steps did nothing to answer the question whether the African reserves were large enough for African needs, and this question was more and more being asked. In 1932 a commission was appointed under the chairmanship of Sir William Morris Carter, Chief Justice of Uganda, to inquire into African grievances over land and to recommend what land should be made available for African settlement. Carter was an experienced man, who had studied African land law in Uganda for many years, and had written on the subject as long ago as 1906. His commission made a thorough study of the subject of land in Kenya. It heard oral evidence from 487 African witnesses and over 200 other witnesses; it received letters from 400 Africans, and considered about 200 statements which Africans made to their district officers, and which the district officers sent on to it. As the commission remarked in its report, it did not suffer from a lack of material.

6 COOPERATIVE SOCIETIES IN EAST AFRICA

A Kenya cooperative society has provided milk for these children

Some of the most interesting parts of the Carter commission's report are those dealing with Kikuyu land: showing the ways in which the Kikuyu obtained their land from the previous inhabitants, and lost some of it again to the Europeans. According to the commission's conclusions, in 1895 the Kikuyu held 1,519 square miles of land, and between then and 1902 they added another 275 square miles; so that their total holding, before European settlement began, was 1,794 square miles. Of this area, about 109 square miles had been alienated to Europeans; but the government had already seen its mistake, and had given the Kikuyu 265 square miles of land in compensation. This new land, however, was less valuable than the land which the Kikuyu had lost, and the commission reckoned that the Kikuyu had lost the value of thirty square miles of good farming land, which it recommended should somehow be restored to them.

The government accepted the recommendations of the Carter commission. The first result was that it added about 2,600 square miles of land to the African reserves, bringing them up to a total of 52,000 square miles. Much more important, the government abandoned the idea that there existed a vague area of Crown land which could be alienated to Europeans; on the commission's recommendation, it fixed the boundary of the White Highlands just as it fixed the boundary of the African reserves. At the time of the report, a little more than 10,000 square miles were actually occupied by European farmers; the total area now reserved for Europeans was fixed at some 16,000 square miles, though a quarter of this was set aside as forest reserve, and farming was prohibited there. Most important of all, the government set up a Native Lands Trust Board, under the chairmanship of the Chief Native Commissioner, to look after the African reserves. The Africans naturally feared that what the Kenya government did by one ordinance it might later undo by another; to guard against this, these various measures were taken not by Kenya ordinances but by a series of Orders in Council, issued in London during 1938 and 1939.

The African 'squatters'

These recommendations of the Carter commission provided, at least for many years to come, a reasonable settlement of the question of the reserves; though sooner or later the African population was sure to increase so that these enlarged reserves were no longer adequate, and the question would then arise once more.

But the reserves were only part of the African land problem. Large numbers of Africans were living on European farms; a census taken in 1945 counted some 200,000 of them. They had gone there to work for the settlers and to have a more or less permanent home on European land. As we have seen, the Resident Natives Ordinance sanctioned this arrangement on condition that the African 'squatters' (as these men were called) worked for 180 days a year for the European settler on whose land they were living.

Even under the conditions laid down by the Resident Natives Ordinance, the squatter system was not wholly bad. Since the European farmer always needed labour, the African squatter was reasonably safe in his holding. It was in the interest of the European employer to keep his people contented by providing decent housing and medical care and schools for the children. Many of the African squatters lived quite comfortably, and in 1937 and later, the employers were compelled by law to pay wages at fixed rates and to provide a specified amount of farming and grazing land for each African family.

But the squatter system had great drawbacks. A man who had to work 180 days a year was a good deal cut off from his family and tribal life. The squatter had no hope of ever acquiring a right to his land; he lost the land when he left his employer. The employer wanted his labour, but did not want his family or his cattle; to the employer, these were a nuisance, part of the price he had to pay to get a useful man. The cattle particularly were unwelcome, roaming freely over the unfenced parts of the European farm, and liable to infect the carefully preserved European cattle. It was not long before the settlers began to protest at the herds of African cattle on their land.

From 1928 onwards, the Europeans had been authorized to set up European district councils to manage their affairs. In 1940 an ordinance allowed a European district council to make by-laws limiting the number of African cattle in its district; and the district councils were not slow to take advantage of this permission. One district council limited the total numbers of African livestock to fifteen sheep per family, with no cattle at all. Another laid down that however many African families might be living on one European farm, they were not to have between them more than forty head of cattle and twenty sheep or goats. Measures like these greatly reduced the attractiveness of the squatter system in African eyes; for what was life without cattle? The Carter commission recommended that the squatters should be encouraged to go back to the reserves; and under these harsher conditions, many of them did go back there. But this of course made it harder for the Europeans to obtain labour; and so there was constant tension between the government, which was trying to make life more tolerable for the Africans; the European farmers, who were trying to obtain the labour which they needed; and the Africans, who wanted more land which they could farm in peace.

This tension was increased by one other recommendation of the Carter commission. The White Highlands had hitherto been reserved for European settlement not by law, but merely by administrative practice. The Carter commission fixed their boundaries, and the government decided that the region should now be reserved for Europeans by law. The commission drew the logical consequences of this decision. If this land, it said, was now to be reserved by law, none but Europeans could have the legal right to live there. But from the earliest days of European settlement, it had been recognized that some land in the Highlands was private land, already occupied by Africans; and these Africans had been protected by law.[5] Their land had not been alienated. They could not be evicted or made to work for a European. Since they were not living on European land, the Resident Natives Ordinance did not apply to them. The Carter commission recommended that these Africans should no longer be allowed to live in the Highlands, and should receive compensation in land and in money. The government accepted the recommendation. About 4,000 Africans were evicted, and they received in compensation about 6,000 acres of good land and about £6,000 in money. (This was before the 1939 war, and £6,000 at that time was worth perhaps £30,000 at present prices.) But no compensation, however generous, can quite reconcile a man to losing his legal rights, especially his right to live on his family's ancestral land.

Thus, along with much good, the Carter commission did some harm. It did all that was possible to ensure that African reserves should be adequate in area, and that Africans should feel secure in them. It gave compensation to the Kikuyu and others who had been dispossessed of their land. But it hardened the division of Kenya into an African area and a European area; and for the first time it became plain that no African farmer, however skilled and scientific his methods, could ever hope to farm land in the Highlands. Before 1932, the sore point in the land question had been the hundred or more square miles of Kikuyu land that had been settled by Europeans. After 1932, the sore point was the 2,000 or so square miles of farm land in the White Highlands, which were lying unoccupied, but on which Africans cast their eyes in vain. It was useless for government agricultural demonstrators to urge Africans to adopt better methods of farming: mixed farming, contour ridging, manuring, rotation of crops, and so on. To all this excellent advice, the Africans had one answer: There is no need for all this. There is plenty of good land lying idle in the Highlands. Why will you not let us go there?

[5] See page 100.

Chapter 6

ADMINISTRATION AND POLITICS IN KENYA TO 1945

The European settlers brought politics with them into Kenya. The government's first political problems were to arrange the affairs of the Europeans who wanted land, and of the Europeans who wanted to exclude the Asians from political power.

EARLY ADMINISTRATION

Before the European settlers arrived, the government was busy in setting up its administration. The East African Protectorate was established on July 1, 1895, and was placed under the British consul-general at Zanzibar. Not until 1900 did the Protectorate receive its own commissioner, with his headquarters at Mombasa.

There could be no question of any agreement, such as the agreements made with Buganda and other kingdoms beyond the Nile. The protectorate was thinly peopled; some of its peoples were nomadic, and none of them had strong kings or chiefs like the Kabaka of Buganda. The government had no revenue and depended on a grant from the British Treasury; consequently it was always short of administrative officers. It would have liked to make use of African chiefs and develop a system of indirect rule, but it could find no chiefs capable of working such a system.

In 1897 the government issued the Native Courts Regulations, which authorized its district officers to cooperate with the courts of elders who tried cases under African customary law. In 1902, the Village Headman Ordinance made an attempt to set up authorities with whom the district officers could deal. Under this ordinance, the government appointed existing chiefs or clan leaders as headmen; if it could find no such people, it appointed headmen of its own. The duties of the village headman were not heavy. He was to help in collecting the hut tax, to supply men to work for the government on public works, and to hand over criminals to the government justice. In spite of the government's attempts to find men who were already recognized by their people as possessing authority, the duties which it laid upon the headman naturally made the people regard the headman as a government official, the district officer's assistant. There were no doubt many cases in which the government appointed the wrong man as headman.

The Native Authority Ordinance of 1912 increased the powers of chiefs and headmen. Each was to hold authority over a fixed geographical area, and was empowered to call up men to do up to six days' work every three months for public purposes in the African reserves. This was a development of the traditional custom of communal labour.

As the European demand for labour increased, chiefs and headmen were more and more called upon to supply it; and this put more power into their hands. A headman could say who must go to work and who need not go; he might be paid a fee by the labour recruiter, and his position could easily become very profitable. It began to seem that too much power was being concentrated in the hands of the chiefs and headmen, and that the elders were being pushed into the background. In 1924 and again in 1933, the Native Authority Ordinance was amended to remedy this. By these amending ordinances, Local Native Councils were established; some of their members were nominated (these were elders holding traditional positions of authority) but most were elected. The councils were authorized to deal with agriculture, education, communications, the registration of marriages and deaths, and other local matters. On these matters they were empowered to make by-laws; but not to make changes in customary law, or to take part in protectorate politics. They had a revenue; they could levy rates and certain fees, and spend the money on schools and other public purposes. In 1926, the Local Native Councils had a total income of £37,000; by 1938 it had risen to £112,000. By that year, the African demand for education was becoming insatiable, and the councils wished to spend all their money on building schools, much to the embarrassment of the Kenya government, which found itself unable to provide trained teachers to staff them.

THE BEGINNINGS OF EUROPEAN POLITICS

As early as 1902, a group of people in Mombasa, both European and Asian, asked the commissioner, Sir Charles Eliot, to set up an advisory council. Eliot refused; but two years later he himself thought that the time had come to set up a formal legislative council, and he encouraged the Farmers' and Planters' Association to hope that the council might include some unofficial members. When this Association renamed itself the Colonists' Association in 1905, it took up this idea and went further: it asked for a legislative council containing not merely nominated unofficial members, but elected. The Secretary of State, Lyttelton, replied that he doubted if the white population of the protectorate would ever be large enough to justify this; on the other hand, he thought that East Africa was the natural outlet for emigration from India. Much more was to be heard of this idea later on.

The 1906 constitution

The Colonists' Association did not accept this rebuff, and went on pressing for elected representation. Under the influence of a group of settlers from South Africa, it demanded forts, an all-white police force, and a militia after the South African pattern. But the government in London refused to allow this imitation of South African ways, and it gave the protectorate in 1906 a constitution of the usual colonial type, with an executive council and with a legislative council consisting of six official and two nominated unofficial members. The commissioner, Sir James Hayes Sadler, was now styled the governor.

Sir James Hayes Sadler submitted to London the names of Lord Delamere and another European, Mr Baillie, for approval as nominated members of the legislative council, and was asked whom he proposed to nominate to represent the Indians. He had not thought of nominating anyone, but he was told to look for a suitable candidate. Sadler did nothing to find one; in 1908 the Indians petitioned for representation, and while Sadler was on leave, his deputy, Jackson, suggested the name of Mr A. M. Jeevanjee, who was duly appointed a third nominated unofficial member.

Sir Percy Girouard arrived as governor in September 1909, before Jeevanjee had taken his seat. He reported that both the official and the unofficial sides of the council needed strengthening. Delamere was not for the moment a member of the council; he had resigned a few months before. Girouard recommended that he should be renominated, but he was doubtful about Jeevanjee. If you nominate him, he said, you will have legitimate demands from the Arabs, who are twice as many as the Indians. It does not seem to have occurred to the governor that if the Arabs were twice as many as the Indians, the Indians were at least ten times as many as the Europeans, so that this was a dangerous argument. He was too late; Jeevanjee's nomination was already gazetted, and he took his seat. But Mr Jeevanjee was not happy as the sole non-European member of the legislative council; his appointment expired in 1911 and was not renewed, and after that date there was no Indian member. Girouard's proposal to increase the number of unofficial members was approved; in 1913 there were four of them, all Europeans.

The Europeans were pressing harder than ever for elections, and in 1913 Delamere pointed out that some of the arguments which had been used against their demand were no longer valid. The country was now self-supporting; by 1912 the railway revenue had risen so high that the Treasury grant was no longer needed, and the government had been able to raise its first loan.[1] Europeans, he pointed out, were now paying a poll-tax. The official members of the council, he said, were able to look after African and Asian interests, but the Europeans demanded the right to elect their own representatives. Though the governor supported this demand, the Secretary of State again refused it; whereupon the Convention of Associations called upon the four unofficial members to resign, and three of them did so.

Then in 1914 came the war, in which Europeans in Kenya earned the right to vote by their war service. The new Secretary of State, Bonar Law, approved the idea in principle, but said that it could not be put into effect until the war was over. It was now a matter of working out the details of a scheme. The Europeans had strong views about keeping all political power in their own hands, and they were alarmed at the streams of Indians who were pouring into the country. They feared that Kenya would soon be an Indian colony; and they demanded that no Indians should be allowed to vote, either for the legislative council or for town councils; that Indians should not be allowed to hold any land, except plots in the towns, to be held on short leases; that Indian immigration into Kenya should be restricted, if not prohibited altogether; and that no Indians should be employed in government service.

The Indian question

Extreme demands like these naturally provoked a reaction. The Indians had already organized themselves in 1914 into an East African Indian National Congress, and the Congress appealed to the government of India to stand by its own people. India was then ruled by Britain, but it had a certain amount of self-government, and the India Office in London had its own Secretary of State, who was not bound to concur with the views of the Colonial Office.

When the Electoral Representation Bill was introduced into the legislative council in 1919, it proposed to give the vote to European men only. An unofficial member moved an amendment, providing that the vote should be given to any non-European British subject who satisfied certain educational requirements, roughly corresponding to the modern School Certificate. This amendment was defeated by thirteen votes to three. Another amendment, giving the vote to European women, was carried. At the same time, two unofficial Europeans were nominated as members of the governor's executive council.

The new council was elected in February 1920; it contained eleven

---

[1] The loan was of £250,000, and the money was used to build a branch railway to Thika and deep-water quays at Kilindini harbour.

elected European members, with a majority of official members. The governor nominated an Indian lawyer, Mr Phadke, as an Indian representative.

In May 1920, the Secretary of State, Lord Milner, sent his comments on the European proposals. He agreed that the Indians should not be allowed to hold land in the Highlands, but said that they must be allowed to hold land elsewhere in the country. There could be no question of restricting Indian immigration, or of refusing Indians the vote, and there should be two elected Indian members of the legislative council. On the other hand, he was prepared to allow segregation in towns; there should be separate Indian and European residential areas, and as far as possible, separate business areas also.

These proposals satisfied nobody. The Indians refused the offer of two elected members; if 8,000 Europeans were to be represented by eleven elected members, the 22,000 Indians needed more than two. They did not ask for an Indian majority, but they did ask for eleven elected members, so that the official members of the legislative council would hold the balance. They asked also for equal representation on the governor's executive council and on town councils; they asked for an end to segregation in towns; for an assurance that immigration would not be restricted, and that Indians should be appointed and promoted in government service on their merits. Finally, they asked for the right to hold land in the Highlands. All this was in flat opposition to the Convention of Associations, and some of the Indian spokesmen used language which the Europeans seized on as evidence that their fears were justified. India was represented at the Peace Conference in 1919, and the proposal was made there that India should be given the mandate over Tanganyika. When this was rejected, some Indians said that Kenya ought to be an Indian, not a British colony, and it could soon be made into a second India. Both Europeans and Indians were clamouring to have Kenya developed in their own interests. Both seemed to forget the interests of the Africans, whose function in life, it seemed, was to earn money from the European employer and spend it at the Indian shop.

The Kikuyu enter politics

All this time, the Africans had remained quiet. But in 1920 and 1921, two associations were formed among the Kikuyu; the Kikuyu Association in 1920 and the Young Kikuyu Association next year. The first was mainly an association of chiefs and headmen, and was concerned mainly with land affairs; the Young Kikuyu Association was the stronger and more active of the two.

The leader of the Young Kikuyu Association was Harry Thuku, a telephone operator in a government office. Thuku began by being strictly moderate. He sent the government a copy of the rules of his association, and assumed that the government would be ready to discuss his grievances and put them right. In June 1921 some senior government officers met Thuku and his associates at Dagoretti. He complained of recent cuts in wages and increases in taxation. He complained that the registration system was bad, and the way in which it was administered made it worse; that men and women were being compelled to go and work on European farms, although the government had promised that this should not happen; that Europeans had written documents for their land, but that Africans had none; that there was not enough African education; and in particular that the government provided no schools of its own, but left education entirely to the missionaries and the European farmers.

Harry Thuku no doubt expected that the government officers there would promise to have all these matters put right. But though they listened sympathetically, the officers knew that it was out of their power to make such promises. All they could say was that they would report to the governor.

Unluckily, the governor was Sir Edward Northey, who was a soldier and believed in discipline, and an administrator who was convinced that the future of Kenya depended on the prosperity of the European settlers. Northey was terribly harassed: the prices of all Kenya produce had slumped; Europeans were going bankrupt; the Convention of Associations was at the height of its campaign against the Indians; the currency crisis was serious. The governor had little time or patience to deal sympathetically with the grievances of a young government telephone operator. His senior officers mishandled the affair. Thuku was a government official, and by regulations was forbidden to take part in politics; the government applied the regulations strictly, and told him to keep quiet or else resign his post. Thuku resigned, and thus became a martyr. Still convinced that the King would give him justice, he sent cables to London appealing against the Kenya government's policy. He used stronger and stronger language in his public meetings, and in March 1922 the government arrested him for sedition. Instead of putting him in prison to await his trial, it put him in the very insecure police barracks. An excited African crowd gathered outside the barracks, the tired and jumpy police fired without orders, and more than twenty people were killed. Thuku was not tried; he was sent away to Kismayu to live under supervision. His Young Kikuyu Association for the time being gave up politics, but did not disband.

This unhappy affair need never have occurred. Many missionaries were sympathetic to Harry Thuku; so were many government officers. The government ought to have noticed two significant things about the new movement: for the first time, the Africans were beginning to take a part in politics, and the young men were beginning to take a line of their own in opposition to their chiefs and headmen. If the government had been wise, it would have realized that here was the beginning of a new political force, which might be the very thing it was looking for to help it to stand up to the Europeans. But even without this, if the government had handled Thuku with ordinary tact and sympathy the bloodshed would have been saved and the Young Kikuyu Association might have been guided into useful activity.

The Indian question continues

Meanwhile, Europeans and Indians were still manoeuvring for position, each hoping to become the controlling force in Kenya. The Indians appealed for help to the Indian government, and the Indian government sent one of its senior officials, Sir Benjamin Robertson, to visit Kenya and see the position for himself. In October 1920 his report was received. He recommended that Indians and Europeans should vote together on one common roll; that Indians and Europeans should live together in towns, Indians not being segregated into separate streets or areas in towns; and that Indians should be allowed to hold land in the Highlands. The Indian government accepted his views, and criticized Milner's proposals of May 1920 accordingly.

This matter of the 'common roll' is of great importance. The common roll of voters is opposed to the communal roll. If voting is on a common roll, it means that all the voters' names are on one list, so that in each electoral district the candidate is chosen by all the voters —of whatever race—voting together. This system will have certain consequences. If there is strong racial feeling, as there was in Kenya in 1920, the Indians and the Europeans will no doubt organize themselves into separate political associations. Then, if there is an Indian and a European candidate contesting a seat and the Indians are in a majority, it will be possible for the Indians to ensure that the Indian candidate is elected. Taking the country as a whole, the legislative council may have an overwhelming majority of Indian members. This is exactly what the Europeans were afraid of in 1920. No one at that time thought of giving votes to Africans; but more than thirty years later, when Africans were to receive the vote, the African leaders demanded a common roll, and the Europeans were afraid of it, for just the same reason.

If voting is on a communal roll, Indian voters' names are put on one list, and European voters' names on another; Indians vote only for Indian candidates, and Europeans only for European candidates. In this way, the council is sure always to contain both Indian and European members. The constitution will decide how many of each there are to be.

Each system has its advantages and disadvantages. The disadvantage of the common roll is that if racial feeling is strong, one race may be unrepresented, or badly under-represented in the council. Its advantage is that as racial feeling dies down, it becomes possible for voters to elect the best representative, without troubling whether he is Indian or European. The advantage of the communal roll is plain where racial feeling is strong. Its disadvantage is that when racial feeling dies down, the communal roll keeps the race question alive in the council; for Indians who would gladly vote for a European, and Europeans who would gladly vote for an Indian, have no opportunity of doing so.

Sir Benjamin Robertson favoured elections on the common roll. The Convention of Associations put out a statement of what it called its 'irreducible minimum' demands. These were: (1) Indians should continue to be excluded from the Highlands; (2) they should be segregated in the residential areas of towns, and as far as possible in the business areas also; (3) there should be no Indian voting, but Indian interests should be represented by two nominated Indian members on the legislative council; (4) Indian immigration should be restricted, and eventually prohibited altogether.

In February 1921, Lord Milner was succeeded as Secretary of State by Winston Churchill, who had already shown himself less sympathetic than Milner to the claims of the Europeans. A few months later, Northey was succeeded as governor by Sir Robert Coryndon, who was transferred from Uganda, and came to Kenya foreseeing that, as he said, he would have 'no more peace'. A few days after the new governor's arrival, he received new constitutional proposals from England. These had been drawn up by the Colonial and India Offices in consultation, and were known as the Wood–Winterton proposals, Wood and Winterton being the two Under-Secretaries of State who had approved them.

The Wood–Winterton proposals were: (1) that there should be no restriction on Indian immigration, and no segregation in towns; (2) elections should be held on a common roll, and there should be a property qualification for the vote so that about one Indian in ten should have the vote; (3) there should be four seats in the legislative council reserved for Indian elected members, and the number of European elected members should be reduced from eleven to seven. The two Under-Secretaries could not agree on the question of the

Highlands, and the India Office reserved its right to reopen this question later.

The Wood–Winterton proposals were not discussed in the legislative council, and were not published; but they soon leaked out. The Indians were still not satisfied, mainly because they were still being denied equal representation with the Europeans, which meant as much to them at that time as 'One man, one vote' meant to the Africans thirty years later. However, they were inclined to accept the proposals, trusting that with a more sympathetic Secretary of State at the Colonial Office, the Wood–Winterton scheme would be a good starting-point for further advance. For this very reason, the Europeans attacked the Wood–Winterton proposals furiously. The Indians, they said, would never be content with this scheme, and before long they would make fresh demands so as to make Kenya an Indian colony.

Relations between Europeans and Indians had recently been much embittered. The all-European Economic Committee of 1917–19 had reported that the Indians were a bad moral influence on the Africans and had an 'incurable repugnance to sanitation and hygiene'. In 1920 a Public Health Bill was introduced, which proposed (largely on these very grounds) to make segregation the law of the land: Indians would be confined to their own areas in towns by law instead of merely by administrative action. The unpleasant opinions of the Economic Committee were repeated in the debates; the bill was bitterly contested, and feeling ran so high that Mr Phadke, the only Indian member, resigned his council seat in protest. The Secretary of State refused to approve the segregation clauses of the Bill, but Mr Phadke did not return to the council.

The Devonshire White Paper of 1923

By 1923, feelings had become so bitter that both the European and the Indian communities in Kenya sent delegations to London to discuss the country's future with the Secretary of State. Again there was a new Secretary of State, the Duke of Devonshire. One of the weaknesses in the British colonial system was that until after the 1939 war, the post of Secretary of State for the Colonies was regarded as one of the less important posts in the government; anyone who did well in it hoped to be speedily promoted to something higher. During the 28 years from October 1903 there were no fewer than thirteen Secretaries of State, an average of only 26 months each in office. All thirteen had to deal with Lord Delamere; even if Delamere had been less tough than he was, he would still have been at an advantage in dealing with this procession of short-lived ministers.

In dealing with the Duke of Devonshire, however, Delamere overplayed his hand. He emphasized that the Europeans had a Christian duty to protect the Africans in Kenya against exploitation by Hindus and Muslims from India. He was unable to show in detail how the Europeans would fulfil this duty; he merely repeated the old claim that Africans would somehow be benefited through working for European employers. On this question of Christian duty, however, Devonshire had at his disposal advisers who spoke with more authority than Lord Delamere. The missionaries in Kenya were represented in London by Dr J. H. Oldham, and he was in close touch with the Archbishop of Canterbury, Randall Davidson. These two distinguished men pointed out that Kenya was an African country, in which both the Indians and the Europeans were immigrant minorities. Britain, they said, had a responsibility to educate and prepare the Africans to take a greater share in the affairs of their country. Indians and Europeans were trying to strengthen their own positions; neither showed much interest in African needs and desires.

The result of these discussions was a document, usually known as the Devonshire White Paper, which gave no satisfaction either to the European or to the Indian leaders. 'Primarily,' it said,

'Kenya is an African territory, and His Majesty's Government think it necessary definitely to record their considered opinion that the interests of the African natives must be paramount, and that if, and when, those interests and the interests of the immigrant races should conflict, the former should prevail.'

Lord Delamere's hopes of responsible government in European hands were firmly negatived; so too were the Europeans' hopes that Indian representation on the legislative council should be by nomination and not by election:

'His Majesty's Government cannot but regard the grant of responsible self-government as out of the question within any period of time which need now be taken into consideration. . . . In no responsible quarter is it suggested that the Indians in Kenya should not have elective representation upon the legislative council of the colony.'

The White Paper went on to emphasize the idea that the government thought of itself as responsible for African development. The interests of Europeans, Indians and Arabs already living in Kenya, it said, must not be injured by any abrupt reversal of government policy.

'But in the administration of Kenya, His Majesty's Government regard themselves as exercising a trust on behalf of the African population, and they are unable to delegate or share this trust, the object of which may be defined as the protection and advancement of the native races. . . . As in the Uganda Protectorate, so in the Kenya Colony, the principle of trusteeship for the natives, no less than in the mandated territory of Tanganyika, is unassailable. This paramount duty of trusteeship will continue, as in the past, to be carried out under the Secretary of State by the agents of the Imperial Government, and by them alone.'

Not by Lord Delamere or the elected European and Indian members of the legislative council!

Having thus laid down some general principles, the White Paper went on to make detailed constitutional proposals. It proposed that the legislative council should contain eleven elected European members, five elected Indians and one elected Arab, but the official majority should be maintained. African interests should be represented by one European missionary, to be nominated by the governor for this special purpose. Indians should be allowed to elect their representatives to town councils.

The White Paper rejected the Wood–Winterton proposal of the common electoral roll, which it regarded as quite unworkable in the excited condition of Kenya at the time. Indians, it thought, would never vote for a European, Europeans would never vote for an Indian. Communal representation was the only practical method. On other matters (immigration, segregation, and the Highlands) the White Paper followed the Wood–Winterton proposals. The India Office had already reserved its right to reopen the question of Indian settlement in the Highlands; the Colonial Office now similarly reserved its right to reopen the question of immigration control if the flood of Indian immigrants seemed likely to swamp the African population and make Kenya into another India.

In Kenya, the Devonshire White Paper pleased nobody. The Convention of Associations had been severely snubbed. The Indians hated the idea of the communal roll and thought five members quite inadequate representation on the legislative council. Hardly any Africans at that time had enough education to understand what the White Paper was saying. The few that had education found its words satisfactory; but it remained to be seen whether fair words would be backed up with deeds. The Indians expressed their disapproval by refusing to register as voters; only about 200 registered out of about 15,000 who were eligible. Until 1926, Indians even refused to accept nomination to the council, but in that year five allowed themselves to be nominated.

Next year, one Indian stood for election and was returned, so that Indians were then represented on the legislative council by one elected member and four nominated members.

THE MOVEMENT FOR CLOSER UNION

During these few years while the Indians were to some extent withdrawing from active politics, the Europeans found themselves faced with a new problem. The government in London put forward the idea that the three territories of Kenya, Uganda and Tanganyika should in some way be joined more closely together. The idea was strongly pressed forward by Mr Amery, who was Secretary of State for the unusually long period of four and a half years, from November 1924 to June 1929. Amery had already put forward the idea before taking office, and in July 1924 a commission of three members of parliament, under Mr Ormsby-Gore, was appointed to visit East Africa. It was not required to report on the possibility of any closer political union; but it was to study the position with regard to African labour and taxation, and to report on the possibility of coordinating some of the public services of the region, such as health, communications, agriculture and cotton production. It was also to report on ways of improving the social position of the Africans and their relations with the Indian and European communities.

Although closer political union was not in the commission's terms of reference, it was known in East Africa that this idea was being discussed in England; and when the commission arrived, it found everyone ready to explain why closer union would not do. The Kabaka of Buganda and his Lukiko objected, for fear that the 1900 Agreement would be affected. The Indians in all three territories objected because they feared that in any scheme of closer union the Kenya Europeans would be dominant. The Europeans in Uganda and Tanganyika were not strongly opposed to closer union in principle, but they had special reasons for not wishing to come under the leadership of Lord Delamere. In Uganda, they felt that Kenya was taking more than its fair share of the railway and customs revenue. In Tanganyika it was known that Delamere wanted to attract as much as possible of Tanganyika's trade to Mombasa; for this purpose he wanted to stop the Tanganyika government from building a railway line from Tabora to Mwanza, and he wanted the Kilimanjaro district to be taken from Tanganyika and added to Kenya. Thus the Europeans in Tanganyika were unwilling to come into closer union with Kenya.

Since most people objected to closer union because they were afraid of the Kenya Europeans, we might have expected the Kenya

Europeans themselves to be enthusiastic at the idea. But even they were cautious, for they too had their fears. Closer union would be very well if it maintained or increased their political power, but they were afraid that it might bring them still more under the control of the Colonial Office. They were inclined therefore to accept the idea of closer union only on condition that the Kenya legislative council should have a majority of elected members.

The Ormsby-Gore commission reported that closer political union was for the moment out of the question, and it did not see much hope of setting up machinery for coordinating public services. It recommended that the governors of Kenya, Uganda and Tanganyika should meet regularly to discuss ways and means of cooperating. This Governors' Conference met first in 1925, and from 1930 onwards it met every year.

The idea of closer union had been shelved for the moment; but Amery was still Secretary of State, and people in East Africa felt that the Governors' Conference was meant to be the first step towards a closer union in the future. In 1925 Amery appointed Sir Edward Grigg to succeed Coryndon as governor of Kenya, and told him to prepare a scheme of closer union. Grigg did so: he proposed to set up a federal council to take charge of customs, railways and harbours and trunk roads, posts and telegraphs, defence and research. Delamere felt that he must guard against the danger. In December 1926 he persuaded his fellow elected members of the Kenya legislative council to make an offer to the government: they would accept a scheme of coordination (even possibly of federation) between the three territories, provided that the elected members of the Kenya legislative council became a majority over the official and nominated members.

But Grigg's scheme found a stronger opponent than Delamere. This was the new governor of Tanganyika, Sir Donald Cameron. Cameron was bent on introducing indirect rule into Tanganyika, and did not want to be hindered in this by the Europeans in Kenya. Moreover, he wanted to build the Tabora–Mwanza railway line to tap the trade of the lake country and bring it down to Dar-es-Salaam. His two fellow-governors, anxious to keep as much traffic as possible for Mombasa, even went the length of sending a telegram to London asking the Secretary of State to forbid Cameron to build the Mwanza line. Cameron was furious, and when he heard of Grigg's plan for a federal council he refused to have anything to do with it, and threatened to resign.

As a rule, a Secretary of State is not greatly perturbed when one of his governors threatens to resign. But Cameron's resignation would have been very awkward. Tanganyika was a mandated territory. The governor's resignation would have to be reported and explained to the League of Nations; and the League would be displeased if the governor seemed to be resigning because he felt that the prosperity of Tanganyika and the interests of its African peoples were being sacrificed to the interests of Kenya and Uganda. So the Secretary of State allowed Cameron to build his railway, and appointed a committee to study Grigg's plan for a federal council.

The committee's views were published in July 1927. They emphasized that from the economic point of view, some form of closer union was very desirable. The frontiers between the three territories were quite artificial, and the three governments could do much better for their people if they acted together than if each went its own way without thinking of the others. But the committee did not try to draw up a scheme for closer union, whether based on Grigg's idea or not; it recommended that this idea should be studied by yet another commission, which should visit East Africa and report.

The Hilton Young commission of 1928

Sir Hilton Young was appointed chairman of the new commission, which visited East and Central Africa in 1928. There had been talk of bringing Northern Rhodesia and Nyasaland (the modern Zambia and Malawi) into one federation with the East African territories; but when the commission visited those countries, it quickly became plain to them that there was no chance of this; the Europeans in Central Africa would much rather join with Southern Rhodesia.

In East Africa, the Uganda government was less hostile than it had been, because it had just made a new arrangement with Kenya over the railway revenues. Uganda had always felt it to be unfair that such a large share of the railway revenue was taken by Kenya and paid over into the Kenya Treasury for the general expenses of the Kenya government. Uganda wanted a larger share of the revenue, and it wanted the railway revenue kept separate from general revenue and spent on extending and improving the railway. Kenya had now agreed to this, so Uganda was feeling happier. In 1928 the new line was opened from Nakuru to Jinja.

But this sort of economic cooperation was a very different matter from political union, and to any closer political union the opposition seemed as strong as ever. Everyone in East Africa was afraid that closer union would give more power to the Kenya Europeans; and the Kabaka and his Lukiko, Sir Donald Cameron, and the Indians in all three territories were united in opposing any scheme that would have this effect. Nevertheless, the commission reported that there was one very strong reason for pressing on with some scheme of closer union.

This was to ensure that the three governments should have as far as possible one and the same policy towards their African peoples. In this, the Hilton Young commission was following up the ideas of the Devonshire White Paper of five years before, which had said very emphatically that in all three countries, the governments' main task was to act as a trustee for the interests of the Africans. In Uganda and Tanganyika, the governments were having some success in this aim. In Kenya, the government was doing its best, but was having great difficulty with its European settlers. If Kenya could be brought into closer relations with the other two countries, the commission thought that its government would have less difficulty in following an enlightened policy of trusteeship. The commission dropped Grigg's idea of a federal council. It recommended that a High Commissioner for East Africa should be appointed, and that the existing Governors' Conference should be ready to give him advice. But as far as African affairs were concerned, the High Commissioner should be able to give the three governors orders.

Nobody in East Africa liked the idea of the High Commissioner. The Kenya settlers saw that it was meant to enable the Kenya government to enforce on them the kind of policy they had always been fighting. The Indians were not interested, for the High Commissioner's attention would be given mainly to African affairs, and all they wanted was equal elected representation with Europeans in the legislative councils. The Kabaka had an agreement with the King, and he would rather deal directly with London than with a High Commissioner in Nairobi. Sir Donald Cameron did not wish to have a High Commissioner to order him to do what he was already doing in Tanganyika without orders.

So for the time being, very little came of the Hilton Young proposals. The Labour government which came to power in Britain in 1929 was inclined to favour the idea of a High Commissioner with special responsibility for African affairs; but before taking any action on the matter it set up a parliamentary committee to study the whole question. The committee was impressed with the evidence it received from the African witnesses from Kenya and Uganda who came before it. Chief Koinange from the Kikuyu and Mr Ezekiel Apindi from Kavirondo demanded direct African representation on the legislative council; they were not interested in the suggestion that African political advance should be made in local affairs, through the Local Native Councils. The Africans made it clear that they would rather remain directly the responsibility of the governor and the Secretary of State than come under the proposed High Commissioner in Nairobi.

Faced with this general opposition, the committee recommended that the idea of the High Commissioner should be dropped, and that the East African territories should be left to develop separately, and to work gradually towards more effective cooperation by means of the Governors' Conference. It would have liked to propose a scheme of direct African membership of the Kenya legislative council, which its African witnesses had asked for. But very few Kenya Africans at that time understood enough English to take part in the debates, so the committee contented itself with recommending the Kenya government to do what it could to increase the representation of African interests. The council already contained one missionary nominated for this purpose, and the government made no change until 1944, when it nominated the council's first African member.

Kenya's years of poverty began in 1928, when all the farms were devastated by locusts. Both Indians and Europeans had far too much to worry over in keeping alive and in business to think much about politics. Lord Delamere died in 1931, and the Europeans thus lost their strongest leader. The Kenya government suffered a great drop in revenue, and had to cut its expenditure. A financial adviser, Lord Moyne, came out from England to examine Kenya's financial situation, and his report threw a doubt on the whole system of the country. He pointed out that the Africans were paying $37\frac{1}{2}$ per cent of the direct taxation, and were getting very little for it in direct government services. The government, he thought, should spend more on African education and should do much more to improve African agriculture. The settlers had always claimed that the best way of improving the condition of the Africans was to employ them on European farms. The Moyne report threw great doubt on this claim, and it had a considerable effect on public opinion in Britain. It did not bring about any changes in government policy before the outbreak of war in 1939, but through those years, public opinion in Britain was turning increasingly against the European settlers and in favour of the hitherto largely ignored African population.

AFRICAN POLITICS REVIVE

During the 1930s, politics among the Indians and the Europeans were quieter than they had been. But among the Africans, and especially among the Kikuyu, political activity became greater and greater. Harry Thuku's Young Kikuyu Association had renamed itself in 1924 the Kikuyu Central Association. It was asking that Thuku be allowed to return from his exile in Kismayu, that Africans should be allowed to grow coffee, that the laws of Kenya should be published in the Kikuyu language, and that a paramount chief should be appointed over the Kikuyu people. In 1931 the government allowed Thuku to return home.

Apart from these grievances, there were two main questions agitating the Kikuyu Central Association at that time. One, it need hardly be said, was the whole question of land, on which the Association sent its new secretary Jomo Kenyatta (the future President of Kenya) to England in 1931 to make its views known there. Mr Kenyatta stayed in Europe for fifteen years, from 1931 to 1946, to represent the views of the Africans of Kenya.

The other question was new: it was the question of female circumcision, which was part of Kikuyu, but not of European custom.[2] In 1929, the Church of Scotland missionaries in Kenya decided that the practice was un-Christian, and they called on all their followers to give it up. The Christian Kikuyu were divided on the matter: some obeyed, but others said that they saw nothing in the Bible to forbid the custom. The KCA took up the matter. It said that it was opposed to any sort of compulsion: if Christian Kikuyu chose to abandon this tribal custom they should be free to do so, but if other Christian Kikuyu wished to keep it up, the missionaries had no right to stop them. Feeling among the Kikuyu rose high, and many Christians began to take part in dances and other tribal gatherings and ceremonies which they knew the missionaries disapproved of. Whatever the rights and wrongs of the question, it was unfortunate that Dr Arthur, who led the protest against the labour circular of 1919, and now sat in the legislative council as a nominated member to represent African interests, also led the missionary protest against female circumcision. The result was that the Kikuyu lost their trust in the missionaries, and put their trust instead in their own political organizations.

In this way, what had begun merely as a matter of church discipline quickly became a political matter. Kikuyu nationalism began to grow at great speed. The KCA and many of the Christian Kikuyu decided to open their own schools in opposition to the schools run by the missionaries, and they set up the Kikuyu Independent Schools Association. In 1938 the Association opened its own training college to supply its schools with trained teachers.

The government now made a mistake which many British colonial governments have made. It thought that the KCA did not really represent African feeling: that it was only a small group of young men, and that the true representatives of African feeling were the chiefs and the older men. The government had some excuse for this

[2] The Kikuyu view of the matter is set out in Mr Kenyatta's book *Facing Mount Kenya*, pp. 130–154.

mistake. The KCA had not many active members, and some of the chiefs violently disapproved of its policy. But although only a small proportion of the Kikuyu were active members of the KCA, many people who did not take the trouble to become active members heard its speeches and were influenced by them. Moreover, the KCA members belonged to an age-set which had just come into authority among the Kikuyu people, and so its influence was growing. The government would have been wiser to try to work with the KCA leaders.

Politics were not confined to the Kikuyu. There was a similar movement among the Kavirondo people, with two branches, a Luo and a Bantu branch. The Kakamega gold-mining dispute caused this movement to become active in 1934. A few years later, the government, which was worried at the over-grazing and erosion of the soil in the Kamba country, tried to persuade the Kamba people to slaughter some of their cattle to be sold for food; the Kamba bitterly resented the scheme and formed the Ukamba Members' Association to resist. Down in Mombasa there was a labour dispute among the dock workers, and here too the KCA stepped in on the side of the workers, many of whom were Kikuyu. In July 1939 the KCA organized a strike in the docks; but a few weeks later the war broke out, and the government then prohibited all political activity so that it could concentrate on the war effort.

On the outbreak of the war, the people of Kenya rushed to join the fighting forces, as they had done in 1914. But the great problems remained, and it was certain that after the war they would have to be solved. The Africans would certainly have to be given political representation, and somehow their interests and the interests of the Europeans and Indians would have to be brought into harmony. African education and other social services were seriously underdeveloped; the government was so short of money that it had very few education officers, and after posting one European for a time to help the Kikuyu independent schools, it had to withdraw him. Some way must be found of developing these social services: of settling the land question: of stopping soil erosion: of developing new sources of revenue. Would coffee, tea and pyrethrum suffice to provide the necessary funds, and could other crops, or minerals, or outside sources of revenue be found to supplement them? While the war lasted, little could be done to answer these questions; they would demand an answer all the more urgently when the war ended.

Chapter 7

UGANDA FROM 1919 TO 1945

Uganda, like Kenya, had its European planters and Indian traders, and because of them it had some of the same difficulties as those we have seen in Kenya. But there were great differences. Uganda's Eastern Province, which was transferred to Kenya in 1902, contained the high land which was most suitable for European farmers; without that province, Uganda as a whole was less attractive to European settlers than Kenya. And whereas large areas of Kenya were thinly inhabited by African peoples who were organized in small clans without powerful chiefs, Uganda was closely populated, and many of its African peoples —notably Buganda—formed solid and highly organized states. Moreover, there was much more education in Uganda than in Kenya: the first secondary school was opened in 1904. Thus, although Uganda had problems of its own, the problems caused by the European settlers and the Indian traders were not nearly as serious as they were in Kenya.

LAND AND LABOUR

Uganda's chief export had been ivory, but by 1903 the ivory trade was rapidly diminishing, and there was nothing yet to take its place. In that year, the government's expenditure was £186,000 and its revenue only £51,000; the balance was made up by a grant from the British Treasury. How was the revenue to be increased so that the Treasury grant could be dispensed with? Two different answers were offered to this question. Some said, 'Bring in European settlers'; others said, 'Try growing cotton.'

Cotton-growing was tried quite early, but for a time it had little commercial success. The first seed was imported by Mr Kristen Borup of the Church Missionary Society, and in 1904 the government imported more than four tons of seed and distributed it to chiefs in Busoga, Buganda, Ankole and Bunyoro. The government built a ginnery at Kampala, and it also distributed many hand ginning machines to enable growers to gin[1] their own cotton before delivering it for export. The plants grew well, and in 1907 Uganda was able to export 650 tons of ginned cotton, as well as a good deal of unginned

[1] To gin cotton means to take out the seeds: a slow and laborious process if done by hand.

cotton, which went to a second ginnery at Kisumu. But the spinning factories in England were not pleased with the quality of Uganda cotton. Three different varieties were being grown, and all three were mixed in the bales, which were often wet and dirty. The spinners wanted bales of clean dry cotton, all of the same variety; they could make very little use of Uganda cotton as it was.

So it seemed that cotton was not, so far, the solution to Uganda's economic problem, and those who believed in European settlement were encouraged to try it. The chief advocate of this policy was Sir William Morris Carter,[2] who was chairman of a committee appointed in 1911 to report on land policy in the protectorate. Carter suggested various ways in which land might be made available for European settlers. He was supported by two governors, Jackson (1912–17) and Coryndon (1917–22), both of whom believed that Africans in Uganda would best help their country by becoming wage-earners on European farms. But anyone could see that Uganda could never compete with Kenya as a country to attract European settlers. Nevertheless by 1914 some 20,000 acres had been occupied by European settlers; coffee was the main crop, but rubber and cocoa were being tried.

Meanwhile, the government was giving attention to the criticisms of Uganda cotton: it was too mixed, too dirty, and not always well ginned. In 1908, after consultation with the chiefs, the government issued a Cotton Ordinance, which gave the governor powers to make rules for the cotton industry. Under the ordinance, the governor, Sir Hesketh Bell, banned the use of hand ginning machines and set up several new ginning factories. The one variety of cotton which seemed best suited to Uganda was kept, and all cotton plants of other varieties were pulled up and burnt. No cotton seed was to be imported into Uganda without government permission, and importers of cotton seed were to be licensed. As a result of these changes, bales of Uganda cotton became well ginned and uniform in quality. The shorter the distance that the raw cotton needs to be carried in head loads, the cleaner and drier it will be when received at the ginnery. It was important to open up the country with roads and railways so as to lessen head porterage. Lack of money was the difficulty here; but Sir Hesketh Bell spent all he could on roads, and with the aid of a government loan from Britain he built a new railway line from Jinja to Namasagali to open up an important cotton-growing area. The line was opened in

[2] The same Carter who was chairman of the commission of inquiry in Kenya in 1932.
[3] It was not until October 1907 that the administrator of Uganda was styled governor; till then he was styled commissioner.

1913, after Bell had left Uganda and been succeeded as governor by Sir Frederick Jackson.

All these improvements would have been impossible without the support of the chiefs all over the protectorate. It says much for the good work of the missionaries and the administrative officers that the chiefs and people should have been so ready to cooperate. Cotton-growing began to spread and flourish. By 1914, when European planters were cultivating 20,000 acres of coffee and other crops, five times that area was occupied by African cotton-growers. Uganda's export of cotton was worth £60,000 in 1909–10, but well over £300,000 in 1913–14.

This increase in cotton-growing did not please the European settlers and those in the government who wanted to see a great extension of European settlement. In 1908 the Uganda chamber of commerce complained to the government that the Europeans were finding it hard to get labour for their plantations, for Africans were all busy growing cotton for themselves instead of coming to grow coffee for the Europeans. But however anxious the government might be to help the European settlers, it could not discourage such a profitable industry as African-grown cotton, which was bringing in so much revenue and making it possible to cut down the British Treasury grant. After the Cotton Ordinance, the Treasury grant tapered away rapidly:

	£		£
1909–10	103,000	1913–14	35,000
1910–11	96,000	1914–15	10,000
1911–12	65,000	1915–16	nil.
1912–13	45,000		

Whatever the position in Kenya, those who believed that European settlement was the best hope for Uganda would have difficulty in proving it in the face of this rapid African progress.

Carter was still in favour of European settlement; but two of his committee were against him: Spire, commissioner of the Eastern Province from 1909 to 1918, and Simpson, director of agriculture from 1911 to 1929. They could not be brushed aside, for both were in a position to know exactly what the African cotton-growers and the European settlers were doing. Their view was that African cotton was doing so well that it was plain that Africans were quite able to grow cash crops successfully without European supervision. More than this: they pointed out that large-scale alienation of land to Europeans would bring about undesirable results in African life. They saw what was happening in Kenya and did not wish to see it happen in Uganda. But Sir Frederick Jackson approved of Carter's views and in 1915 recommended them to the Secretary of State, Bonar Law, who replied chillingly, 'I am not satisfied that the arrangements contemplated are in the best interests either of the peasants or of the development of the territory.'

There, for the time being, the matter had to rest. After the war, the government appointed a development commission, which (unlike the Kenya development commission) had Indian as well as European members. They made the sort of recommendations that might be expected: that Kampala should have a municipal council elected on a common roll, and that there should be no segregation in the business areas of towns, though the Indians were willing to accept segregation in residential areas. On the other hand, since both Indians and Europeans were interested in farming, the commission recommended that much more land should be alienated, and that chiefs should be pressed to supply labour for Indian or European settlers.

These recommendations were made in 1920, and the governor, Coryndon, supported them. But he was too late. Immediately afterwards there came the currency crisis and the fall in the prices of East African produce. Cocoa and rubber had never been very successful. Coffee had been; but Europe was the only market for it and its price fell from £180 to £60 a ton. Cotton on the other hand could be exported to India, where there was a growing spinning and weaving industry. Thus the African cotton-growers were paid in rupees at the full rate, whereas the European coffee-growers were paid in devalued British pounds. Many European farmers were ruined, and the European farming community ceased to be an important factor in Uganda politics. Uganda was not to be a white man's country.

The European settlers were unlucky; but some Indian settlers who experimented with sugar from 1924 onwards were very successful, for two reasons. One was that they themselves lived much more simply and cheaply than the Europeans; the more important reason was that they did not have to send their sugar to Britain or India, but could sell all they grew in Uganda and Kenya, where Africans were eager to buy it. Thus they did not have heavy transport costs.

So after 1921, Uganda was no longer troubled by the question of European settlers' demands for labour. In July 1922 Coryndon wrote to the Secretary of State, admitting that Carter's policy of large-scale land alienation was no longer practicable, for no Europeans now wanted to take land in Uganda. The Duke of Devonshire accepted this change of policy, and this question was now settled.

Chief and Tenants
Nevertheless, the Uganda government still had a land problem, though

one which concerned only the Africans: the problem of adapting ancient African custom to the new situation in which land produced not merely food crops, but cash crops: not merely food, but money.

The general custom was that tenants should pay their chief a tribute or rent, consisting partly of labour, and partly of a share in the produce of their farms. The amounts varied: in Buganda it was usual for the tenant to pay a labour tribute (*busulu*) of 28 days unpaid labour a year, and a tribute (called *envujo*) of about one-tenth of the food and beer produced on the land. When people began to grow cotton and other cash crops, the landlords claimed envujo on these too. In 1920, the Lukiko of Buganda passed a law fixing the rate of envujo on cotton at ten per cent, but the governor thought this too high, and vetoed the law. Six years later, the Lukiko tried again; this time it suggested ten per cent for most crops, but twenty per cent for coffee, and no less than 35 per cent for cotton. Again the governor vetoed the law; and the provincial commissioner of Buganda suggested a compromise figure, which both the governor and the Lukiko reluctantly accepted. It was an important part of this busulu and envujo law of 1927 that as long as the tenant paid the rent he could not be turned out of his land.

All this haggling shows how old African ideas were being modified by the contact with new economic conditions. In the old Africa, land can hardly be said to have any value. There was land for everybody, and every family was entitled to a share. The customary tribute was paid to the chief, partly to acknowledge his position as trustee of the land, and partly to enable him to exercise hospitality, as every chief must. But now cotton land had become valuable, and at once there arose a conflict of interests between the chief and his tenants: the chief demanding more, the tenant unwilling to pay. From the government's point of view, the busulu and the envujo of the old days had strictly speaking ceased to be necessary, because since 1900, chiefs had been paid a salary. Chiefs and others who held freehold land were entitled (according to European ideas) to charge a rent to their tenants; but the rent should be reasonable.

It now seemed to the government that the Lukiko represented the interests of the chiefs, and that the chiefs were a privileged class, and the poorer people needed to be protected against them. Many of the chiefs were becoming rich. They were responsible for collecting the poll tax, which in 1921 was fifteen shillings a year in rich areas and from six to ten shillings elsewhere. As payment they were allowed to keep some of the money for themselves, sometimes ten, sometimes as much as 30 per cent. In addition, many chiefs used their busulu labour to grow cotton. To the government it seemed that if men were to be compelled to leave their own farm and go to work without pay on someone else's, it made no difference whether they were compelled to work for a European settler or for an African chief. The system placed a great temptation in the way of the employer, and the government set out to remove this temptation. In 1923 in Toro, in 1927 in Busoga, and gradually during the next ten years everywhere else, it converted the chiefs' personal tribute into a local tax; the tax was paid into a central fund, and the fund was used to pay the chiefs a fixed salary, as Buganda chiefs were already paid. The chiefs naturally disliked the change; it reduced their authority among their people and made them appear merely as salaried servants of the government. But they nearly all accepted it; only in Busoga did the lower-grade chiefs refuse the salary and prefer to keep their traditional authority among their people.

The demand for mailo land

The Buganda agreement of 1900 differed from the later agreements with Ankole and Toro in one important respect. In Buganda, nearly half the land was declared to be freehold land; not only were freehold estates reserved for the Kabaka and great chiefs, but a thousand 'chiefs and private landowners' were given 8,000 square miles of land between them. In Ankole and Toro, there was no such mailo land; the only land reserved was the estate of the paramount chief and his family. But in these two states, and also in Bunyoro and Busoga, the chiefs had not yet given up hope that the mailo system might yet be introduced. Mailo land was popular, because it could be leased or sold, whereas land held in the traditional way could never be sold, and could not so easily be leased. In all four states, the paramount chief had granted land to members of the ruling class, and in 1919 they hoped that the protectorate government would recognize these grants and declare the land to be freehold. The Morris Carter committee supported this request, on the grounds that it would be a good thing to have the same land policy all over the country: that the freehold land would please the chiefs and make them loyal and friendly to the government: and that some chiefs might sell or lease their freehold land to Europeans—which, as we know, Carter always thought desirable.

The provincial commissioners however disapproved. They thought that the chiefs had quite enough power already, and that the government's duty was to protect the rights of the poor tenants, not to help the rich to grow yet richer. In 1924 the government made up its mind; it announced, 'The mailo system which is in force in the kingdom of Buganda will not be introduced except in so far as the government is bound by the Toro and Ankole agreements.'

The decision naturally caused the chiefs great disappointment. The government tried to make what concessions it could without abandoning the principle. In 1933 it gave Bunyoro a formal agreement so as to put it on a level with Ankole and Toro; the agreement did something to restore the Banyoro people their self-esteem. As for Busoga, in 1930 the government offered Busoga too an agreement, and it went so far as to offer to include in the agreement a provision of 85 square miles of freehold or mailo land. But the Busoga chiefs rejected this offer. They thought they could bargain with the government and make it give them much more than 85 square miles. However, the government refused to bargain with them; and in 1935, when its offer had been open for five years and was still being rejected, the government withdrew the offer, so that the Busoga chiefs got nothing.

The Bataka land question

Until the 1914 war, the land settlement in Buganda was generally accepted. The peasants continued to cultivate their old farms, and many of them were becoming prosperous through their cotton sales. There was only one group of the Baganda who were dissatisfied. This was the heads of clans, called *bataka*, who represented the old order of things in Buganda; they had ruled the people hundreds of years ago, before ever there was a Kabaka. These men were trustees of the land which had been set aside by the clan as a burial ground. Their own political standing had been diminished by the growth in the power of the great chiefs, and some of their trust land had been taken from them by the Lukiko and distributed as mailo land. The bataka protested, but the Lukiko paid no heed.

In 1918, the bataka renewed their protests, and three years later they formed a Bataka Association to press their claims. The Kabaka Daudi Chwa had now come of age, and he listened to them. He agreed that they had a just grievance, and he suggested to the Lukiko that it should pass a law to remedy it. Any bataka who could prove that he had lost his trust land should be granted a piece of màilo land; and he could exchange this mailo land for his clan's traditional land, provided the present occupier agreed. It was an agreement which could not have been carried through without goodwill, but with goodwill it would have been quite workable. However, the Lukiko rejected the Kabaka's proposal by three to one, which shows two things very clearly: first, that the Lukiko had taken over a great deal of the power which had formerly belonged to the Kabaka; second, that the Lukiko represented the rich and great, and had little thought for old traditions and the rights of the humble.

Rejected by the Lukiko, the Bataka Association applied to the protectorate government. The government appointed a commission to inquire into the matter, and the commission recommended that a special land arbitration court should be set up. The business of the court should be to investigate all bataka claims, and to restore to its rightful trustees any land that had been wrongfully taken. In other words, an adjustment which the Kabaka proposed to make if everyone concerned agreed, the commission proposed to make even if there were disagreement: a very different matter. The governor, Sir William Gowers, passed on the committee's suggestion to the Secretary of State, but in 1926 Mr Amery rejected it as impracticable. However desirable it might be to remedy an injustice, it is plain that there were many arguments against this proposal. For one thing, the government had entrusted the land settlement to the Lukiko, and had not thought of providing for any appeals against the Lukiko's decisions. The Lukiko's settlement was now nineteen years old, and the court would find it very difficult to arrive at the truth amid conflicting evidence on what had happened during those nineteen years. Once such an inquiry were started, everyone who had any land dispute of any kind would claim that bataka land was involved. People might have bought bataka land quite innocently; they would have to be compensated, and the compensation would be ruinously expensive. If the inquiry succeeded, Buganda would have a very complicated system of land tenure: Crown land; freehold or mailo land, which could be leased or sold; and bataka land, which could not be transferred in any way. Perhaps the government should not have allowed the Lukiko to make the distribution of land without reserving to itself a right of supervision, so that anyone aggrieved could appeal. But if in 1900 the government had taken up this attitude, would it have secured the agreement?

POLITICS AND ADMINISTRATION

In Uganda, as in Kenya, the protectorate government had to deal with the Asian and European immigrants, who demanded political concessions such as representation on a legislative council: and also with the African states, who for a long time showed no interest in the idea of a united Uganda, and asked only to be protected against the immigrants and to be allowed to develop in their own way.

The legislative council

In October 1920, the government of India wrote to the Secretary of State for India in London, commenting on Lord Milner's despatch of May 1920,[4] in which he gave his views on the government of Kenya

[4] See page 130.

and Uganda as if conditions in both countries were alike. The Indian government pointed out that conditions were very different. There was no high land in Uganda especially attractive to European settlers. The Uganda development commission contained Indian as well as European members, and did not press for segregation in business areas of towns, though it accepted segregation in residential areas. There was no elected municipal council, and there was not even a legislative council. For all these reasons, it said, the position of Indians in Uganda must not be considered as similar to their position in Kenya.

A small group of European farmers and businessmen in Uganda had already proposed that Uganda should have a legislative council. As Secretary of State, first Milner and then Churchill agreed that the unofficial Europeans must certainly share in the responsibility of government, and so, if possible, should the Indians. They approved a council of five official members, with two nominated unofficial European members and one nominated Indian. But Uganda resembled Kenya in one respect: the Indians there greatly outnumbered the Europeans. This being so, it is not surprising that the Indians refused to accept this ratio of one Indian member to two Europeans; as in Kenya, they wanted equality. The council first met in 1921, but it met without an Indian member, for the Indians refused to accept nomination. It was not until 1926 that an Indian allowed himself to be nominated for membership. In 1933 the governor persuaded the Secretary of State to agree to add a second Indian member; and this small and peaceful council (so different from the turbulent legislative council of Kenya) of five official and four nominated unofficial members lasted until 1945.

There were no African members. The Kabaka and the Lukiko were nervous of the whole idea of a legislative council, for it seemed to them likely to weaken the basis of the agreement. They feared that if any Baganda sat as members of the council, they might find themselves out-voted. If this happened, it would be much harder for Buganda to appeal against the council's decision than to appeal against a decision taken by the governor. Buganda was better off as it was. If the Kabaka disliked any action of the protectorate government, he could always take his stand on the agreement and appeal to the Secretary of State. Meanwhile, the Kabaka alone was the spokesman of his people; if the government wished to know what the Baganda thought, they had only to ask him.

This attitude was never challenged by the protectorate government until 1945. The government accepted a responsibility to push ahead with social, economic and administrative development: but not with political development. The upheaval of the second world war brought other people to the front, who refused to accept whatever the Kabaka and the Lukiko said. It was only then that the protectorate government set out on the task of encouraging political and constitutional development.

Native administration in Uganda

On the surface, Uganda appeared to be an excellent example of the British system of indirect rule. Buganda, Ankole, Toro and (after 1933) Bunyoro had their agreements. The northern peoples had no agreements, but the government made a point of ruling them through African chiefs or agents, and apparently hoped that one day they might organize themselves into states on the lines of Buganda. But this appearance of indirect rule was deceptive; it did not correspond to the facts.

The kingdom of Buganda was the most completely organized state in the protectorate, with its strong central government and its three-tier arrangement of *saza*, *gombolola*, and *miruka* chiefs.[5] But Buganda had in fact, though not in appearance, lost some of its self-government. The Kabaka Daudi Chwa (1897–1939) was a child when he came to the throne, and did not come of age till 1914. For seventeen years, Uganda was under the rule of the three regents, headed by the katikiro Sir Apolo Kagwa. During this time, the district commissioners got into the habit of consulting directly with the saza chiefs, without always troubling to keep the central government informed. All this time, the regents depended on the British government's support, for they were politicians who had taken a prominent part in the turbulent political life of Buganda, and they could not hope to command the loyalty that was given to the Kabaka. Thus, because of its agreement, Buganda was more independent than most African states (for example the emirates of Northern Nigeria) under British colonial rule; and yet, in spite of the agreement, the British district commissioners were accustomed to dealing directly with the saza chiefs in a way which would be impossible in Northern Nigeria. The British were not particularly anxious (as by the theory of indirect rule they should have been) to develop Buganda and the other states into efficient self-governing local authorities. They were much more anxious to develop them into efficient local agents of the central protectorate government.

In the north, British authority grew out of the work of the Muganda general Semei Kakunguru, who conquered the land north of Lake

---

[5] The *miruka* chief was a village headman; several villages were grouped into a *gombolola*, and *gombololas* again were grouped into the *saza* or county.

Kioga and set up his own administration over it. When the British took over this country, they continued for a time to recognize the Baganda chiefs whom Kakunguru had appointed there. The government's report of 1913–14 says,

'The undoubted administrative gifts of the Baganda have been utilized in these districts by their employment as government agents to educate and supervise the local chiefs: a system which is open to obvious objections, but which in its ultimate results has been incontrovertibly successful. This method of administration is however only tolerable under the closest supervision by district officers. The local chiefs have now made sufficient progress to enable the greater number of these agents to be withdrawn.'

This 'closest supervision by district officers' was unlikely to develop into a genuine system of indirect rule.

All this administration outside Buganda was codified by three ordinances, all made in 1919. The Native Authority Ordinance gave official recognition to chiefs of different grades. It sanctioned any order which a chief might make in accordance with native customary law, and listed the matters on which he might make orders. A chief was empowered to call on his people to provide labour for thirty days a year without pay, and for sixty days with pay. A chief who was neglectful or who disobeyed the government might be fined or imprisoned. The other ordinances were the Courts Ordinance and the Native Laws Ordinance. The Courts Ordinance defined the jurisdiction of the chiefs' courts and defined the district commissioner's powers of supervising the working of the courts and of revising their judgements. The Native Laws Ordinance gave the governor power to recognize a district council, and gave the district council power to make recommendations for changing customary law and for inflicting penalties on those who offended against the law. This legislation is very similar to that in Kenya and in other African territories. It shows how the government was hoping to work through the chiefs and other traditional authorities, and to make their courts and the customary law part of the judicial system of the protectorate.

The government no doubt believed that in all this it was working towards self-government, which might be remote but which one day would arrive. Its weakness was that it would not leave people alone to learn by their mistakes. Chiefs whose tribute was converted into a cash salary seemed to their people to be merely sub-officials of the British government. The district commissioner administered native authority funds, and it was rarely that the local finance committee ventured to oppose his suggestion on how the money should be spent. Outside Buganda—even in Ankole, Bunyoro and Toro—chiefs were appointed, promoted, and dismissed by the governor on the district commissioner's advice. No doubt the district commissioner consulted the senior chiefs of the district before making his recommendation to the governor, but it was his recommendation that counted.

It is understandable that in Buganda itself the government officers should have slipped into the way of dealing directly with the chiefs during the Kabaka's long minority; but it was unfortunate that when the Kabaka came of age the government should wish to continue the habit. The Kabaka and his katikiro, Sir Apolo Kagwa, felt that it diminished their status and the effectiveness of their administration. They were able to quote the 1900 agreement in their favour. Section 9 said, 'On all questions but the assessment and collection of taxes, the chief of the county will report direct to the king's native ministers, from whom he will receive his instructions.'

In 1925 the protectorate government and the government of Buganda came into direct conflict. The occasion was a quite trivial matter: the issue of licences to sell beer in one district of Kampala. It became a question of principle when the chief who was involved asked the provincial commissioner to support him against the orders of the katikiro. The provincial commissioner, Postlethwaite, supported the chief, and thought that this decision of his should settle the matter. But the katikiro, Sir Apolo Kagwa, thought this a matter for the Buganda government, not the British. He regarded himself as the head of a partly independent government in alliance with Britain; he was hurt at being treated in this way by the provincial commissioner, who was a much younger man; and he was angry with his subordinate chief for going to the British instead of coming to him. The matter went to the governor, who thought that Postlethwaite had decided wrongly on the particular question of the beer licences; but the governor upheld the general principle that British officers must be able to deal directly with the Baganda chiefs. The matter ended in Sir Apolo Kagwa's resignation.

This unfortunate affair showed how weak the Buganda government was in its relations with the government of the protectorate. The Lukiko was an assembly of chiefs and of members nominated by the Kabaka; there were no elected members. On the whole it represented the class of great landowners and officials, and it would need a good deal of help and guidance if it was to become an efficient parliamentary assembly. The protectorate government saw this, and felt that it had a responsibility towards the ordinary people; it ought not to leave them without protection against the Lukiko. In 1926, after much criticism of the Lukiko's inexperience in handling public money, the Kabaka himself asked for help in reforming the administration of the Buganda treasury. As time went on, the educated young men of Buganda began more and more to criticize the Lukiko for its conservative ways, and to demand that the Buganda government should find some means of taking their views into consideration. This raised in Uganda the question which is raised sooner or later everywhere in Africa: what can be done to replace a government which is composed of the chiefs, the old men, the holders of traditional offices, by one which will represent all classes of the community, young as well as old, educated as well as uneducated, poor as well as rich, the humble as well as the mighty?

Constitutional changes, 1935–44

In 1935 a newly arrived governor, Sir Philip Mitchell, found a minor constitutional crisis developing in Buganda: the Kabaka and the Lukiko were in open disagreement. The Lukiko was distressed to find that some owners of mailo land were leasing it to Indians; and in 1933 it passed a resolution to the effect that mailo land should never be leased to any but Africans. The provincial commissioner approved of the resolution, but the Kabaka disagreed; the Kabaka published a pamphlet of his own, saying that mailo owners should be completely free to lease their land to anyone they chose. In May 1934 the Lukiko passed another resolution confirming its previous decision. This time, the Kabaka did not send the resolution to the provincial commissioner until February 1935. Even then, he sent it only because the provincial commissioner asked him for it; and he sent it on without signing it.

The agreements had not contemplated the possibility that the Kabaka and the Lukiko might openly disagree. Section 11 of the 1900 agreement provided that when the Lukiko forwarded to the Kabaka a resolution which had been carried by a majority vote, 'The Kabaka shall further consult with Her Majesty's representative in Uganda before giving effect to any such resolutions voted by the native council, and shall in this matter explicitly follow the advice of Her Majesty's representative.' It was plain from the 1900 agreement that the Kabaka and the Lukiko together made laws for Buganda, subject to the governor's approval. The Kabaka seems to have thought that if he disapproved of a Lukiko resolution he could veto it simply by omitting to forward it to the protectorate government. The government thought he was mistaken; it took the agreement to mean that he was bound to forward the resolution, whether he approved or disapproved, and must follow whatever advice the government gave him. This was rather a fine point, and Mitchell and the Colonial Office decided not to rely on it, but to fall back on Section 6 of the agreement, which required the Kabaka to cooperate loyally with the protectorate government. But the government would clearly find itself in a difficult position if disagreements between the Kabaka and the Lukiko became frequent, and the government had to support now one side and now the other.

Mitchell's remedy was for the protectorate government to withdraw from its detailed supervision of the Buganda administration, and to leave the Kabaka and the Lukiko with the responsibility of making indirect rule a real thing. He transferred the judicial powers of the district commissioners to a judicial adviser, and restyled the provincial commissioner the Resident. Outside Buganda, Mitchell found that most chiefs derived almost all their real power from the protectorate government; many of them had no traditional authority whatever. In Busoga and the Western Province, he separated the officially appointed chiefs from the traditional chiefs, and in the Eastern Province he added elected members and traditional chiefs (and sometimes religious leaders also) to the local councils, which had hitherto been composed entirely of officially appointed chiefs. We may sum up by saying that all over Uganda he found real power coming to depend not on holding traditional office but on appointment by the government; and he made a brave effort to bring back the traditional chiefs into the administration and thus make indirect rule a reality.

According to Lugard's formula, the success of indirect rule would depend not only on keeping power in traditional hands, but on educating the traditional chiefs and elders so that they could rise to their modern responsibilities. Mitchell felt that his attempt to make indirect rule in Uganda a reality could not succeed without a big increase in education. At his request, the Secretary of State set up a commission to advise the government on the development of higher education.

Compared with some African countries, Uganda was well supplied with education. Both the Catholic and the Protestant missionaries worked hard to establish schools. At first they used the Luganda language, not only in primary schools but even in training teachers; and in 1901 the Bible became available in Luganda. But in 1903 the decision was taken to use English in teacher-training and in secondary education, and, in 1904, King's School Budo was founded. Secondary education, however, developed but slowly. The government gave grants to the missions but opened no schools of its own till after the 1914 war. Then, in 1922, it opened a technical school at Makerere, which later developed into a secondary school and teacher-training college. The government concentrated its attention a good deal on developing Makerere, which (like Achimota in Ghana) was one result of the British government's new interest in education which developed after the 1914 war.

Mitchell's education commission, headed by Lord De La Warr, recommended that Makerere College should be developed as fast as possible into a university college, and that there should be a great expansion of secondary education so as to provide the university college with students. A new educational programme was set in motion to carry out these recommendations. During the five years of Mitchell's governorship, the number of full primary schools (which were needed to provide pupils for the secondary schools) was increased from 23 to 78, the pupils enrolled in secondary schools increased from 226 to 1,335, and the government's expenditure on education rose from £79,000 to £386,000.

In September 1939 the second world war broke out, and two months later the Kabaka Daudi Chwa died, still a comparatively young man. He was succeeded by his son Edward Mutesa, who was only fifteen years old, so once again Buganda had to be governed by regents. Next year, Mitchell was succeeded as governor by Sir Charles Dundas, who, like Mitchell, had been a successful administrator in Tanganyika under Sir Donald Cameron, and, like Mitchell, believed in leaving Buganda to govern itself with as little interference from the protectorate government as possible.

Dundas was soon faced with trouble. In 1940, the Anglican Church in Uganda handed over to the protectorate government the rights to any minerals that might be found on its land. This caused a good deal of resentment. The land had been given to the Church by the chiefs and people, and there was a general feeling that if the Church did not want the mineral rights, it should return them to the original owners, not to the government. This well-meaning action raised the suspicion that the bishop and the governor were plotting somehow to deprive the people of their land.

Next year there was worse trouble. Daudi Chwa's widow, the mother of the young Kabaka, wished to remarry. This was contrary to the custom of Buganda. Nevertheless, she was supported by the katikiro, Martin Luther Nsibirwa, who had held his office since 1928; and with his approval she asked the bishop to sanction her marriage. The bishop knew that it was contrary to Buganda custom; but there was nothing in Church law to forbid the remarriage of a widow, and if the katikiro and others approved, he felt it was not for him to disapprove. When he sanctioned the marriage, there was an outcry, and the Lukiko demanded that the katikiro should resign. True to his principle of allowing Buganda to run its own affairs, the governor agreed. But this did not end the matter. Nsibirwa was the leader of a group of chiefs who for many years had been governing the country with British support. They had their rivals; and when the governor allowed Nsibirwa to fall, their rivals were encouraged and the ruling group felt betrayed.

In 1944, Dundas pressed on with his reorganization. The district commissioners in Buganda had already lost their judicial powers, which had been transferred to the judicial adviser; Dundas now withdrew the district commissioners altogether from Buganda, and appointed two assistant Residents. The Resident and the assistants would advise the Kabaka and his ministers; but it would be the responsibility of the Kabaka and his ministers, not of the protectorate government, to supervise the chiefs in Buganda. This transfer of real power from the protectorate government to the government of Buganda is just what Sir Apolo Kagwa had wished for twenty years earlier. It would have been more successful in his time than it was in 1944. If indirect rule in Buganda was to succeed, something had to be done to modernize the Lukiko. Dundas realized that the Lukiko was an assembly of wealthy and powerful land-owners. All its members were appointed by the Kabaka, and nothing had been done to give the ordinary citizens of Buganda any direct representation. Dundas suggested to the Kabaka and the Lukiko that they should work out a scheme to strengthen the Lukiko by adding elected members. But his time was short, and nothing was done before he left the country.

Dundas left the country in 1944. In January 1945 there were serious riots in Kampala and elsewhere in Buganda; they were directed hardly at all against the protectorate government, but almost entirely against the government of Buganda. There were several causes. There was a new group of young educated Baganda who felt angry at having no voice in the government of their country. Everyone knew that rival groups of chiefs in the Lukiko were intriguing against one another. The government had good reason to believe that some ambitious chiefs supported the riots in order to overthrow their rivals. There were of course other grievances which could always be used to work up trouble: such as rising prices, and the ancient fears of losing land and of being somehow handed over to the mercy of the Kenya Europeans.

The main demand of the rioters was that the treasurer of the Buganda government, Serwano Kulubya, should be dismissed. He resigned, and Kawalya Kagwa (son of Sir Apolo) was appointed in his place. But the protectorate government took prompt action against the rioters. The new katikiro and a few other chiefs were deported from Buganda, and others were dismissed; Nsibirwa was reinstated as katikiro. The new governor, Sir John Hall, decided that the Mitchell–Dundas policy had failed; he again stationed assistant Residents at the old district headquarters to supervise the chiefs as the district commissioners had formerly done.

Shortly afterwards another storm blew up. The city of Kampala had grown closely round Makerere College, and if Makerere was to grow into a university college, as the De La Warr commission advised, it must somehow acquire more land. In Britain, the law allows the government to compel land-owners to sell their land for such public purposes, and there is special machinery for settling the price to be paid. No such law existed in Buganda, and the Resident urged the Buganda government to make one. The katikiro Nsibirwa supported the proposal, and the Lukiko reluctantly agreed. Next day, Nsibirwa was murdered on the steps of Namirembe cathedral. Again the government acted swiftly. More chiefs were dismissed and deported. Kagwa, the treasurer, replaced Nsibirwa as katikiro. The old system of close government supervision was set up once more.

So the protectorate government entered the post-war period, still hoping to find chiefs who were efficient administrators and also politically acceptable to their people. It believed that the mass of the people were content to live under British rule, and would remain so for many years to come. The government, it thought, would have plenty of time to make gradual progress in extending education, and in guiding the chiefs towards modern methods of administration. Little did the government think that in less than twenty years British rule in Uganda would be at an end, and Uganda would be an independent state.

Chapter 8

TANGANYIKA TO 1945

When the British took over Tanganyika after the 1914 war, they had to make a fresh start, with very little to build on. They held the country on a mandate from the League of Nations. During the war, the British Labour Party suggested that the whole of Africa from the Sahara to the Zambesi should be transferred to the League of Nations to be administered as one state. But the British, French and Belgian governments would not listen to this idea. On the other hand, the British government was not anxious to take over Tanganyika. It pressed the United States to accept the mandate, but the United States refused.

Early in 1919 Sir Horace Byatt was appointed administrator of all the territory occupied by the British; and when Ruanda and Urundi were allotted to Belgium in 1922, Byatt became governor of the British mandated territory of Tanganyika. He faced an enormous task. Much damage had been done to public buildings of all kinds, and railways, roads and bridges had been systematically destroyed by the retreating German army. The population had been reduced by the killing of soldiers and carriers in action and also by famine and a severe epidemic of influenza. The tribes had been broken and scattered by the war. The governor had very few British administrative officers, and all his staff were new to the country. Ruanda and Urundi, now administered by Belgium as parts of the Congo, had been two of the richest provinces, and the government could ill afford to do without their revenue. The British Treasury gave Tanganyika a grant of £330,000 a year.

In July 1920 an Order in Council established an executive council of four senior officials, but there was no talk yet of a legislative council. Two months later a director of education was appointed to work out an educational programme. The British were impressed with the high quality of the German schools. But because of the war there was a great shortage of teachers, and the schools had the difficulty of changing over from German to English; so that the professional problems facing the education department were as great as those facing Byatt himself.

Like all British administrators, Byatt believed in working through the African chiefs if he could. He retained the German division of the country into 22 administrative districts, and for the time being, wherever Byatt found the akida of a district at his post, he found it convenient to keep him there. But clearly the government would sooner or later have to choose between the akida and the chief; it could not revive the tribal authorities as administrative units as long as it employed as its agent an akida who was an outsider.

In 1921 and 1923 the government issued two Native Authority Ordinances on the usual lines. The governor was empowered to recognize a chief or headman or a council of elders as a Native Authority, and when a Native Authority had been so recognized, it was empowered to issue orders and to hear cases in its courts. But similar powers were given to the akidas, so that the system was somewhat of a muddle. Byatt left the country in 1924, and a conference of his senior officers recommended that a regular system of indirect rule should be introduced. This would involve getting rid of the akidas and working solely through the native authorities. The 22 districts, they proposed, should be grouped into provinces, and a Secretary for Native Affairs should be appointed to supervise the development of indirect rule.

LAND AND LABOUR

There had been some German and other European settlers in Tanganyika before the war. After the war was over British and other settlers came trickling back, though it was not for some years that Germans were allowed into the country. There was a proposal to set up a soldier settlement scheme like the one which brought about the alienation of Nandi land in Kenya,[1] but Byatt would not allow it. His land policy was intended to protect African interests. His Land Ordinance of 1923 provided that all land, occupied or not, was to be public land, and was to be controlled by the governor for the benefit of the African people. African villagers as well as European or Asian settlers were to be tenants of the Crown; but existing titles and African customary rights were to be maintained, and the governor was to have regard to African customary laws. No title to land was to be valid without the governor's approval. No new freehold grants of land were to be made, and no land was to be leased for more than 99 years; no European or Asian was to be granted more than 5,000 acres without the approval of the Secretary of State. Byatt was plainly determined to have no Lord Delamere in Tanganyika, and he was of course much criticized by European settlers and would-be settlers.

European criticism was increased when one of Byatt's district commissioners, Charles Dundas, encouraged the Chagga people living on the slopes of Kilimanjaro to plant high-quality coffee[2] under the shade of their banana trees. The Chagga people took kindly to the idea, and in 1924 they formed the Kilimanjaro Native Planters' Association, which soon grew to be a very big and successful organization, employing skilled European technical staff and producing excellent coffee in spite of what the European planters said.

[1] See page 115.

[2] There are two main species of coffee, *arabica* and *robusta*. *Arabica* is native to Ethiopia, and produces the best coffee; *robusta* is native to other parts of East Africa, and was already being much grown in the Bukoba district. The Europeans did not mind Africans growing *robusta* coffee in districts away from European farms; but they said that Africans ought not to be allowed to grow *arabica*, for they took it for granted that Africans would not take proper care of the plants, and European coffee plantations would become infected with disease.

The Tanganyika government was enlightened in its labour policy. The Masters and Servants Ordinances of 1923 and 1926 were planned to protect the interests of the African workers. The 1923 ordinance provided that any labour contract which caused a man to travel far from home must be put into writing and witnessed by a magistrate or a district commissioner, so that the man knew exactly what he was undertaking; and no one was to be away from his home for more than six months at a time. The 1926 ordinance extended this period to twelve months; but on the other hand it laid down minimum conditions of housing, food and health services which the employer must provide, very much on the lines of the Kenya ordinance of 1910.

The government was still worried about the condition of the workers, and in 1924 it appointed Major Orde Browne to investigate labour conditions all over Tanganyika. He found much that was unsatisfactory. The workers were weakened by malaria and other diseases, and most of them were under-nourished. Many of them walked long distances—sometimes hundreds of miles—from their homes to the mines or the plantations where they worked. The government accepted his report, and set up a special Labour Department, with Major Orde Browne at its head. The department began putting up labour camps along the routes, where men might rest and be well fed and medically cared for while on their journey. Tanganyika's example in this was followed by other British colonies.

Byatt left Tanganyika in 1924 without having the satisfaction of seeing the country's revenue balance the expenditure; this balance was not reached for another two years. But he had done solid work in repairing the destruction of the war and getting the administration going again. He was criticized for being too cautious, and for doing things himself without consulting other people first. But he had everything to do, and a very small staff and very little money to do it with. It must be for his successor to lay down bold outlines of policy.

SIR DONALD CAMERON AND INDIRECT RULE

Byatt's successor was Sir Donald Cameron, who had been Chief Secretary of Nigeria under Lugard, and was a whole-hearted believer in the Lugard idea of indirect rule. Before leaving London, Cameron discussed Tanganyika's problems with Ormsby-Gore, the leader of the commission which visited East Africa in 1924. Cameron thought that the time had come for Tanganyika to be given a legislative council of the usual colonial type; and the Secretary of State and the Ormsby-Gore commission agreed. The new legislative council met for the first time in December 1926; it contained thirteen officials and seven nominated unofficial members, five Europeans and two Indians. Cameron thought it too soon to appoint African members. There were special difficulties in Tanganyika. Very few Africans yet understood English. Men educated under German rule understood German, and those who spoke English were young men whom Cameron thought as yet unacceptable to their people as their representatives in the council. Until these young men had grown older and could speak with authority on their people's behalf, thought Cameron, African interests must be looked after by the governor and his senior officials.

Meanwhile, Cameron hoped that other machinery would enable Africans to take part in politics. Following the Lugard tradition, he hoped to develop regional councils of native authorities. Later on, these regional councils would send delegates to what he called a Central Native Council, where delegates from all over Tanganyika would discuss African affairs together. And not so long afterwards, this Central Native Council would be developed into a General Council, in which members of all three races would sit together as a legislative assembly. Thus, Cameron thought of his legislative council of 1926 as nothing more than a beginning; but it must suffice for the time being. In 1929 two more nominated unofficial members were added, one European and one Indian.

It was not only Cameron's experience in Nigeria that made him anxious to try indirect rule in Tanganyika. When he arrived in the country he found another reason. Byatt's administration had already arranged that the customary tribute which Africans paid to their chiefs should be commuted into a money tax; the tax was to be paid into a central fund, from which the chiefs were to be paid salaries. It thus was important for the government to know who was entitled to a salary and who was not; and this the government was still far from knowing. Cameron set his district commissioners hard at work making inquiries. They found that in spite of the German system of direct rule through the akida, the people everywhere still recognized their chief or clan head, and were prepared to pay the customary tribute.

Encouraged by this, Cameron pushed ahead with the organization of indirect rule. His Native Authority Ordinance of 1926 revised the 1923 ordinance. The chief duties of the native authority were to maintain law and order, and to collect the taxes: the hut tax, the poll tax, and the tax in commutation of the tribute. The native authority held a court of customary law, which brought it some revenue from court fees and fines. It had an additional source of revenue: as in other British territories, it received from the central treasury in Dar-es-Salaam a share of the taxes which it collected in its area.

So far, Cameron was working on lines familiar to all believers in indirect rule. But with his Native Courts Ordinance of 1929 he struck out a new path. In one important respect, the ordinance amended a Native Courts Ordinance of 1920. That ordinance provided that appeals from a decision of a native authority court could be made first to the district commissioner's court, and from him to the High Court at Dar-es-Salaam. Cameron disapproved of this. He thought that the learned judges of the High Court were not the best people to determine cases which (because they began in the native authority court) were primarily matters of African customary law. More questionably, he thought it would weaken the administration if people saw an administrative officer's decision being reversed by the High Court. He therefore removed the appeal to the High Court, and substituted an appeal to the court of the provincial commissioner. Outside the administration, Cameron's advisers thought him wrong. The Chief Justice protested, and so did all the unofficial members of the legislative council. Cameron overrode all protests, and carried the Bill through the council by the official majority. He made only one concession. He had intended that appeals from the courts of the Muslim *liwalis* at the coast should also go to the provincial commissioner's court, but he agreed to allow these appeals still to go to the High Court.

Cameron was not completely successful with his schemes for developing regional councils of chiefs. In 1927 and 1928 the Sukuma and Nyamwezi federations were recognized as superior native authorities. Soon afterwards the people of Mwanza province elected a paramount chief, and two sections of the Ngoni people agreed to combine. But it soon appeared that these developments were not working out quite as Cameron hoped. If the Sukuma or Nyamwezi chiefs happened to disagree with a decision of their federal council, they did not consider themselves bound by it; so in 1930 the government had to relieve these councils of their executive powers, though it left them their common treasuries and courts of appeal. In Mwanza province the people did not mean their paramount chief to have any power over the other chiefs; he was merely the president of the council. The Ngoni did not elect a paramount chief; the two sections remained under their own chiefs, but they appointed an executive officer to act for them both.

Elsewhere, Cameron had even less success. He could not persuade the Gogo people to federate at all. In the Masasi district there were no strong chiefs, only clan elders; and here, as in the Ibo country of Nigeria and the Kikuyu country of Kenya, the British found it difficult to make indirect rule work. The government thought that the laibon of the Masai was a chief, and recognized him as such; but he was not a chief, and the Masai continued to run their affairs in their own way. The European settlers criticized Cameron for taking so much trouble to push ahead with native administration; they thought he would have done better to spend his energies on opening up the country for European settlement. But Tanganyika was so large, and so desperately poor, that there was nothing else that Cameron could do to develop national feeling. At that stage in the country's development, to group districts into provinces and to group small tribal units into larger units gave the best hope for the future of a united Tanganyika. Cameron was on the right path. Indirect rule in Tanganyika, as elsewhere in Africa, broke down later, because the British failed to bring the young educated men and the chiefs and elders together in an effective partnership. But that was long after Cameron's time, and it was not his fault.

As for opening up the country, Cameron did a good deal. In spite of opposition from Kenya and Uganda, he built the railway line from Tabora to Mwanza. He extended the northern railway line from Moshi to Arusha. He developed communications across Lake Tanganyika with the Congo. Revenue increased greatly, and by the end of Cameron's time as governor, the government was able to spend far more than before on health, education, and other services.

THE SLUMP AND THE WAR

Then came the slump of the 1930s, in which Tanganyika suffered like every other country. The country's chief export was sisal, and the price of sisal dropped from £32 to £12 a ton. The revenue from the hut tax dropped from £750,000 to £45,000. Africans who were beginning to grow cotton and groundnuts and other cash crops for export were discouraged. Cameron's successor, Sir Stewart Symes, had to apply again to the British Treasury for a loan to help the country through its difficulties, and the expansion of education and other services had to be stopped. Europeans and Asians were more heavily taxed, and the salaries of all government officials were cut. It was a bad time for everyone, but Tanganyika came through it better than the government feared. This was largely because the farmers, both European and African, went on growing cash crops and improving their quality so as to be ready to take advantage of higher prices when the slump ended. Two new crops, tea and sugar, were introduced. In 1939 the cotton crop was the highest on record.

In one respect Tanganyika was luckier than Kenya; it did not depend entirely on agriculture. In 1922, gold was discovered, and by 1939 it had become the country's most important export after sisal.

In 1940 diamonds were discovered, and by the end of the war in 1945 they were being exported to a value of more than £600,000 a year.

Education was the country's weak spot. There were no native authority schools. Education was provided by the government and by the voluntary agencies, such as the Christian missions and the Hindu and Muslim committees. By the end of the war in 1945, only 7·5 per cent of the children were receiving any schooling at all, and few of these went beyond standard four. There were twenty-two industrial schools, but not all the carpenters and fitters and masons who were trained in them were able to find paid jobs. There were very few secondary schools, and none that prepared their students for the Makerere entrance examinations. Makerere was not yet a university college, but it provided higher education than any institution in Tanganyika, and in 1938 the Tanganyika government contributed £100,000 to Makerere so as to be able to send students there.

For a few years immediately before the 1939 war, the German leader, Adolf Hitler, was hinting that Germany should have her former colonies restored to her. There were people in Britain who were ready to consider doing this. Many German settlers had returned to Tanganyika, and one-third of the alienated land was held by Germans, all of whom looked forward to coming again under the rule of their own country. But the war broke out before any serious plans had been made, and all talk of giving Tanganyika back to Germany then ceased.

THE BEGINNINGS OF POLITICAL ADVANCE

While Cameron and his successors were pressing ahead with native administration and indirect rule, there was already beginning a new political movement among the young educated Africans. In 1929 a group of young men formed a Tanganyika African Association; it was never a large body, but as often happens, it had much more influence than its small numbers might suggest. Thus in Tanganyika, as in other territories of British Africa, national politics were beginning not (as Cameron hoped) in regional councils of chiefs, but in small groups of educated young men in the towns. Indirect rule did not make a chief popular among his people. He received a government salary, and one of his main duties was to collect government taxes; he came to seem more and more like a government official. Still more was this so during the war, when many European officials were away, and more and more government work was piled on to the African chiefs.

In 1939 Africans joined the army in large numbers; no fewer than

87,000 men from Tanganyika served in the war. The government hoped that when they came home again, these young men would take an interest in native administration; they would bring their experience into the councils of elders and help the native authorities to develop so that national life would grow upwards from the villages. But the government was disappointed. When the ex-servicemen and other young men began to take an interest in politics, they wanted to work through their own organization and gain control of the central government. The idea of working through the village or regional councils did not appeal to them at all. It happened like this all over British Africa. Whatever advantages the British method of political advance may have had, it had one fatal disadvantage: it was slow. After the war, Africans were not willing that their political advance should move at the pace of the ox. They preferred the pace of the motor-cycle.

Chapter 9

AFTER THE SECOND WORLD WAR

The second world war did not produce the same spectacular economic results as the first. There was nothing like the rapid rise of prices in 1920 and the rapid fall in 1921; nothing like the muddle over reparations and war debts; nothing like the disastrous slump of the 1930s. The statesmen of the world were able to avoid some of these troubles because they had learned by their bitter experiences. They understood, for example, how to manage their currency so as to avoid rapid changes in its value, and they knew that it was impossible to make the defeated nations pay for the whole cost of the war.

The most spectacular results of the war were not economic but political. Germany was divided into two. Italy lost all her colonies. Eastern Germany and other countries in Eastern Europe were persuaded or compelled by Russia to accept communist governments. The world became dominated by two giant powers, Russia and the United States. Each of these powers possessed the atomic bomb and the power to inflict immense damage on the other. Compared with them, Britain was no longer a great power, and could only look on while Russia and the United States manoeuvred in rivalry against each other.

Rising prices

From the economic point of view, the chief result of the war was that a great stimulus was given to industry, not only in the older industrialized regions but all over the world. There came to be a huge demand for manpower and for raw materials. Every office and factory was short of labour, and so wages began to rise. With higher wages, people were able to buy more food and manufactured goods, and so the demand for these increased.

Thus as far as Africa is concerned, the most noticeable economic result of the war was a jump in the prices of all the materials that Africa produced. The prices rose high, and they stayed high, bringing the African governments much bigger revenues in customs and export duties. It is true that the cost of living rose as well, so that many people did not directly benefit from selling their produce at higher prices. But the governments benefited, for they had much more money to spend on all kinds of development than they had before the war.

African ex-servicemen

They had much more, but they still had not nearly enough; and this brings us to the political results of the war. Even larger numbers of Africans served in 1939 than in 1914, and there was a great difference in the fighting. The African troops in the 1914 war fought in Africa: in Togo, the Cameroons, and in Tanganyika. They fought almost entirely against other Africans: it was a case of African troops under British officers fighting against African troops under German officers. But in the 1939 war, the African troops fought alongside British and Indian troops against Italians in Ethiopia and against Japanese in Burma, and they were able to measure themselves against their British and Indian allies and against their Italian and Japanese enemies. In this way, many thousands of men who, but for the war, would have stayed quietly at home and would have had no wider experience than a visit to Kampala or Nairobi or Dar-es-Salaam, went over the seas and saw the world. They came home determined that Africa was not to go on in the same old way and at the same slow pace. When the war ended in 1945 they were not perhaps yet thinking of independence; but they were thinking of much more education, and of much faster constitutional progress, than there had been hitherto. In 1945 Kenya for example had only one African secondary school, and one African member of the legislative council. This state of things had to be changed, and changed quickly.

The question was, would Britain respond to this demand? One of the changes which the war had brought about in Britain was a change in the way in which people there thought about colonies. There had been for many years a group of people who thought that the colonies would one day have to be given their independence, and that it was Britain's duty meanwhile to prepare them for it. This way of thinking produced the Devonshire White Paper. Unfortunately, few people in Britain cared or knew anything about the colonies; not many members of parliament attended debates on colonial affairs; the enlightened group in Britain had a hard struggle against this indifference. But the war helped it, for many people in Britain were impressed with the fighting record of African troops.

The United Nations and colonies

Moreover, the League of Nations was now replaced by the United Nations, and there was a general feeling in the United Nations that all colonies should become independent as soon as possible. The United States had not been a member of the League, but it was a member of the UN; and the United States, having been at one time under British colonial rule, was always hostile to the colonial system. So were all the countries of Latin America; so were all the communist countries. The UN went further than the League had done. The League was interested in mandated territories, but not in colonies, which it regarded as the private concern of the administering power. But the UN Charter contained a clause inviting every administering power to send annual reports on the progress of its colonies. More than this: the UN laid down the lines on which the reports were to be drawn up, and asked very detailed questions; and before long the assembly of the UN set up a special committee to examine the answers which the administering powers gave. The administering powers were not compelled to answer the questions, and Portugal never did answer them. But Britain, France and Belgium all felt it would be unwise for them to take this line; they answered the questions every year, and before long they found themselves sending delegates to the UN headquarters in New York to defend their work in the colonies against criticisms made by other member states.

In this way, British thinking on colonial matters was strongly influenced by world opinion. But even before the end of the war and the establishment of the United Nations, the enlightened group of British thinkers had won an important victory. The biggest problem in British colonies was poverty. Colonies remained as colonies because they were poor: too poor to afford the schools, hospitals, research stations, communications and surveys they needed. They could never hope to raise themselves without spending far more money than they had available to spend. Where was the extra money to come from? The only possible answer was that it must come from Britain; and during the war, the enlightened thinkers in Britain convinced parliament of this.

The Colonial Development and Welfare Act of 1945

There had already been Colonial Development Acts in 1929 and 1940, which provided modest amounts of money for projects (such as railways or harbours) which would bring increased revenue. But in 1945 parliament passed a Colonial Development and Welfare Act which provided money not only for such projects as these, but also for such things as schools and hospitals, which would not directly increase the revenue. The sum of £120 million was provided, spread over ten years. Every colonial government was invited to draw up a scheme of capital development and then to apply for assistance under the Act. This sum was worth much more then than it would be today, and it was increased by subsequent Acts. But it was not nearly enough to satisfy all the demands. Over six million pounds were spent in building and equipping university colleges (Makerere among them), and large sums too were spent on higher technical education. Scores of new secondary schools and training colleges were built, as well as hospitals and clinics. Much was spent on roads, airfields, railways and harbours, and on searching for new minerals. Over two million pounds were spent on scholarships for further study in Britain: scholarships given not only to provide young people with university or higher technical education, but given also to older people so that they could gain practical experience and go home to take up higher posts. One can always lament that the sum was not bigger, and that the Act was not passed forty years earlier. But it was money well spent, and it produced a great effect in Africa. To take one example alone: Kenya had but one African secondary school in 1945; in 1958 it had thirty-one such schools. Such an increase as this would have been impossible without the money provided by the Colonial Development and Welfare Acts.

British plans for constitutional advance

The British government perhaps expected that the African people would be content with this visible spurt in social and economic development, and would be willing to wait for constitutional development to proceed gradually. The British saw that the Colonial Development and Welfare Acts would bring independence nearer; but they did not at first realize that the African people were impatient and would not wait for their independence till Britain thought them ready for it. It was in 1948 that the British first realized this, when there were riots in the Gold Coast (now Ghana), and for the first time the Gold Coast people began openly calling for independence. The Gold Coast was the richest colony in Africa, and it was free from many of the problems that caused trouble in East Africa. The shock in London was all the greater. If this could happen in the Gold Coast, thought the officials, much worse things could be expected elsewhere. African independence was evidently coming soon, whether Britain thought the African people ready for it or not. If so, the governments must push ahead with preparations for independence; in particular, they must increase the number of qualified Africans by building more schools and colleges in Africa and by providing still more scholarships for study in Britain.

Apart from this, the method which the Colonial Office proposed was to increase the African share in the legislative and executive councils. First, additional unofficial members were added to the executive council, and the number of elected members in the legislative council was increased until they formed a majority over the official and the nominated members together. Under the old colonial system, policy was laid down by the governor on the advice of his senior departmental officers, and the legislative council could criticize the policy, but could not compel the governor to change it. If the elected members were increased in number so that they formed the majority of the legislative council, the danger would arise that they could, if they wished, block all government business and bring public affairs to a standstill. To avoid this danger, two measures were taken. One was to give the governor some 'reserved powers' for use in such an emergency; for example, if the legislative council got quite out of hand and took such an extreme step as refusing to vote the necessary funds, the governor was empowered to declare the budget passed in spite of the council's opposition. These reserved powers were hedged round with safeguards to ensure that they were never used unless in such a serious emergency; and in fact hardly any colonial governor in Africa ever did use them. The second measure, much more positive, was to give the unofficial members a share in laying down policy. A member was given ministerial responsibility for one department, with the power of overriding the professional advice of the British departmental head. This was a difficult situation, for the departmental head was a professional man who had been responsible for making and for carrying out his own policy, and he now had to be ready to take orders from a minister who was not a professional man. In the British African colonies as a whole, both the unofficial ministers and the British members of the Colonial Service deserve credit for the way in which they worked together during this transitional period.

The next stage in the advance towards independence was to change the relationship between the executive and the legislature. Policy was still laid down by the governor, though he now acted not on the advice of his departmental officers but on the advice of his ministers. In the old days, if the legislative council (even with an unofficial majority) disapproved of departmental policy, they could do nothing effective. They could not make the departmental head resign; and if they refused to vote the departmental budget, they might find the governor passing it by virtue of his reserved powers. Under the new ministerial system, the legislative council had more power; it could compel the minister to resign. But if one minister resigned, it made no difference to his colleagues; they carried on. The greatest step towards independence was taken when all the ministers were made collectively responsible to the legislature: when the governor's executive council was transformed into a cabinet. To bring this about, the governor was required to appoint as prime minister the leader of the strongest party in the legislative council, and to invite him to choose his own ministers from among the members of his own party. When this stage was reached, the governor no longer had any control over policy; policy was made by the cabinet, which was responsible to the legislature. The governor lost his reserved powers and became a purely ceremonial head of the government; the real head was the prime minister.

This was the process of constitutional advance which the British government planned, and which it thought might be completed in perhaps thirty years from the end of the war. In actual fact, the African leaders were not prepared to wait so long, and the British government found it wiser to grant the African colonies their independence sooner than it intended. Ghana became independent in 1957, only nine years after the riots which so startled the Colonial Office; by 1967, every British territory in Africa was independent except one: Rhodesia.

Difficulties in the way
This rapid progress was made in spite of certain difficulties. The first difficulty was that the British attached great importance to administrative efficiency. They liked things to run smoothly, and it was painful for an experienced and well-qualified Englishman to hand over his department to an African of less experience and qualification. Africans thought efficiency less important; to them it was more important to have their own people in control, even if things sometimes went wrong. This caused misunderstandings: Africans sometimes thought that it was for selfish reasons that the British clung to power, and the British sometimes thought that the Africans had selfish reasons for wanting to take it from them.

The second difficulty was the British system of indirect rule. The British were looking for national leaders, but they hoped to find them among the chiefs. They tended to distrust the political leaders who arose among the educated men in the towns, and it took them some time to accept these leaders as true representatives of the people.

The third difficulty was that the East African countries were multi-racial, and the British spent much time and thought on devising schemes for protecting the European and Asian minorities. The African leaders naturally wanted power to be given to the African majority; and they suspected that in protecting the minorities and resisting the cry of 'One man, one vote', the Colonial Office was really trying to keep control in its own hands.

The fourth difficulty was tribalism. Political parties in Britain are divided by disagreements over policy: Shall we, or shall we not nationalize the steel industry? Shall we, or shall we not keep a naval squadron in the Indian Ocean? But when political parties first arose in Africa, they were almost always based on tribal loyalties, not on differences of policy. There was as yet very little national feeling. People followed their tribal leader because he spoke their language and knew their customs, and because if he came to power, he would see to it that men from his tribe would have a good share of public office, and that a good share of the new roads and schools and hospitals would come to their part of the country. This was very natural, but it worried the British. They did not see how democratic government could work under these conditions, and they tended to hold back and wait for new parties to emerge which, like the British parties, would not depend on differences of language or customs, but on differences of policy.

The East Africa High Commission

Another result of the war was to encourage the countries of East Africa to work more closely together. There were fresh proposals like those which had been made through the movement for closer union,[1] and they produced very similar reactions.

The Governors' Conference had been meeting since 1926. In 1932 the postal services were joined into one. The East African governments had also agreed to have the same customs duties; and in 1940 they came to work yet more closely together in an East African Economic Council, though this was intended only as a war measure.

In 1945 the Colonial Office published a White Paper which said that the loose organization of the Governors' Conference would no longer be enough for the needs of East Africa after the war. The conference had only a small staff, and things were beginning to move so fast that the governors had sometimes to take decisions without giving their

[1] See pages 137–9.

legislative councils time to discuss them properly. The White Paper proposed to set up an East African High Commission, with a legislative body of its own. The commission would still consist of the three governors, but it would have a much larger executive staff as well as a central legislature. The White Paper proposed that the legislative council should consist of 24 members. The legislative councils of Kenya, Uganda and Tanganyika should each elect two European and two Asian unofficial members. The governors should nominate two members from each territory (Africans if possible) to represent African interests, and a final group of six members from anywhere in East Africa; two of this group should represent Arab interests.

This proposal met with a mixed reception. The Asians welcomed the proposed legislature, because it was to have as many Asian as European members. The Kenya Europeans rejected the scheme for this very reason. African opinion was mixed. The Kenya African Union approved, but it hoped that all six of the members nominated to represent African interests would be Africans. Buganda on the whole feared the scheme because of the danger from the Kenya Europeans; Africans in Tanganyika felt the same.

After considering these opinions, the Colonial Office produced a modified scheme. The central legislature was now to consist of seven officials from the central executive, plus one official from each of the three countries, a total of ten. Against these, there were to be thirteen unofficial members, some nominated and some elected; of these thirteen, six were to be European and at least three African. This modified scheme was accepted by the Kenya Europeans, but Asian and African opinion was against it. However, it was carried through the three legislative councils, and the East Africa High Commission was formally established at the beginning of 1948.

The commission took over from the separate countries several departments of government in which one large authority was likely to be more efficient: such as posts and telegraphs, railways and harbours and international air services, customs, defence, income tax, higher education, statistics, currency, locust and tsetse-fly control, and certain scientific services. Everyone could see that such a central body was useful, but Uganda and Tanganyika were always afraid that the commission was but the first step towards a political union which would place them at the mercy of the European settlers in Kenya. The commission was set up in the first place for three years. In 1951 its life was extended for four more years, in 1955 for four years again, in 1959 for three. But before these three years expired, Tanganyika became independent, so that a commission of three governors was no longer workable. The commission was replaced by a new body, the East Africa Common Services Organization, which began working in 1961. Some people hoped that when all three countries were independent, and there was no longer any need to fear the European settlers in Kenya, the Common Services Organization might gradually develop into a federal government of East Africa. But this has not yet happened.

Chapter 10

TOWARDS INDEPENDENCE IN KENYA

Whatever the European settlers in Kenya may have thought, the African people and the Kenya government were agreed that the most urgent problem at the end of the war was to extend African education.

EDUCATIONAL ADVANCE

Education is one of the most difficult problems for a poor country like Kenya, especially when the revenue goes up and down from year to year. Bridges and power stations may be expensive to construct, but once they are finished, they cost little to maintain. But a school is useless without a staff of teachers; consequently, before deciding to build a new school, a poor country has to think carefully whether it will be able to afford the annual salary bill.

Africans today are so enthusiastic for education that it is hard to imagine a time when they were not so. But in Kenya, as in other African countries, when the missionaries first opened their schools they found it difficult to persuade parents to send their children. Kenya education in the early days consisted of many small schools, each run by a European missionary with one or two African assistants whom he himself was training. There were very few government schools; and although after the first world war a few leaders like Harry Thuku were beginning to ask for government schools, there was no general demand for them. In Harry Thuku's time there were fewer than 100,000 children attending school, and the numbers rose only slowly until the 1930s.

Then, as we have seen, the Kikuyu people began putting their energies into education, and the demand for schools rose swiftly; by the end of the second world war there were more than 200,000 children in school. The Kikuyu especially had realized the political importance of education. Kenya is not alone in this. The demand for education developed similarly in West Africa, very slowly at first and with a sudden jump in the 1930s.

It should have been the duty of the Kenya government to build government schools and teacher training colleges in order to supply this new demand for education. Unfortunately, the new demand co-incided with the economic slump. The missionary societies found that the Christian churches in Europe which supported them were unable to keep up their subscriptions fully, and some missionaries had to give up their work and leave Africa. The Kenya government found its revenue so badly hit that instead of increasing the strength of the education department it was forced to reduce it; some government education officers, like the missionaries, had to leave Kenya. Kenya would have been better prepared for independence if the government had been able, as it wished, to appoint additional staff to help and encourage this new African demand for education.

The Beecher commission

During the 1939 war, the demand for education went up and up. People built schools and called on the government to find them teachers. At the end of the war, there were immense numbers of children in school; most of the teachers were quite untrained, and there were only fourteen government education officers available for the work of training African teachers and supervising African schools. The Kenya government sent to Britain and brought out large numbers of experienced British teachers to expand the staff of the education department; and it appointed a commission, under the chairmanship of Archdeacon (later Archbishop) Beecher, to draw up a programme of educational expansion.

The situation was so bad that it could not be quickly remedied. Half the children who entered school left it after two years, having learnt nothing useful in that short time. The Beecher commission reported in October 1949. It proposed that the government should first concentrate on making sure that half the children entering school should stay for four years; this period, it was thought, would give the children permanent literacy. The government should do what it could to extend primary education from four years to eight, and to build more secondary schools and teacher training colleges. But the most urgent task was to get half the children to stay at school for four years instead of two. The second stage of the plan was to see that *all* town children, and most country children, stayed for the four years, and that a high proportion of them stayed for a second four-year course. Gradually, the commission hoped, a full eight years primary course would become available for all.

With financial aid under the Colonial Development and Welfare Acts, this Beecher scheme made good progress. In twelve years, the number of trained teachers rose from 1,980 to 10,500. The children in the first four-year school course increased from 200,000 to 504,000, and those in the second four-year course from 7,000 to 68,000. Before the Beecher scheme began, Kenya had one African secondary school with 400 pupils; twelve years later it had 31 schools with 4,500 pupils.

But from the political point of view, the Beecher scheme came too late. If it could have been begun in 1935 it would have kept abreast of the African demand; now, Africans thought it miserably inadequate. They saw that all European children in Kenya were receiving a full primary education, and that they had generous opportunities of secondary education. Europeans had demanded education for their children from the beginning, and were willing to pay school fees. The government could afford to provide education for European children, because the numbers concerned were so small. But the Africans now said that if the government provided so much education for European children, it ought to provide as much for African.

Moreover, the Beecher plan was misunderstood. In the early years, it often happened that the government opened a new primary school, but did not for the time being allow it to continue beyond the fourth year; this further development must wait for a later stage in the programme. Many Africans concluded that the purpose of the Beecher programme was to limit African education permanently to a four-year course. This was one of the grievances that led to the Mau Mau movement. As time went on and the Beecher plan was carried out, its true purpose became plain; but the damage had been done.

POLITICAL ADVANCE

Educational programmes take time to produce their results, but the governments in Nairobi and London had no intention of waiting to see the full results of the Beecher programme before pushing ahead with political advance. In 1944 the first African, Mr E. W. Mathu, was nominated as a member of the legislative council. In 1948 four Africans were nominated instead of only one, and the number of official members was cut from twenty to seventeen. This meant that the official majority disappeared, and the unofficial members had a majority of four over the government. The European unofficial members had been hoping that they by themselves would have a majority; but the governor, Sir Philip Mitchell, so arranged it that the unofficial majority depended on African and Arab votes. In 1951, the four African members were increased to six, but at the same time the total size of the council was increased. There was still an unofficial majority, but of two only. And at that point the government had to give its attention to the Mau Mau movement.

The Mau Mau

Nobody knows what the name Mau Mau means. Perhaps the most likely explanation is that a European policeman who did not understand the Kikuyu language misheard the Kikuyu word *muma*, an oath.

In 1946, Mr Mathu founded a new political organization, the Kenya African Union. In that same year, Mr Kenyatta returned from his long stay in Europe. He at once became chairman of the KAU, and also took over control of the Kikuyu independent schools association. Mr Kenyatta told the governor, Sir Philip Mitchell, that he would like to take an active part in politics; the governor, perhaps not understanding what sort of a man Kenyatta was, advised him to begin by joining his Local Native Council. Mr Kenyatta preferred to become the acknowledged national leader not only of the Kikuyu but of all the Africans in Kenya. While Mr Kenyatta and Mr Mathu were advising the government to push ahead with constitutional advance and to reach a satisfactory settlement of the land question, others of the Kikuyu were more impatient, and were ready to use force.

They had many grievances. Many men returning from the army could not find employment, and did not wish to go back to their old life of subsistence farming. There was a great shortage of housing in Nairobi, and the city was full of Kikuyu and other Africans who had come there to find work, but who could find neither work nor homes, and who dared not go back to their villages and admit that they had failed. The Beecher programme of education was another grievance, for it was only just beginning, and the Africans thought, as we have said, that the Beecher commission meant to limit African education to the four-year course. And always there were the two great permanent grievances: European settlers were occupying African land, and many of them were treating Africans as if they were inferior beings and must always remain so.

The more impatient among the Kikuyu began using violence. They took oaths binding themselves to kill whenever their leaders called on them to do so. They began maiming cattle and killing people who were opposed to them. They stopped African farmers who were terracing their fields, because they were doing so on the advice of government agricultural officers. Kikuyu chiefs and other leaders who dared to speak against the Mau Mau were murdered. By 1952 thousands of young men had gone into the forest to form the 'Kenya Land and Freedom Army'. In October 1952 the government banned the KAU and all other political organizations; it declared a state of emergency, arrested Mr Kenyatta and nearly a hundred other leaders, and asked for British troops to fight the Mau Mau. Mr Kenyatta was tried and convicted on a charge of being the real leader of the Mau Mau, and was sent away to the north of the country to serve a seven-year sentence.

The government hoped that by arresting so many men who might have provided the Mau Mau with skilful leadership, it had struck the movement a heavy blow. But the Kikuyu were accustomed to organizing themselves in small units; and in spite of the efforts of large numbers of British troops with artillery and air support, they kept the war going in the forest for over four years. On the other hand, the Mau Mau never looked like overthrowing the government or conquering the White Highlands. Very few of their leaders were men of education. They had no broad plan of campaign. They seem to have thought that they would be fighting merely against the European settlers, and were surprised that the Kenya government could call on such strong support from Britain. The Mau Mau men killed 58 European and Asian civilians, and 2,000 Kikuyu civilians. When it came to fighting in the forest, they killed about 1,000 government troops in action, but their own losses were far heavier. One by one the Mau Mau leaders were hunted down and caught, and by 1956 the worst of the trouble was at an end.

One of the biggest reasons for the defeat of the Mau Mau is that it lost the support of the mass of the Kikuyu people. In the beginning, probably the majority of the Kikuyu agreed with the aims of the Mau Mau. After a number of chiefs and other leading men had been murdered for daring to speak out against its methods, there was not much open opposition. The Kikuyu people lived in small family settlements scattered over the countryside. It was easy at first for the Mau Mau men to persuade or compel the people in these isolated settlements to give them food and information. But as time went on it became harder. The government made the Kikuyu leave their isolated homesteads and come together into large compact villages fortified with stockades; and the men living in these villages formed themselves into a home guard to protect their village against Mau Mau raids. The leaders of the Land and Freedom Army hoped to gain the support of the whole Kikuyu people in their struggle, but they failed. In January 1954, twenty-three Kikuyu leaders (including Harry Thuku and both the Kikuyu members of the legislative council) made a public appeal to their people to abandon the Mau Mau; they said that its oaths were contrary to Kikuyu custom and that its methods could not possibly lead to independence. In the end, the mass of the Kikuyu people decided to withdraw their support; and when that decision was made the defeat of the Mau Mau was only a question of time.

The Mau Mau emergency is so recent, occupied so much attention, and caused so much suffering, that it is easy to over-estimate its historical importance. The British government did not need such a sharp warning, for it had already made up its mind that Kenya must be developed into an independent multi-racial state. The Kenya government went ahead with its plans as if there were no emergency. In 1954 it set up a Council of Ministers, and in 1957 it held elections to the legislative council, in which Africans voted for the first time. In 1958 it increased the number of African members of the council, and next year it promised to hold a constitutional conference. From 1953 to 1955 a Royal Commission was touring Kenya studying the country's economic problems, and in 1954 the government adopted the far-reaching Swynnerton programme of land reform. We cannot say that the Mau Mau emergency speeded up the government's efforts. In fact, in one respect it slowed down progress, for until all the danger was over, the government would not allow the formation of African political parties on a nation-wide basis. It feared that the Mau Mau leaders would gain control of any such parties and use them as a means of spreading Mau Mau activities all over Kenya.

Perhaps the greatest importance of the Mau Mau episode is that it put an end to the old claim of the Kenya Europeans that they understood Kenya and its needs better than the government in London. The Moyne report had thrown a good deal of discredit on this claim before the war; after the Mau Mau, no one outside Kenya believed it any longer. The Mau Mau movement was a strong protest against what we may call the Delamere policy. It was now plain that that policy was dead. There were still some European settlers who clung to the old idea of European domination and of the White Highlands. But a large section of the Europeans, led by Mr Michael Blundell, saw as clearly as the government in London that Kenya must quickly become an independent multi-racial state.

Another result of the episode, which the government certainly did not foresee, was that the long-drawn trial of Jomo Kenyatta established him in the eyes of the world as a national statesman. The court proceedings were widely reported in the Press. Mr Kenyatta was himself an orator, and he had a brilliant counsel to defend him. He was convicted, it is true; but the speeches for the defence had the effect of putting the Kenya government and the whole of the British record in Kenya on trial. The government might send Mr Kenyatta away to the arid north, but he would surely one day return as the national leader of Kenya.

The Lyttelton proposals

Kenya already had a system by which certain unofficial members of the legislative council were appointed to take a special interest in some particular branches of the administration. This rudimentary ministerial system had been in force since 1945. In 1954 the Secretary of State, Oliver Lyttelton, proposed that Kenya should have a fully developed ministerial system. There should be a Council of Ministers, consisting of six official members of the legislative council and six unofficial members (three European, two Asian, and one African) with two extra ministers nominated by the governor. The governor and his deputy would attend meetings of the council. There was to be no immediate change in the legislative council, but Lyttelton recognized that it was time to have elected African members, and he asked the Kenya government to work out a scheme for African elections to be put into effect two years later.

The British government at that time was far from the idea of 'One man, one vote'. Britain herself had taken over a century—from 1832 to 1948—to reach this idea; during this period a series of laws had been made which gradually widened the electorate, always on the assumption that the vote should be given only to those who could be trusted to use it properly. The government was prepared to compress this process in Kenya to within twenty years or so; it meant to extend the vote more widely as education developed. But it still held the view that it would do Kenya no good to give the vote to millions of people who understood nothing of the problems of modern government. The view was natural in the light of Britain's own history, and the government was not taking this line merely to protect the interests of the white settlers. But since all Europeans in Kenya had the vote, the government's line was not practical politics. The government soon found out that the Africans would be content with nothing less than 'One man, one vote', and, as we shall see, that they had means of enforcing their demand.

For the moment the only subject for discussion was Lyttelton's proposed council of ministers. The Arabs with some hesitation decided to support the scheme. The Asians had no objection from their own point of view, but they thought it insufficient to have only one African minister, and they advised the Secretary of State to reconsider this. The Europeans were divided. Of the fourteen European elected members, eight (headed by Mr Michael Blundell) accepted the scheme; three more said that they would accept it provided the electors in their constituencies agreed; the other three rejected the scheme altogether.

The Africans would have nothing to do with it. They said there should be at least two African ministers, and preferably three. But the African members' organization said that although it disliked the scheme, it would not boycott it; if any African was prepared to take office, he was free to do so. The scheme was put into effect, without modification, in April 1955. An African, Mr Ohanga, was appointed Minister of Community Development, and two Africans were nominated as members of the executive council.

In June, six of the European elected members, headed by Michael Blundell, formed themselves into the United Country Party, with a policy of working towards multi-racial government. The party was opposed to all racialism, it supported all schemes for African progress, and it wished Kenya to develop an efficient modern system of local government. It saw that the Lyttelton constitution was only the first step, but it supported it because it seemed a step in the right direction.

After two years' study, the Kenya government produced its scheme for African voting, which was approved by the government in London. It was a scheme of direct voting[1] by secret ballot. The vote was given to all men of twenty-one or more who qualified in any one of seven ways: (a) he had completed eight years of schooling; (b) he was earning £120 or more a year, or possessed property worth £500; (c) he had long government service; (d) he was a village elder or was forty-five years old; (e) he had a university degree or some professional qualification; (f) he was, or had been, a member of the legislative council or of a local government body; (g) he had been decorated by the government. A man might qualify in more than one of these ways; if so, he might be given extra votes, up to a maximum of three.

This cautious scheme produced an African electorate of 126,811 registered voters; no doubt there were some who did not trouble to register. Elections to the new legislative council were held in October 1956 for the Europeans and Asians, and in March 1957 for the Africans. Only two of the eight African members of the old council kept their seats. The election brought Mr Tom Mboya into the council; he was general secretary of the Kenya Federation of Labour, and quickly

---

[1] In direct voting, you vote to choose your own representative. In indirect voting, you vote for some wise man who will sit in a committee, and he will choose your representative for you.

7   MODERN AFRICA: THE PARLIAMENT BUILDING IN NAIROBI

became the effective leader of the African members. Of the European seats, six were won by the United Country Party; the other eight went to members who disliked the whole idea of appointing ministers according to race, and said that they should be appointed on 'merit and ability'—which in their view would probably mean that for a long time to come they would all be Europeans. The new council contained 29 elected members out of a total of 59: 14 Europeans, 3 Hindu and 3 Muslim Asians, 1 Arab, and 8 Africans.

As soon as they had taken their seats, all eight African members declared that they regarded the Lyttelton constitution as null and void. They demanded an additional fifteen seats for elected African members, which would give them a majority of two over all the other elected members together. Until this demand was granted, they said, they would not accept ministerial posts or take part in the work of the council.

This was the first time that the Africans had used the weapon of the boycott, and a powerful weapon it was. From March to November 1957 the African members took no part in the council's work, and the Lyttelton constitution stood idle. In October 1957 the African members put out a full statement of their demands: (a) the existing limited scheme of votes for Africans must be swept away, and all men and women of twenty-one should vote on a common roll; (b) constituencies must be geographical, not racial; there must be no seats reserved for members of any particular race; (c) Kenya must not be given independence until the Africans were adequately represented in the legislature and could influence public affairs; (d) there should be a maximum limit set to the size of land-holdings, and all unoccupied land in the Highlands must be opened to African farmers; (e) trade union rights must be protected; (f) there must be eight years schooling for all; (g) all schools must be open to pupils of any race; (h) Africans must be effectively represented in local government bodies; (i) all races must be liable for jury service; (j) the state of emergency which had been declared because of the Mau Mau must be ended.

In this programme it is easy to see the hand of Mr Mboya. There was nothing in it that the Kenya government and the United Country Party would not accept as desirable; the only difference of opinion would be over the question of timing. Some of the African demands, such as eight years schooling for all, could not be achieved by a stroke of the pen; you cannot have schools without teachers, and it takes time as well as money to produce the teachers. Other demands, such as universal adult voting, could have been granted, but the government thought it wiser to work towards them gradually.

The Lennox-Boyd proposals

Still, things could not be left as they were; and in October 1957 Lyttelton's successor as Secretary of State, Lennox-Boyd, came to Kenya to see what could be done. He quickly agreed that the Lyttelton constitution was unworkable, and he made fresh proposals. The eight elected African members should be increased to fourteen, and there should be two African ministers instead of one. There should be a special Council of State to see that no law was passed which did not apply equally to all races. The legislative council should be enlarged by twelve unofficial cross-bench[2] members, four from each race; these members should not be directly elected by the voters, but should be nominated and elected by the council itself. Lennox-Boyd promised that whenever the legislative council was again enlarged, there should be no new communal seats; all additional members should be elected on a common roll.

The Asians welcomed what one of their leaders called 'this fine example of sagacious statesmanship'. The Africans, though with some reluctance, rejected the proposals. They did not trust this policy of gradual constitutional advance, carried out by the governments in London and Nairobi as a series of compromises between what the Africans were demanding and what the European settlers could be persuaded to concede. They wanted a constitution to be worked out at a constitutional conference in London and imposed on Kenya by the authority of the British government.

In spite of being thus rejected by the Africans, the Lennox-Boyd constitution was brought into effect in April 1958. Mr Mboya protested that it was unfair to have fourteen members to represent 50,000 Europeans, and only fourteen to represent six million Africans. For this and other reasons, the African members boycotted the Bill to raise the number of African seats from eight to fourteen, but it was of course carried without them, and the six additional members were duly elected in March 1958. All fourteen African members then declared themselves opposed to the new constitution, and when the legislative council proposed to elect the twelve cross-bench members, they took no part. This did not prevent the council from electing the twelve; and one of the four African cross-bench members, Mr Musa Amalemba, became Minister of Housing.

A year later, in April 1959, the elected members of the legislative council sorted themselves into three groups; they could not be called parties, for the emergency was not yet ended and the government was not yet permitting political parties on a national basis. Michael Blundell formed the New Kenya Group of ten European members. He looked forward to a representative parliament with responsible self-government, and he hoped that there would be 'a steady and intentional development' towards this end. He approved of the common roll,

---

[2] These members were free to support the government or the opposition as they chose. In the British parliamentary tradition, such independent members sit on benches at right angles to the benches on which party members sit. But there are hardly any independent members in the British parliament nowadays.

and he thought the cross-bench system should be extended so as to accustom Kenyans to the idea of voting for men of other races. Land, he thought, should not be regarded as a tribal or racial reserve. He was in favour of non-racial schools, and of a great extension of African education.

The second group was the Constituency Elected Members Association, led by Dr Kiano. This group consisted of all fourteen directly elected African members, all six Asian elected members, one Arab, and one European. The CEMA was friendly towards the New Kenya Group; it entirely approved of the Group's aims, but it disliked the Group's policy of gradual advance, and wanted rapid change. The CEMA wanted twelve more elected African members; it wanted politics in Kenya to be run on a basis of party, not of race; and it wanted to take the decisive step forward from a colonial constitution to a constitution with a responsible cabinet like that in Britain.

The third group was the small group of four Europeans, led by Group Captain Briggs, who would have nothing to do with Blundell's progressive ideas; they rejected the common roll, non-racial schools, and African intrusion into the White Highlands.

This beginning of party politics was a healthy sign, and it was especially welcome that the CEMA included members from all three races. Nevertheless, the Africans disliked the Lennox-Boyd constitution. They appealed to Lennox-Boyd to abolish the council of state and the cross-bench members. But he appealed to them in return to try his constitution and see how it worked; they could discuss with the governor any changes they wanted, but how could they condemn a constitution as unworkable when they had not tried to work it? This attitude of 'Try it and see how you get on' is characteristically British, and most Englishmen felt that in declining to 'try it' the Africans were being unreasonable. But the Africans saw that while the government in London wanted them to try its ideas, it was unwilling to try theirs; it was just as ready to say that in the Kenya of 1959 the common roll and 'One man, one vote' were unworkable as Mr Mboya was to say that the Lennox-Boyd plan was unworkable.

The Africans knew that it was settled policy in London to push ahead with constitutional advance as fast as possible, and that there was much more sympathy in Britain for the cause of African independence than for the interests of the European settlers. Partly for this very reason, the Africans wanted negotiations to be conducted in London instead of in Nairobi, and they hoped that Lennox-Boyd would accept their idea of a constitutional conference. But it was not till April 1959, after another three months of boycott, that he accepted it; and then Mr Oginga Odinga led a Kenya delegation to London to make plans for a full constitutional conference to be held later.

A few days before this April meeting in London, Mr Kenyatta and four others were released from detention, but they were still compelled to live in the north and were forbidden to take part in politics.

In July the government at last allowed national political parties to be formed, and the New Kenya Group became the New Kenya Party. Among the Africans there was a good deal of movement. Without Mr Kenyatta, African politics had an air of unreality. All the Africans wanted the same things, they all regarded Mr Kenyatta as the national leader; without him, parties split and re-formed over matters of detail.

The first Lancaster House conference

The long-awaited constitutional conference met at Lancaster House in London in January 1960. It had a difficult task, for the views of Briggs's party and of the Africans were quite irreconcilable, and all the skill and patience of the new Secretary of State, Iain Macleod, could not produce a constitution which was acceptable to all. But a large majority of the delegates agreed on a new constitution which was a great advance on the constitution of 1958.

The legislative council was to have 53 members elected by direct vote on a common roll, and 22 cross-bench members elected as in the Lennox-Boyd constitution. Of the 53 directly elected seats, 33 were open, and the other 20 reserved for minority races: 10 European, 8 Asian, 2 Arab. These 20 seats were to be filled by a system of two elections. In an Asian seat, for example, there would be a first election in which only Asians voted, and any candidate who did not win one-quarter of the votes was rejected. Then would come a second election in which voters of all races voted for the remaining candidates.

The number of African voters was greatly increased, though the government still clung to the idea that the vote should be restricted to those who understood how to use it. The complicated list of qualifications was greatly simplified. All Kenyans were given the vote if they satisfied any one of four conditions: (a) they were literate in their mother-tongue, (b) they were 40 years old or more, (c) they had an income of £75 a year or more, (d) they had held public office. By 1960 the Beecher educational programme had been running for ten years, and illiteracy among young Kenyans was rapidly falling, so that more and more Africans would soon qualify for the vote through literacy.

The council of ministers was to consist of 8 unofficial ministers and 4 officials. Of the 8 unofficial ministers, 4 were to be Africans, 3 Europeans, and 1 Asian; this was an advance on the Lyttelton scheme of 1 African minister and the Lennox-Boyd scheme of 2.

The constitution was to include a Bill of Rights, a statement of the rights belonging to every citizen of Kenya, much on the lines of the Declaration of Human Rights which had been issued by the United Nations.

This Lancaster House constitution of 1960 did not give responsible government, and it fell short of what the Africans were demanding. Mr Ronald Ngala said that it was a big step forward, but he disliked the clause in the Bill of Rights which declared that every Kenyan had the right to keep and enjoy property. Was a farm in the Highlands, for example, to be regarded as property, and did this clause mean that European claims to the Highlands were to be protected by the constitution? Nevertheless, the constitution was much too good to be boycotted; the thing to do was to work it and try to get it improved. The Africans asked Ngala, Kiano and two others to join in a temporary government to hold office while the new elections were being prepared. The other African members remained in the legislative council as an opposition party, and continued their policy of using the council as a platform for their speeches.

African political parties

The elections were to be held early in 1961, and the new register of voters included 20,000 Europeans, 60,000 Asians, and 1,300,000 Africans. The African members split into two groups. The stronger called itself the Kenya African National Union; its main strength was among the Kikuyu and the Luo. In Mr Kenyatta's absence, Mr Gichuru was chairman of the party, Mr Odinga vice-chairman, and Mr Mboya secretary. But the strength of KANU was so formidable that it raised fears among other African peoples, and other small groups were formed, all of them frankly local or tribal. Four of these were the Masai, Somali, Kalenjin, and Coast parties; the fifth was the Kenya African People's Party, which was the old CEMA without its European and Asian members. Five small parties have no chance in an election against one large one. It was clearly prudent for the five parties to combine, and they did combine into a party which called itself the Kenya African Democratic Union, with Mr Ngala as chairman and Mr Muliro and Mr Arap Moi as prominent members.

In the 1961 elections, KANU was returned as the strongest party with 18 seats; KADU had 10, there were 14 independent members, and 11 members representing four other small parties. The governor, Sir Patrick Renison, called on the strongest party, KANU, to form a government, but KANU would form no government unless the governor released Mr Kenyatta, and this the governor refused to do. The governor then turned to KADU, but the KADU leaders took just the same line as KANU. In April 1960 the governor gave way, and agreed that a house should be built for Mr Kenyatta at Gatundu in the Kiambu district. In return for this, KADU agreed to form a government, and invited KANU to join it in a coalition. No KANU members would take part, but Blundell and Havelock of the New Kenya Party accepted office under the leadership of Mr Ngala.

All this time, Mr Kenyatta was the real leader. A joint delegation of KANU and KADU members visited him in the north, and agreed to set up a committee to work for independence in 1961. Kenyatta made it clear that he did not favour either party; he advised both parties to carry on for the time being as they were, KADU forming the government and KANU being in opposition.

In August 1961 the house at Gatundu was ready, and Mr Kenyatta came down from the north and re-entered politics. He presided over a joint committee of KANU and KADU, which put out a statement asking for immediate internal self-government, and for another constitutional conference which should prepare for full independence on February 1, 1962. The governor welcomed the statement, but he said it would be impossible to make all the arrangements in so short a time. It soon proved that he was right; for when constitutional talks began, disagreements arose between KANU and KADU which even Mr Kenyatta could not heal. KADU, as was natural from its origin as an amalgamation of small tribal groups, wanted a federal system with a great deal of power reserved to the regional governments. KANU wanted a unitary system with a strong central government. Finding it impossible any longer to hold the two parties together, Mr Kenyatta accepted the leadership of KANU and became for the time being a party leader, rather than a national leader.

The Second Lancaster House conference

In January 1962 Mr Kenyatta was returned unopposed as a member of the legislative council, one KANU member having resigned his seat so as to make this possible. Next month the constitutional conference opened in London, the Kenya delegation consisting of 31 KANU members led by Mr Kenyatta, 27 KADU led by Mr Ngala, and 11 others. It was difficult to bring about a compromise between the views of KANU and KADU. But in the end the conference agreed that (as KANU wished) there should be a strong central government led by a prime minister who commanded a majority in the lower house of parliament. On the other hand, as KADU wished, there should be regional assemblies with both legislative and executive powers; they should derive their authority from the constitution, not from the central government. The lower house, the House of Representatives, was to consist of 117 members elected on a common roll with universal adult suffrage, and 12 cross-bench members. The upper house, the Senate, was to consist of 41 members, 1 from each district and 1 from Nairobi. The regional assemblies were to have a good deal of control in agriculture, education, health, and local government.

Independence

After the conference, a fresh council of ministers was appointed; there were 7 KANU and 7 KADU ministers, and 2 officials. New elections were held in May 1963 in accordance with the new constitution. The lower house contained 67 KANU and 40 KADU members, with 5 independents; 5 seats remained empty because the Somali people in the north-east of the country boycotted the elections. The KANU leader, Mr Kenyatta, became prime minister, and chose a cabinet of 14 African members of KANU and 1 European.

It seemed as if all that remained was to fix the date of independence. Tanganyika and Uganda were already independent, and in June 1963 their prime ministers, Dr Nyerere and Dr Obote, visited Nairobi and discussed with Mr Kenyatta the possibility of setting up an East African federation. The discussions went well, and the three statesmen agreed to set up the federation before the end of 1963. It thus became important for Kenya to become independent before then. The date finally fixed was December 12, and it was agreed in London that the British troops should be withdrawn from Kenya within twelve months from independence. At midnight on December 11, 1963 the British flag was hauled down and the new flag of independent Kenya was hoisted in its place; Mr Kenyatta was the prime minister of a free and independent country within the Commonwealth. The governor was invited to become governor-general, a non-executive head of state, and to remain as the Queen's representative.

THE LAND QUESTION AFTER 1945

Land has always been the biggest problem in Kenya politics. It was a problem far too important to be discussed merely on a political basis, with the Europeans asking, 'Why cannot the government provide us with more African workers?' and the Africans asking, 'Why will not the government allow us to farm in the Highlands?' Kenya has hardly any minerals. Everybody in Kenya depends on the land. The more fertile the land, the more it can be made to produce, the more prosperity there will be for all. Old customs which stand in the way of increasing production must be changed. The African custom was to give each family a small patch of land for subsistence farming, and allow it to graze as many cattle as it liked on the village land. The European custom was to give a family a very large farm, and to leave land uncultivated because no European farmer was available to cultivate it and African farmers were not allowed in the area. Customs like these must go.

There was no longer plenty of land for all. Modern medicine was

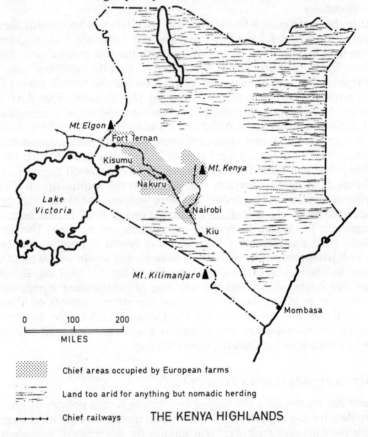

Mt. Elgon

Fort Ternan

Kisumu

Nakuru

Mt. Kenya

Lake
Victoria

Nairobi

Kiu

Mt. Kilimanjaro

Mombasa

0   100   200

MILES

Chief areas occupied by European farms

Land too arid for anything but nomadic herding

Chief railways   THE KENYA HIGHLANDS

Notice how the European settlers clustered near the railway lines. The shaded area was not solidly occupied, and there were African reserves in the Highlands. The 'White Highlands' were only a small part of Kenya, but they were a much larger part of the habitable area of Kenya. Moreover, much of the well-watered land along the coast and around Lake Victoria was infested with tsetse-fly, and the Highlands were free of the fly keeping alive both people and animals who in the old days would have died. When a man's farm was divided between his sons, there were more sons living than formerly, so each got a smaller share. When the soil was tired and the family farm was moved, there was less bush land available, and so the farm had to be brought back to the old place before the soil was properly rested. Similarly with the cattle: in some places there were so many cattle that they were grazing the land bare. Land in the Highlands must not be left unoccupied when there was this land hunger in the African areas. But to throw all the Highlands open to African subsistence farming would be no permanent solution. If this were done, in thirty or forty years these lands too would be exhausted, and Kenya would be facing the old problem of land hunger once more.

This was the true land problem, as it was seen by the government's agricultural advisers. If the population went on increasing, and old ideas and customs remained unchanged, the time was not far ahead when the soil of Kenya would become a desert. Somehow or other, old ideas and customs must be changed before things went so far.

The Swynnerton scheme
After the war, the government received advice from two sources. The first was from its assistant director of agriculture, R. J. M. Swynnerton. He presented a report which pointed out that most of the African people were living in areas which had enough rainfall to make them suitable for intensive or semi-intensive farming: that is, farming which aims at growing the heaviest crops that the soil can produce without becoming exhausted, as opposed to the African method of subsistence farming, in which each family aims at growing only enough food to support itself, or very little more. Most of the African cattle, on the other hand, were being grazed in semi-arid areas, where the rainfall was not enough for intensive agriculture; Swynnerton reckoned that African herds totalled about six million animals.

Swynnerton estimated that on the average, an African family produced about £10 worth of crops a year more than it needed; he thought that this £10 of surplus could be increased to £100. Similarly, the average value of a cow was £2, and it should be possible to raise this to £10 or £15. If African cattle-owners could be persuaded to sell about 650,000 animals a year for slaughter, this would provide much more wealth and keep down the size of the herds to a figure which the grass could support. Swynnerton knew the difficulties. He knew Africans were reluctant to slaughter their cattle; he knew African farms were small and were made up of several scattered strips; the improvements he wished for would be impossible unless Africans could be persuaded to look at their land and their cattle in a new way. Above all, the government must overcome the Africans' natural fear that any new proposal about land must be some trick in the interests of the European settlers.

The first problem was to persuade the African farmers that these changes were possible. They must be encouraged to grow not merely food crops, but cash crops such as coffee, cotton, sugar, pyrethrum, the very crops which the European settlers had so long wished to keep for themselves. Another 170 agricultural advisers would be needed to help the Africans with these new ideas, and Swynnerton hoped that the government in London would help to pay for them. And somehow or other, said the report, the government must overcome the African custom of breaking farms into small pieces. A man should be able to have all his land in one block, so that he could fence it round and keep his cattle on it and improve it as he wished; and a farm must be big enough to be worth improving.

The Swynnerton scheme was put forward during the Mau Mau troubles, and in one respect these troubles helped it. To make it harder for the Mau Mau men in the forest to get food and information from the scattered Kikuyu homes, the government made the Kikuyu leave their homes and come and live in large villages where they could be better protected. This gave it the opportunity to lay out the farm land round these villages in blocks; and in this way many Kikuyu farmers came to see the advantages of having their farm land in one block instead of scattered strips, and of keeping their cattle in fenced kraals instead of letting them roam in the bush. In May 1954 the Swynnerton scheme was adopted by the legislative council; the African Land Board approved of it; and the British government gave £5 million to put it into operation.

In February 1954 the Kenya government received the report of a committee which it had set up to look into the question of African wages and labour. African wages, said the committee, were too low. About half the African workers in towns, and a still larger proportion in the rural areas, were not being paid enough to keep them well fed and healthy. The traditional system of migrant labour was bad: Kenya must break away from the idea that a man's real home was in the reserves, and that when he came to work on a European farm or in an office or factory in town, he was merely a temporary visitor there. A man ought to be able to live and make his permanent home in the place where he worked; and the government ought to change its laws and regulations about housing so as to make this possible.

The Royal Commission on Land and Population

Soon afterwards, the government received similar advice from a still more authoritative source. The British government had appointed a Royal Commission to go round the whole of East Africa and study land and population problems. In June 1955 the commission produced a long and detailed report, which stressed that in East Africa as a whole, not only in Kenya, people thought about land and population problems in ways that were hopelessly old-fashioned, and they must modernize their ideas if the region was to have any hope of prosperity. They were hampered by the results of their past actions. In Kenya, for example, Africans still felt bitter because the government had deprived them of their right to live in the Highlands, and fresh bitterness was being brought about by the sight of land lying empty in the Highlands while the African reserves were overcrowded.

The commission said that the idea of cutting Kenya into tribal reserves must be abandoned. The Europeans must no longer behave as if they were a tribe hanging on to its tribal territory. People must no longer think, 'This is Nandi land, this is Kikuyu land, this is European land, this is Kamba land.' All the people of Kenya must realize that the land belonged to the nation, and in the national interest it must be improved and made to produce as much as it could. This would mean giving up the old idea that land belonged to the tribe or the clan, and adopting the European idea that land belonged to an individual. If a man had to buy his farm, he would see to it that the farm repaid him by its produce; in this way, individual ownership of land would be in the national interest.

Like Mr Swynnerton, the commission recommended that African subsistence farming should end, and that Africans should farm their land on a commercial basis. They should grow cash crops, as the Europeans did; they should use fertilizers and farm machinery, and they should form cooperative societies, both for buying these things and for grading and marketing the crops. The small scattered strips of an individual's farm should be consolidated into one compact holding.

All this of course would bring about new problems. Under the old African system, everyone lived on the land. Under the new system, one man driving a tractor could cultivate as much land as a hundred working with their hoes, and the land would produce more. But the other ninety-nine men would not be needed on the land. They could go to the towns and work there in offices or factories, and could buy their food in the market. In the end, most people in East Africa, like most people in Europe, would have no land of their own except a small garden. A change like this could not be made suddenly; people must be given time to adjust themselves to the new system. But sooner or later the change must come, if the countries of East Africa were to develop into modern industrial states.

The commission went on to say that African education and health services must be improved. Many African workers were weakened by disease, and it was no good releasing people from agriculture if they had not the strength or education to fit them for work in the town. And the towns themselves must be improved. It had always been assumed that the towns were mainly for Europeans and Asians: that the Africans were village people who did not look on the town as their home, so there was no need to make the town home-like for them. In the future, more and more Africans would be living and working permanently in the towns, and they must be able to make their homes there; there must be better housing, better water and electricity supplies, and more comforts of all kinds.

If these proposals of the commission were acted on, the new East Africa would be very different from the old. Both Africans and Europeans would have to change their ideas, and many of them would not understand and welcome the changes. In July 1956 all three East African governments accepted the recommendations of the commission, though they added that everything would depend on how they could persuade the Africans to accept these changes.

As far as Kenya was concerned, there was no hope of persuading Africans to accept them while large areas of land were lying empty in the Highlands. Any scheme of reform must include proposals for making land in the Highlands available for African farmers. But this was a matter which was certain to rouse opposition among a section of the Europeans. The government must move carefully, so as to gain as much support as possible from the moderate section of European opinion.

In 1959 the legislative council passed two ordinances of the type that Swynnerton and the Royal Commission wanted. They were the Native Lands Registration Ordinance and the Land Control (Native Lands) Ordinance. These two new laws made it possible for African farmers to exchange their scattered strips of land with one another, so that each man had all his land in one block; the boundaries of the block were then surveyed and recorded, and the farmer received a written certificate of ownership. In that same year the government abandoned its policy of reserving the White Highlands, and in 1960 it put out its first scheme for establishing African farmers in the Highland area. It proposed to buy land from the European settlers, and to establish 8,000 family holdings of 50 acres each. Any African applying for one of these holdings would be trained in modern farming methods.

This was only a beginning, and of course the African leaders said it was on far too small a scale. Next year the government revised its scheme: the 8,000 holdings were to be increased to 20,000, but the size of the holdings was to be cut from 50 acres to 25. From 1960 onwards, these two processes of land reform went on side by side. The government in London provided large sums of money so that European estates in the Highlands could be bought and opened up for African farmers; and in the old African reserves the scattered farm strips were consolidated into blocks. As early as January 1961 nearly 250,000 Kikuyu farms had exchanged their strips and received title-deeds for their consolidated farms. Since then, both these processes of land reform have spread outside Kikuyu land to other parts of Kenya.

THE COASTAL STRIP OF KENYA

As Kenya approached independence, the question arose: What was to be done with the ten-mile coastal strip which still belonged in theory to the Sultan of Zanzibar? Since 1887 the strip had been administered as part of Kenya, first by the Company and then by the Kenya government; but under the 1887 agreement, the Sultan still received revenue from it. In 1961 the British government appointed Sir James Robertson, formerly governor-general of Nigeria, to study the problem and make proposals.

He reported in December 1961 that from the historical point of view, the claims of the Sultan and his Arab people were strong; the strip had been part of the Sultan's dominions for a very long time. But times had changed. The present population of the strip was 300,000 Africans, 48,000 Asians, 37,000 Arabs, and 7,000 Europeans. Its revenue amounted to less than two million pounds a year, which was insufficient to cover the expense of administration. Thus, the strip contained a strong majority of Kenya Africans, and the rest of Kenya was helping to administer it. It contained Kenya's principal port, Mombasa, and the best thing to do was to make the strip part of Kenya; it was not practical politics to set it up as an independent state. If an independent Kenya government would not continue the existing arrangement with the Sultan, and preferred to annex the coastal strip altogether, Sir James suggested that £675,000 would be a fair compensation to pay the Sultan. In any case, it should be administered as a separate region; there should be proper safeguards for Muslim law and customs; and the Kenya government should remember that the port of Mombasa was important for the trade of Uganda and of northern Tanganyika as well as for Kenya trade.

In April 1962 a special conference was held to consider the Robertson report. It approved the general principles laid down, but agreed to leave it to the independent governments of Kenya and Zanzibar to negotiate the transfer.

Chapter 11

TOWARDS INDEPENDENCE IN UGANDA

When the war ended in 1945, Uganda had its own problems; but it was not troubled, as Kenya was, by the problem of European-owned land and the problem of European domination in the legislative council. In Uganda, the main problem was the position of the kingdom of Buganda. This arose from the 1900 agreement, which placed Buganda in a privileged position, which the Kabaka and the Lukiko were anxious to retain. The British government wished to develop the protectorate as it was developing other territories: by adding more African members to the legislative council and by extending the system of elections until the council became entirely composed of elected representatives from all parts of the country. But the Kabaka and the Lukiko were opposed to this, because they regarded it as dangerous to Buganda's position and therefore contrary to the agreement.

EDUCATIONAL DEVELOPMENT

Another important problem was how to extend education. In 1944 the British government set up a royal commission, the Asquith Commission, to make recommendations about the development of higher education in the colonies after the war. The commission recommended that university colleges should be set up in Nigeria, the Sudan, Jamaica, Uganda, and Malaya, with money from Britain set aside under the Colonial Development and Welfare Acts. The college in Uganda should be based on Makerere, which would need to be greatly enlarged and developed; it should serve as a university college for the whole of British East Africa. The British government accepted these recommendations, and in March 1950 Makerere became a university college, linked with the University of London. Mr Bernard de Bunsen was the first principal.

This was satisfactory; but at once the question arose, where were the university students to come from? The secondary schools then existing in Uganda and East Africa could not provide very many, and they could not be greatly expanded until the primary schools had been improved. Money for educational expansion could be found from funds available under the Colonial Development and Welfare Acts, but the protectorate government was a good deal criticized for not acting more energetically to build up primary and secondary education so as to provide a solid foundation for the university college. In 1951 the Colonial Office sent a commission of expert educationists from Britain to tour East Africa and make proposals for speeding up educational development all over the region. When their report was received, the governor of Uganda, Sir Andrew Cohen, appointed a local committee under the principal of Makerere to work out a detailed programme for Uganda. Then at last Uganda began to move ahead.

POLITICAL DEVELOPMENT

In October 1945 the protectorate government began to act on its plan of appointing Africans to be members of the legislative council. One was appointed from Busoga and one from Bunyoro, and the governor wished to appoint also the katikiro of Buganda. The Lukiko hesitated; as usual, it feared that this might weaken Buganda's position under the agreement. But the governor agreed that if the katikiro accepted a seat in the legislative council, anything he said there should be taken as his own personal opinion, and not as the opinion of the Kabaka or the Lukiko. On this understanding, the Lukiko allowed the katikiro to accept nomination.

The Bataka Federation

Most African people at the time were not very interested in having more African members sitting in the legislative council. In Buganda, people were much more interested in having members elected to the Lukiko. After the riots of January 1945, the Buganda government saw that such a change would have to be made, and elections were held. In March 1946, 31 elected members took their seats in the Lukiko alongside the 89 traditional members. But some people in Buganda were not satisfied with this. They wanted the Lukiko to be mainly, if not entirely elected, and they wanted the Kabaka and the Lukiko to govern strictly in accordance with the wishes of the people. Those who asked for this great change revived the old Bataka Federation, which had been so effective in 1918. The Buganda government protested that these young men were not heads of clans, and so had no right to call themselves Bataka. The young men did not care; to them, the name Bataka conveyed the idea of the common people standing up against the Kabaka and the Lukiko, and so it was a good enough name for their purpose.

The so-called Bataka Federation found allies among the cotton farmers. In Uganda, as in many other countries, there was a government marketing organization, which bought all the cotton and kept back some of the profits in a good year, so as to protect the farmers against a fall of prices in a bad year. The farmers did not like to see their money being held by the marketing organization, and for this and other reasons, the African Farmers Union entered politics and opposed the Buganda government.

In 1948 and 1949 there was trouble. The Bataka were opposed to the establishment of the East Africa High Commission, and they were angry with the Buganda government for not fighting the scheme more strongly. The three Buganda ministers and sixteen of the saza chiefs met together and condemned the Bataka, which they said had no claim to speak for the people of Buganda. When the Lukiko met early in 1949, the Bataka declared that this meeting of three ministers and sixteen chiefs had no constitutional importance, for the elected members of the Lukiko should have been present also. They demanded that the Kabaka should dismiss his ministers and the saza chiefs who had attended the meeting, and that all chiefs in future should be elected by their people instead of being appointed by the Kabaka. When the Kabaka refused to dismiss the men, there were serious riots against the Buganda government: shops were looted, houses were burnt, eight men were killed, and troops had to be called in to help the police to restore order. The protectorate government banned both the Bataka Federation and the Uganda Farmers Union, and the Buganda government sentenced some of the riot leaders to imprisonment.

The legislative council again enlarged

Meanwhile, the British government continued to make progress in its own way. In December 1949 the legislative council was again enlarged. A fourth African member had recently been added from the Northern Province. Under the new scheme, the 4 African members were to be increased to 8, the 3 European and 3 Asian unofficial members were increased to 4 each, and the official members were increased from 10 to 16. The official and unofficial sides of the council were thus equal at 16 each, but the official majority was secured by the governor's casting vote.

The Lukiko's alarm increased. Buganda was to have two representatives: one nominated by the Kabaka, the other chosen by the governor from a list submitted by the Lukiko. The Kabaka nominated his man, but the Lukiko refused to draw up a list, and for a time the second Buganda seat in the council remained empty, until the Kabaka agreed to nominate this second Buganda representative also. It was plain that the protectorate government was facing two serious difficulties. The first was the Buganda government's dislike of anything like a national legislative council, in which Baganda members might come to be regarded as speaking on behalf of the Kabaka and his people, and in which they might be outvoted by members from other regions. The other difficulty was that the Buganda government was still regarded as unsatisfactory by some of the Baganda people; the machinery of local government needed to be overhauled.

Sir Andrew Cohen Governor
The British government tackled local government reform by appointing Mr A. C. Wallis as a commissioner to study the problem and make proposals. He recommended sundry changes, notably the establishment of elected local councils; but he did not report on local government in Buganda, as this could not be dealt with apart from the general question of Buganda's place in the protectorate.

This difficult question could never be settled unless the Kabaka and the governor understood and trusted each other. Sir John Hall was retiring; to succeed him as governor came Sir Andrew Cohen, who was head of the African division of the Colonial Office. Cohen was known to be an energetic and liberal-minded man, who regarded it as his life's work to help the African colonies forward to self-government. If anyone could overcome the fears of the Lukiko, it was thought, surely he could.

The new governor arrived in September 1951, and quickly stimulated his government to a new urgency. A commission was set up to work out educational plans. Money from the cotton marketing board's profits was used to set up an African Development Fund. For two years, work had been going forward on the Owen Falls dam at Jinja, and electric power would soon be available from it. A workable deposit of iron ore was found at Sukulu near Tororo, and the governor hoped that with power from the Owen Falls and with money from the African development fund, it might be possible to start an iron and steel industry. This Sukulu scheme was later abandoned, for the technical difficulties were found to be greater than had been expected. But it was a pleasant change to find a colonial government prepared to take risks, even if it was not always successful.

Cohen's idea was that the Buganda government should take over much of the work then being done by the protectorate government, including primary schools, junior secondary schools, hospitals and animal health. The Kabaka should appoint 3 additional ministers, and the elected members of the Lukiko should be increased from 31 to 60. Much of this new work would be carried out by the saza councils, the central Buganda government keeping a general supervision.

The Kabaka's Case

For a time, the governor and the Kabaka worked well together. But the traditional members of the Lukiko did not like these new developments. Everyone knew that many people in Uganda were hostile to the powerful chiefs. In Buganda itself, a new political party had just been started, called the Uganda National Congress, and its leader, Mr Musanyi, was saying that all the peoples of Uganda should unite and work together for self-government. The new governor was talking of adding yet more African members to the legislative council.

At this critical moment, some words were spoken in London which changed the situation. The Secretary of State, Oliver Lyttelton, was invited to address the East Africa Club in London. In Britain his speech passed almost unnoticed, but in East Africa it caused great alarm. The background to the speech was the new Federation of Rhodesia and Nyasaland. In March 1953, the British government carried through parliament its bill for establishing this new federation, in spite of intense opposition by all the African leaders in the area. When Mr Lyttelton made his speech to the club, he referred to the federation, and said, 'Nor should we exclude from mind the evolution, as time goes on, of still larger measures of federation of the whole of the East African territory.' In East Africa, people took these words to mean that the government in London, having established one federation against the wishes of the African people, was now proposing to establish another, and to place effective political power in the hands of the Kenya Europeans. Was the East Africa High Commission, they asked, intended as the basis for an East African federation?

The Kabaka and the Lukiko at once took fright. The Kabaka made two demands. He wanted the Colonial Office in London to hand over Buganda affairs to the Foreign Office, to show that Buganda was an independent state, and he wanted the British government to draw up a timetable of the stages for granting Buganda its full independence.

The Lukiko repeated these two demands, and asked for an assurance that Lyttelton's speech did not mean that federation was being actively planned.

This assurance was quickly given. But there were now other causes for uneasiness. In August 1953 the governor announced his plans for a further enlargement of the legislative council. The new council, like the old, was to have equal numbers of official and unofficial members: 28 of each instead of 16. Fourteen of the unofficial members were to be Africans: 3 of them from Buganda, the others from other parts of the protectorate. Eleven of the unofficial members (6 Africans, 4 Europeans, 1 Asian) were to form a 'cross-bench': they could speak and vote as they wished on most matters, but if the governor considered a Bill so important that it must be passed at all costs, the cross-bench members must vote for it. The government hoped of course that such Bills would be rare.

The Kabaka is deported

For three months, the governor and the Kabaka talked matters over, but they could not agree. The Kabaka accepted the assurance that federation was not being planned, but he still pressed his two demands. It seemed to him and the Lukiko that the government was trying to build a Uganda after the wishes of the Uganda National Congress, and so to break down the privileged position of Buganda. Nothing that Sir Andrew Cohen could say would move him. On November 30, 1953 the governor decided that the end had come. He told the Kabaka that acting under the terms of the agreement, he had decided to recognize Sir Edward Mutesa II as Kabaka of Buganda no longer. An aeroplane was ready, the Kabaka was put on board, and a few hours later he was in London as an exile.

The news was as great a shock to the Baganda as to the Kabaka himself. The Uganda National Congress might perhaps have seen some political advantage to itself in the removal of the Kabaka; but even the Congress declared that the Kabaka had been insulted; it called on the people to keep calm, and it demanded an inquiry. There might have been serious trouble if the Baganda had not remained calm and kept their dignity.

The Lukiko sent a delegation to London, where its members saw both the Kabaka and the Secretary of State. They said that they welcomed two assurances they had received from Mr Lyttelton: that no East African federation was being planned, and that Uganda would be developed as an African state. On the other hand, independence for Buganda need not, they thought, mean splitting up the protectorate. An independent Buganda might join with the rest of Uganda in a

federal system. But these discussions were of no avail. Mr Lyttelton
said that Mutesa could not be allowed to go back to Buganda as
Kabaka, and this decision was final. The Lukiko's delegation returned
sadly home. But the Baganda were determined to have no Kabaka but
Mutesa; they remained calm, and they brought an action in the
courts to test whether the governor's action in deporting the Kabaka
was legal.

In January 1954 the newly enlarged legislative council met. In March,
Lyttelton announced that he would send out an expert adviser, Sir
Keith Hancock, to discuss these difficult constitutional problems with
the Buganda government. From June until the middle of September
he and the Buganda government's delegates sat at Namirembe discussing the constitution of Buganda and the relations of Buganda
with the protectorate government.

The court action

Meanwhile, everyone in Buganda was waiting to hear the result of the
action which the Lukiko had brought in the High Court to test the
legality of the governor's action in deporting the Kabaka. The legal
arguments in the case turned on the interpretation of two clauses of
the 1900 agreement. On November 4, 1954, the Chief Justice gave
judgement. He held that the agreement did empower the governor in
certain circumstances to take such a step. On the other hand, the
governor had been ill advised. He had claimed to be acting under one
clause of the agreement, but that clause did not justify his action,
though the other clause might have done. The judgement was not
completely satisfactory to either side, but it was much worse for the
governor than for the Lukiko. Mr Lyttelton and Sir Andrew Cohen
were agreed that in view of the judgement the Kabaka must be restored
to his people as soon as possible; but it was highly desirable that some
workable agreement should be reached before the Kabaka returned.

The Namirembe recommendations

The Namirembe conference gave hopes that such an agreement might
be reached. Towards the end of 1954, Sir Keith Hancock and the
Buganda delegates produced a long string of recommendations.

Articles 1 to 29 concerned the constitution of the kingdom of
Buganda. The kingdom was to continue as part of the Uganda protectorate. The Kabaka was to be the symbol of Buganda unity, and
was to keep his traditional styles and dignities. When a Kabaka died,
his successor was to be chosen in the traditional way from the royal
family and elected by the Lukiko, but the British government's
approval was to be necessary before he could take office. The Kabaka

was to govern through six ministers, who were to be elected by the Lukiko, approved by the governor, and formally appointed by the Kabaka.

The Lukiko was to be elected for five years, and the ministry too would normally remain in office for five years. But the ministry would be compelled to resign if defeated by a two-to-one vote in the Lukiko on a matter of importance; and in certain circumstances the ministry might be dismissed by the governor, acting with the approval of his executive council.

It is to be noted that under these articles, the Kabaka would no longer have the absolute power which his forefathers had. He would become a constitutional monarch, ruling with the advice of a Lukiko which was mainly elected, and with ministers who were nominally responsible to him but in fact responsible to the Lukiko.

Articles 30 to 47 dealt with the relationship between the governments of Buganda and of the protectorate. They confirmed the agreement of March 1953 under which the Buganda government was to take over from the protectorate government certain functions in education, health, community development, animal health, and other matters. Joint committees were to be set up to see that Buganda policy in these matters did not diverge too far from policy in other parts of the country. Article 48—which, as things turned out, was important— laid down that no major change in the constitution was to be made for six years. Article 49 declared that, except as amended by the Namirembe articles, the 1900 agreement was still in force.

The British government promptly accepted the Namirembe recommendations; the Lukiko appointed a committee to study them.

The Kabaka returns

All this time, the Kabaka was still in exile. The British government may have hoped to see the people of Buganda choose a new Kabaka, but it could have had no hope of this after November 1954, when the Lukiko resolved that it would have no Kabaka but Mutesa. All the British government could now hope for was that the Lukiko would accept the Namirembe recommendations without too much amendment; if this happened, the government could announce that a new situation had arisen, and abandon its 'final decision' never to let Mutesa return as Kabaka.

Meanwhile, the governor felt encouraged to press ahead with his plans for developing the protectorate constitution, which was a matter outside the scope of the Namirembe conference. The 3 Buganda representatives on the legislative council were increased to 5, and the government side was increased to correspond; thus the council now contained 60 members, the unofficial side consisting of 18 Africans, 6 Asians and 6 Europeans. A more important development was that a ministerial system was introduced. There were to be 7 ministers, 5 of them Africans; though only 2 (1 African and 1 other) were to have full executive responsibility for their departments. The governor undertook that there should be no further major constitutional change until 1962; and he again promised that no East African federation should be introduced until the Buganda government and other authorities throughout Uganda had been fully consulted.

In April 1955 the Lukiko's committee reported on the Namirembe recommendations. It accepted them, subject to some minor amendments, which the British government readily agreed to. The Lukiko accepted its committee's report; 77 Lukiko members out of 86 voted in its favour. After this, there was little difficulty in arriving at a settlement. In August, a new Buganda ministry was formed; early in September the five Baganda members were elected to the legislative council; and in the middle of October the Kabaka arrived back from his exile and signed the new agreement with the governor.

And so the Kabaka's case was officially ended, after causing both the British government and the Baganda people a great deal of inconvenience. Could wiser statesmanship have avoided it? Even if the Secretary of State had never made his speech, the crisis would have arisen sooner or later. The whole situation in Uganda had changed since the agreement was made in 1900. Then the British government wanted to establish its position in Buganda, Ankole and Toro. It was content to leave the east to Kakunguru, and it had hardly begun to look farther north. The Baganda in 1900 wanted to ensure that nothing should alter the relationship between the Kabaka and the British governor. Provided the position of Buganda was secure, it was nothing to them what arrangements the British made for governing other peoples.

But as soon as the British began to work towards a legislative council, in which the representatives of other peoples sat and voted on the affairs of the protectorate as a whole, the Baganda felt their position threatened. If they refused to send Baganda representatives to the legislative council, it meant that the voice of Buganda was not heard there; if they did send them, they feared the British would listen to them instead of coming to listen to the Kabaka. The situation was becoming impossible. If the British concentrated their attention on Buganda, the other peoples of the protectorate complained that they were being neglected, and that the British were using the agreement as an excuse to retain power. If the British tried to help the rest of the country towards self-government, the Kabaka and the Lukiko complained that they were acting contrary to the agreement. No governor and Secretary of State, no Kabaka and Lukiko, however well-meaning and sympathetic, could have avoided this contradiction.

The problem of elections

The Kabaka's case was closed, but the contradiction remained. In April 1956 Cohen announced that in next year's elections the representatives of the other three provinces would be chosen, as before, by the district councils; but he hoped that in Buganda, representatives might be chosen directly by the people. And he would like the newly elected council to consider plans for holding the 1961 elections throughout the country on a common roll, with safeguards to ensure that minority groups should not go unrepresented. His proposal of direct elections was accepted; but all African opinion was opposed to any minority safeguards, such as seats reserved for European or Asian members. To give more time for discussion, the government postponed the elections until 1958, by which time Cohen had been succeeded as governor by Sir Frederick Crawford.

The 1958 elections

The problem of drawing up a scheme for the elections was now considered by the legislative council, and in August 1957 the council unanimously approved a scheme drawn up for it by a committee. The vote would be given to all men and women of 21 years old who satisfied one of the following conditions: (a) he owned or occupied land; (b) he could read and write his mother-tongue; (c) he had worked for seven years in agriculture, commerce or industry, or in government service; (d) he had property worth £400 or an income of £100 a year. The government reckoned that this scheme would give the vote to nearly four men out of five, and to one woman out of five. Direct elections would be held on this basis all over the country except in Karamoja.

So far, the government had been successful: the legislative council had been unanimous, and the Lukiko approved of direct elections in Buganda. But then the agreement broke up. The government proposed that the 1961 elections should be held on this agreed basis and on a common roll, but that some seats should be reserved for Europeans and Asians. This government proposal was carried in the legislative council by 34 votes to 20, but not a single African member voted for it, and two African members resigned from the council in protest.

The government was facing the old question whether Uganda was to be developed as a multi-racial state, or as an African state. All African opinion held that it must be an African state; Africans were nervous of unofficial Europeans and Asians and feared that Uganda might become another Kenya.

Since this thorny question of reserved seats would not arise until 1961, the government thought the way was now clear for the elections of 1958 to be held on the basis agreed in August. As a preliminary step, a small increase was made in the African representation in the council. The governor and the Resident of Buganda left the council, and three additional African members were nominated. The legislative council then consisted of 15 Africans, 14 Europeans and 3 Asians on the government side, and 18 Africans, 6 Europeans and 6 Asians on the representative side. Surely, the governor (Sir Frederick Crawford) thought, the Africans would be pleased to see the European official element in the council thus weakened and the African membership strengthened.

The governor received an unpleasant surprise. When the elections were held in November, direct elections were held in only ten of the eighteen constituencies. Ankole preferred to choose its representatives in the old way, by indirect election. Buganda and Bugisu boycotted the elections altogether. The Buganda government protested that the recent change in the legislative council, though small, was important. It had been agreed that there were to be no more important constitutional changes until 1961; the protectorate government had now broken this agreement, so the Buganda government was no longer bound to arrange for the election of members to the legislative council.

It may seem strange that the government of Buganda should regard the replacement of two European official members of the council by three Africans as so serious a matter. But confidence between the Baganda people and the protectorate government had been badly shaken by the deportation of the Kabaka, and people were ready to suspect evil motives for any government action. The government had proposed to set up a system of reserved seats for European and Asian members in the legislative council, and the proposal had not been withdrawn. The governor was now removing himself and the Resident from the council; would his next step be to provide large numbers of reserved seats, so that European and Asian unofficial members would always be able to outvote the Africans? We can now see that these African fears were unjustified; but they were reasonable in the light of what their leaders then knew.

The Wild committee
The new legislative council met in November 1958, and the governor announced that he proposed to set up a committee to draw up detailed recommendations for the 1961 elections. The chairman was a senior

official, Mr J. V. Wild, and he had with him 2 Asians, 3 Europeans, and 10 Africans. Since both Asians and Africans were opposed to a system of reserved seats, it was certain that no such system would be recommended by this committee. The Wild committee sat from February to December, 1959. It sat in troubled times.

The Lukiko of Buganda, like the legislative council, was due for fresh elections. On the eve of the elections in December 1958, the old Lukiko resolved to ask the British government to end the agreements of 1900 and 1955 and to grant independence to Buganda. In January 1959 the newly elected Lukiko confirmed the resolution by 80 votes to 1, with 6 abstentions. The request was forwarded to London. The reply came that the Secretary of State would not advise the Queen to end the agreements. He suggested that the Buganda government should appoint a delegation to discuss these difficult matters with the governor's representatives.

The Lukiko considered this reply, and agreed to send a delegation. But they did not like the suggestion that the discussions should be held in Kampala. Like the African leaders in Kenya at the same time, they much preferred to have them held in London, with the Secretary of State himself in the chair. The Secretary of State, however, refused to hold a conference in London, as he refused a similar request made about the same time from Kenya. He took the view that the governor was the Queen's representative, and that constitutional discussions should first be carried on with him.

Political parties and another boycott
Meanwhile, there was disagreement among the African leaders. In December 1958 there was a split in the Uganda National Congress; a section broke away under the leadership of Dr Milton Obote. Dr Obote's followers at first called themselves the Uganda Nationalist Movement, but they changed their party's name more than once. Like Dr Obote himself, many of them came from outside Buganda, and they were becoming weary of the Buganda government's constant talk about the agreements. The movement tried to speed up constitutional development by calling for a boycott on trade with non-Africans, and in this it received much support, especially in Buganda. As in earlier boycotts, there was some beating, burning and looting. The boycott caused much hardship, not only to the Asian traders but to their African customers. It also hit the government revenue hard, for importers refused to bring into Uganda goods which they could not hope to sell, and they could not afford to buy Uganda produce, even if the producers were willing to sell it to them. As a result, the protectorate government lost the revenue which it would have drawn from

duties in imports and exports. Many people who suffered from the boycott became angry. In July there was fighting between two crowds, one supporting the boycott and the other hostile; seven people were killed. The Kabaka and the Lukiko condemned the violence which accompanied the boycott, but they refused to condemn the boycott itself. The government declared the whole of Buganda a disturbed area, and prosecuted and punished some of the leaders in the boycott for violent acts. Nevertheless, the boycott went on right through 1959 and into 1960.

New political parties were springing up after the 1958 elections. In Buganda, there was the Democratic Party, led by Mr Benedicto Kiwanuka; this party opposed the Lukiko and was anxious that Buganda should elect its representatives to the legislative council. In the west there was the Uganda People's Union. Dr Obote's wing of the Uganda National Congress was based mainly on the north and east; and in March 1960 it joined with the Uganda People's Union to form a new party called the Uganda People's Congress, under Dr Obote's leadership. A few months later, Mr Kiwanuka tried to bring his Democratic Party to join the UPC, but he could not get his members to agree, and the proposal was dropped. In the middle of 1960 there were two strong parties in Uganda: Dr Obote's UPC, drawing most of its strength from outside Buganda, and Mr Kiwanuka's DP based mainly in Buganda but opposed to the Buganda government. During 1960, Mr Kironde, who was Minister of Works in the protectorate government, formed what he called the United National Party, which was mainly composed of Baganda who supported the Kabaka and the Lukiko against Mr Kiwanuka and his Democratic Party.

The Wild committee's recommendations

It was against this background of disturbance and hardship that the Wild committee produced its recommendations in December 1959.

The committee recommended that the legislative council should be replaced by a National Assembly of at least 79 members. Three senior officials should have seats, and there should be 76 members directly elected on a common roll: one each from Jinja and Mbale, two from Kampala, and the others from rural constituencies. It would be useful if the assembly had a few additional members who were not directly elected, but the committee could not agree on how they were to be chosen: the majority of the committee proposed that the assembly itself should elect them, the minority proposed that the governor should nominate them, on the advice of the leader of the majority party in the assembly.

On the question of safeguards for minority groups, the committee was clear and decided: there should be none.

The committee then discussed the executive side of the government. It proposed that the governor's executive council should be replaced by a council of about twelve ministers: nine members of the majority party in the assembly, chosen by the party leader, and three senior officials. The committee could not agree what powers the council of ministers should have. Most members thought that it should have full cabinet powers; it should be responsible directly to the assembly, so that if defeated there, the whole council would have to resign. Some members of the committee thought the time had not yet come for such a big step; for the time being, the council of ministers should be advisory to the governor, as the executive council had been. Both sides of the committee were agreed that the governor should have certain reserved powers.

The committee ended with some general observations. It agreed that the traditional rulers in Uganda should retain their status. It preferred that Uganda should remain a unitary state, not federal; but it said that the important question of federation should be discussed in a special conference. Lastly, the committee said some wise words on the subject of political parties. Englishmen are so accustomed to their system of two political parties which disagree on matters of policy, that they find it difficult to imagine parliamentary government working successfully in any other way. It worried them in Uganda, as it has done in other parts of Africa, to see political parties developing which differed very little from one another in policy, and which worked for their aims by boycotting elections and trade and by walking out of councils when they did not get their own way. But all this, explained the Wild committee, was natural. Uganda had a government which the people could not control or overthrow. Whatever its opponents might say, the government acted as it thought best. No matter how wise the speech, no matter how many voted in support, the government was free to ignore it. If a political party could not control the government by its votes in council, it was natural that it should try to gain control by other means, such as a boycott. Make the government responsible to the voters, said the Wild committee, and then you will see responsible parties developing, parties which are divided by disagreements over policy.

How the report was received
Dr Obote's party, the Uganda People's Congress, immediately accepted the Wild recommendations, and declared that it would be satisfied with nothing less than the adoption of the whole programme as a plan

of action. The Buganda government took only a day or two to reject them, on the familiar ground that they would weaken the position of Buganda and were contrary to the agreements. Buganda, it said, would accept a suitable scheme of federation, in which Buganda would be able to live its own life; but it would not agree to become merely one province of an independent unitary state. Rather than that, it would insist on independence for Buganda.

The Wild recommendations had been accepted by the congress and rejected by Buganda; what would the protectorate government say? That government, after several weeks' silence, announced a cautious compromise, somewhat on the lines of the minority in the Wild committee. It agreed that the legislative council should have a majority of elected members, that elections should be held on the direct method and on a common roll, and that there should be no reserved seats. It announced a franchise scheme which would give the vote to four adults out of five. It agreed that a special commission should be appointed to study the position of Buganda.

On the question of the executive, the government did not adopt the bold proposals of the Wild majority. It agreed that the governor's executive council should have an unofficial majority, but it decided that the council should continue to be advisory to the governor and that there should be no chief minister. Responsibility for government policy would still lie with the governor, and the executive would in no way be responsible to the legislature.

These government proposals satisfied nobody; they adopted too much of the Wild report to please the Kabaka and the Lukiko, and too little to please the Congress.

The 1961 Elections
During 1960, a new Secretary of State, named Iain Macleod, took office in London. In June 1960 Dr Obote went to London leading a delegation of six African and five European elected members of the legislative council. He explained that they were disappointed at the governor's decision: they wanted votes for all, a Chief Minister, and a strong council of ministers as proposed in the Wild majority report. He hoped that Uganda might become independent in June 1961 after the new elections.

This visit to London by Dr Obote and his colleagues alarmed the Buganda government, and the Kabaka himself led a delegation to London to present his government's point of view. The Buganda delegation stayed more than a month, but while it was in London the Secretary of State received telegrams, not only from the Congress, but from the chief ministers of the other kingdoms, warning him that if he reached any agreement with the Buganda delegation, they would not hold themselves bound by it.

It was now certain that the elections would be held in 1961, and the parties began collecting their strength. The Congress and the Democratic Party, and somewhat later the United National Party also, urged all their members to register as electors. The Buganda government decided to boycott the elections, and those of the Baganda who obeyed it refused to register. The Lukiko again resolved that unless the British government promised Uganda a federal constitution, the kingdom of Buganda should declare itself independent on January 1, 1961.

The Secretary of State was not to be moved. He replied that all these constitutional problems would be considered by a new commission, under the chairmanship of Lord Munster. The commission's proposals would be fully considered at a conference, and if the Buganda government felt strongly on the subject of a federal constitution, it had better appear before the Munster commission and argue its case there. So the year 1960 ended in deadlock: the government determined to go ahead with the elections, the Congress and other parties busily preparing to seize power in the new legislative council, Buganda boycotting the elections and grimly demanding either federation or separate independence. It was in this tense atmosphere that the Munster commission began its sittings in November.

In spite of the Buganda government's decision to take no part, the elections were held in March 1961. About 35,000 Baganda voters defied their government and went to the polls. Most of them belonged to Mr Kiwanuka's Democratic Party, which won 20 out of the 21 Buganda seats. The result of the elections was:

	Seats	Votes
Democratic Party	43	407,000
Uganda People's Congress	35	488,000
Independent	2	56,000
Uganda National Congress	1	32,000
Vacant	1	—
	82	983,000

It will be noticed that the DP obtained most seats, though the UPC obtained more votes. This was because the UPC was not very strong in Buganda, and all but one of the Buganda seats went to the Democratic Party. When the legislative council met, its members elected 9 additional members, 6 of whom belonged to the DP and the other

3 to the UPC. The governor nominated 6 members: 3 African women, 2 European businessmen, and 1 European lecturer from Makerere. As the leader of the majority party, Mr Kiwanuka became the official leader of the assembly; Dr Obote became leader of the opposition.

If the government had followed the majority recommendations of the Wild committee, Mr Kiwanuka would have been asked to form a government; but the governor had not accepted these recommendations. The governor's executive council was transformed into a council of ministers; the governor presided, and there were three senior officials, nine African ministers, and one Asian. The government had fulfilled its promise that there should be an unofficial majority.

The Lukiko was furious, for it had gained nothing by boycotting the elections. Instead of the twenty-one Buganda seats in the assembly remaining empty, they were all filled, and filled with members who were opposed to the Lukiko's point of view. All the Lukiko could do was to resolve that Buganda would not be bound by any laws made by this new government, and that the Lukiko itself would take no part in any discussions with the new ministers. The Lukiko was moving into an impossible position, in open conflict not only with the protectorate government but with all the rest of the protectorate.

The Munster report
From this position, the Lukiko was rescued by the report of the Munster commission in June, which went a good way in support of the proposals of the Buganda government. The commission said very firmly that Buganda must not be allowed to secede and become a separate independent state. This, the report said, 'plainly leads towards disaster both for Uganda and Buganda'; there was strong opposition to the idea elsewhere in the protectorate, and even in Buganda itself, and if Buganda tried to enforce its independence, there might be 'grave danger of civil war as in the Congo'. The Congo, Uganda's neighbour, had become independent in 1960, and one province, Katanga, had declared itself a separate independent state, whereupon a bloody and disastrous civil war had ensued. In making this comparison with the Congo, the commission was uttering the gravest warning.

The commission recommended that Uganda should be developed as a democratic state with a strong central government, but it supported the Buganda government in recommending that Buganda and the central government should have a federal relationship with each other. Some powers (especially foreign affairs, nationality, defence, police, and central taxation) should be reserved to the central government, others reserved to the Buganda government. A third set of powers might be exercised by either, provided that if there were any disagreement, the legislation of the central government should prevail. The central government would have no power of altering Buganda's constitution, and no power of veto over any Buganda legislation which was within Buganda's constitutional rights. The position of Ankole, Bunyoro and Toro should be semi-federal: they should have some powers reserved to them by the constitution, but not as many as those of Buganda.

Having supported Buganda's desire for federalism, the commission proposed that Buganda should elect representatives to the national assembly, but that it should be left to the Buganda government to choose whether to elect them directly or indirectly. The Lukiko should be directly elected; there should be no saza chiefs sitting ex-officio. The Kabaka should withdraw from politics and rule entirely by the advice of his ministers. The semi-federal states should not be allowed to choose, like Buganda, whether to elect their representatives in the assembly directly or indirectly; only direct election should be allowed.

Uganda should be governed by a single-chamber assembly, elected by universal adult suffrage on a common roll for a period of five years. All the members should be elected; there should be no official or nominated members. The commission rejected the idea of a council of State as suggested by Ankole.

INDEPENDENCE NEGOTIATIONS

The commission made these proposals in June 1961, and Iain Macleod, the Secretary of State, had promised that they should be fully discussed at a constitutional conference in London. The conference met on September 18, 1961 and sat till October 9. There were many anxious moments, many threats and protests, and some walk-outs. But in the end, the conference unanimously agreed on the new constitution. There was to be a national assembly of 82 elected members with a Speaker. There were to be no nominated or official members, but when the 82 members first met, they were to elect 9 additional members. Elections should be on a common roll with universal adult suffrage. The governor should remain responsible for foreign affairs and defence, but all other matters should be controlled by a prime minister and a cabinet, responsible to the assembly.

As for Buganda, the conference agreed with the Munster proposal that it should stand in a federal relationship with the central government. It should be left to the Buganda government to decide whether its 21 representatives in the assembly should be directly or indirectly elected. If Buganda preferred indirect election, the Lukiko itself should be the electoral body. The Lukiko should consist of 68 members directly elected by the people, 6 nominated by the Kabaka, 20 saza chiefs and 6 ministers, a total of 100 members. The conference had thus made a concession to Buganda, for the Munster commission had proposed that all members of the Lukiko should be directly elected. One difficult matter was left undecided until after independence had been granted: the Buganda government claimed that the Kabaka must always be Head of State in an independent Uganda, but this was not acceptable to the others.

The Kabaka Yekka

Everything, it seemed, was now agreed in good time for the beginning of internal self-government on March 1, 1962, the date suggested by the Munster commission and accepted by the conference. In February, the new Lukiko was elected. Its election was an overwhelming victory for a new party called the Kabaka Yekka, 'the Kabaka alone'. This party was formed in November, shortly after the London conference, by the constitutional committee of the Lukiko, in alliance with the UPC, the Uganda National Congress, and others. The Kabaka Yekka won 65 out of the 68 elected seats in the Lukiko; the other 3 seats (all of them in the 'lost counties') were won by the Democratic Party. The Lukiko voted in favour of indirect elections for the National Assembly.

On the promised date, March 1, 1962, Uganda received full internal self-government on the lines agreed at the London conference. Mr Kiwanuka became prime minister, and he formed a cabinet of 1 European, 1 Asian, and 11 African ministers. The new elections for the National Assembly were fixed for April 25, and the Buganda government agreed to encourage all its people to vote.

One immediate problem was that of the 'lost counties'. Bunyoro was demanding that Buganda should restore them, and in some of them there was a good deal of unrest and violence. The British government appointed a special commission under Lord Molson to look at the problem and make recommendations.

Meanwhile, Mr Kiwanuka, the new prime minister, was not satisfied with the semi-federal status of Ankole and the other kingdoms, and he proposed that they should be given the same status as Buganda, so that Uganda would become a fully federal state. In this he was supported by Dr Obote and the opposition, so that he was able to transmit the request to London as one supported by all parties concerned. There are practical difficulties in having a fully federal system of government in such a small country as Uganda, but the new Secretary of State, Mr Maudling, felt that if all parties in Uganda wished to have it so, it was not for him to stand in the way. He gave his agreement in principle, though there was not time to work out all the details before the elections to the assembly.

The elections were held on April 25, the Buganda representatives being chosen by the Lukiko. Outside Buganda, 60 per cent of the electors voted. After the 82 elected members of the assembly had met and elected the 9 additional members, the state of the parties was:

Uganda People's Congress	43
Kabaka Yekka	24
Democratic Party	24
	—
	91

The Uganda People's Congress, led by Dr Obote, was thus by far the strongest party in the assembly, but it numbered less than half the members, and needed support from another party. It allied itself with the Kabaka Yekka, so that Mr Kiwanuka's Democratic Party government was heavily outvoted. Mr Kiwanuka resigned, and Dr Obote became prime minister at the head of a cabinet composed of UPC and Kabaka Yekka members, including one European and one Asian.

The Molson commission

A few days later, the Molson commission reported on the problem of the 'lost counties'. These were the six counties which had been taken from Bunyoro in 1894 and transferred to Buganda. The transfer had been confirmed in 1900; and although Bunyoro had several times asked to have the counties restored, the British government had always refused to reconsider the matter. The Molson commission thought that there would always be trouble where a Baganda minority ruled as chiefs or landlords over a Banyoro majority. The population figures were:

	Baganda	Banyoro
Buyaga	2,300	33,000
Bugangazzi	4,200	16,700
Buwekula	21,700	4,800
All the others	75,600	3,500

The commission recommended that the two counties of Buyaga and Bugangazzi, in which the great majority of the people were Banyoro, should be returned to Bunyoro; but the other counties should remain within Buganda. The commission recognized that it would not be pleasant to Buganda to hand back two counties which it had governed for nearly seventy years, but it hoped that for the sake of peace the Buganda government would show itself generous and agree.

In this hope, the commission was disappointed. On the very next day, the Kabaka announced that Buganda would never agree to the transfer. No decision was taken, and the Molson commission's proposals were laid before the final conference which sat in London in June 1962 to settle the final details of the independence constitution.

The conference found no difficulty in working out the details of the federal constitution, in which Ankole, Bunyoro and Toro received the same federal status as Buganda, and Busoga nearly the same. But the problem of the 'lost counties' was insoluble. In the end, the Secretary of State himself suggested a compromise. Buyaga and Bugangazzi should continue to be regarded as part of Buganda, but they should be administered by the central government for two years at least. At some convenient time, after the two years were ended and angry feelings had calmed down, the people in those two counties should be asked to vote whether they would prefer to be governed by Buganda, or Bunyoro, or the central government. Both the disputants, Buganda and Bunyoro, immediately rejected this proposal. But Dr Obote said that no ideal solution was possible; this was the best that could be achieved, and he accepted it. And so it was decided.

Independence

On October 9, 1962, Uganda became a fully independent federal state, with Dr Obote as federal prime minister. The retiring governor, Sir Frederick Crawford, was appointed governor-general; a year later he was replaced by the Kabaka, who became Head of State. On October 25, 1962 the new state was admitted as a member of the United Nations.

Chapter 12

TOWARDS INDEPENDENCE IN TANGANYIKA

Tanganyika was the poorest of the countries of British East Africa. Much of it was too dry for successful agriculture and uninhabitable for cattle because of the tsetse fly. It produced some sisal and a little gold, but the government was desperately poor. It was a thinly peopled country of great distances. No reliable census figures existed, but it was believed in London that the population was about five million; this figure was later found to be much too low. In such a country, there could be no hope of developing health and education and other social services until communications could be improved and more money found.

The beginnings of economic development

In the years immediately following the 1939 war, some economic progress was made. In 1946 Dr Williamson, a Canadian geologist, discovered a diamond deposit at Mwadui near Shinyanga. The diamond mine was a welcome addition to the country's wealth, though it never became one of the world's major suppliers. Ten years after opening, the mine was producing some £3 million worth of diamonds a year, and in 1958 the mine was bought by the Tanganyika government and the De Beers Corporation of South Africa in equal shares.

Tanganyika's ten-year development plan was launched with the help of over £5 million of British government money voted under the Colonial Development and Welfare Acts. The plan concentrated on laying the foundations for economic development: over £4 million were spent on roads, £2 million on railways and harbours, and £3 million on developing the country's natural resources. Smaller sums were spent on social services.

In 1947 it seemed as if Tanganyika would be greatly helped by another development scheme. There was a world-wide shortage of fats and oils, and the British government produced a scheme for clearing the bush over five million acres in the Kongwa district of southern Tanganyika and growing groundnuts there with the aid of modern machinery. The groundnuts were badly needed in Europe; they would be a welcome addition to Tanganyika's scanty list of exports; and the scheme included a new seaport at Mtwara and a railway, which would help to open up southern Tanganyika for other development. Both were built, but the scheme had been hastily planned, and was not a success. The hard rocky soil and the tough tree-roots wore out the machines; the soil and the climate did not suit groundnuts; and the crop failed. In 1950 the project was abandoned. Millions of pounds had been spent in vain, but it was British money, not Tanganyika's; and though Tanganyika was disappointed of its hopes for a new export trade in groundnuts, at least it had its new harbour and railway. The British government also paid to have a route surveyed for a new railway line which would link the Tanganyika railway system with that of Northern Rhodesia, the modern Zambia. But nothing came of this and the projected railway line was not built.

Tanganyika a Trust Territory

In October 1946, the newly formed United Nations agreed with Britain that the former mandated territory of Tanganyika should become a trust territory under the United Nations. This change had results which perhaps the British government at the time did not foresee. The Mandates Commission of the League of Nations had been a group of individuals, many of them experienced administrators, who were nominated by their governments but did not represent them. Lord Lugard for example was a member of the commission for many years, but he did not mind whether the British government of the day agreed with him or not. The Mandates Commission made careful inquiries into the condition of the mandated territories, and the governments of the territories had to send representatives to appear before the commission and be questioned on their work. But the members of the commission sympathized with the difficulties of the colonial official, and did not press him too hard. Moreover, the League was dominated by Western Europe. The United States was not a member, and the Soviet Union did not join until 1934; the membership contained only three African[1] and five Asian states.

The Trusteeship Council of the United Nations was different. Its members were spokesmen of their governments; whatever their personal views, they had to say what their governments told them to say. Nearly all governments, especially those of the communist countries, were anti-colonialist; they regarded it as the first duty of a trustee government to prepare its trust territories for independence, and they were not very sympathetic when the trustee government explained that progress must be slow. Not content with receiving detailed annual reports and examining the representatives of the trustee governments at the United Nations headquarters, the Trusteeship Council developed a practice of sending teams of inspectors to visit the trust territories and see things for themselves. Any citizen of a trust territory could petition the United Nations at any time, and his petition and the government's reply were always carefully investigated.

Thus, the replacement of the League of Nations Mandates Commission by the United Nations Trusteeship Council brought about an important shift of emphasis: political and constitutional development became much more important, with independence as the goal. The

---

[1] Ethiopia, Liberia, South Africa; Egypt joined in 1937 but Ethiopia dropped out after the Italian conquest.

Trusteeship Council was much less willing than the Mandates Commission had been to accept the view of the British government that independence would come in good time, but that there was a great deal of work to be done first. It sometimes tended to ask why the British could not set a fixed date for independence and keep to it.

CONSTITUTIONAL DEVELOPMENTS

In 1949 Tanganyika received a new governor, Sir Edward Twining, who sympathized with the attitude of the Trusteeship Council. Twining had served in Uganda as a commissioner of labour, and his experience there had convinced him that Africa was capable of producing responsible statesmen. When he came to Tanganyika, he found very little political activity there: at least, not of the kind that most British governors looked for. The official British view was that nationalism ought to develop from local councils and native authorities; and in Tanganyika there seemed no likelihood of this happening for many years. The village people and the district councils thought only of their local affairs. Ex-servicemen and educated men took little interest in local government; they preferred to form political groups in the towns. The Tanganyika African Association was still in existence, but it was small and had no very wide influence. Twining was dissatisfied with this state of things, and was determined that something must be done to stir up an interest in politics. He had the support of the government in London, which took warning from the Gold Coast riots of 1948 and was anxious that educated men should somehow be drawn more into political life.

There had already been a little constitutional advance before Twining arrived. Two Africans were nominated as members of the legislative council in 1945, and two more were added shortly afterwards. The legislative council at the time of Twining's arrival contained 14 unofficial members: 7 Europeans, 4 Africans, and 3 Asians. Twining formed these 14 men into 3 committees, and sent them to travel round the country to discuss with the people and make proposals for constitutional advance.

The Twining Committee
Having completed their travels and discussions, the 14 men sat in committee together, and reported in August 1951. They said that the aim must be to achieve responsible self-government, with an unofficial majority in the legislative council. But this aim could not be achieved quickly. Most people, they said, were not yet thinking of Tanganyika as a country or a nation; they were thinking of their own local con-

cerns, and would need much more political education before anything like self-government could become possible. The first step should be to appoint an African to the governor's executive council. Then the country should be divided into regions, each region to have an inter-racial regional council; many of the powers and duties now in the hands of the central government should be handed over to the regional governments. Lastly, the 14 unofficial members of the legislative council should be increased to 21, 7 from each of the 3 races. The council should keep an official majority. One great difficulty was that there were so few Africans at that time with sufficient education to serve on the legislative council. To meet this difficulty, the committee proposed that African civil servants should be allowed to resign their posts temporarily (keeping their pension rights) and enter the legis-lative council. The committee did not think it possible yet to hold elections, for so few Africans would understand what was happening. For the time being, the members of the legislative council would have to be nominated, and the question of elections could be discussed in the new council.

The Tanganyika government accepted the report, and the Africans and Asians welcomed it. The president of the Tanganyika European council said that its recommendations came 'at least 25 years too early'. As a first step, Chief Kidaha Makwaia was appointed to the governor's executive council.

The governor now asked the Colonial Office in London to approve the proposals in principle, and to send an expert adviser to work out the details. The Secretary of State gave his approval and appointed Pro-fessor W. J. Mackenzie.

The Mackenzie constitution

Professor Mackenzie visited Tanganyika and reported in May 1953 that the ultimate aim must be common-roll elections, with safeguards for minorities; but he agreed with the Twining committee that common-roll elections were not yet possible for the whole of Tanganyika, though he suggested that they might be tried in Dar-es-Salaam and Tanga. Elsewhere, African representatives should for the present either be nominated by the governor, or (where possible) indirectly elected. There should be 3 members for each constituency, 1 from each race; and each elector should have 3 votes. All men and women over the age of 21 should vote, and there should be no restriction by means of an educational or a property qualification except in the two common-roll constituencies, Dar-es-Salaam and Tanga.

Mackenzie felt something must be done to improve local govern-ment, but he did not agree with the Twining committee's proposal to set up regional administrations. Mackenzie proposed that the 54 administrative districts of Tanganyika should be grouped into counties; each county should have its county council, with powers to levy local taxes. They should exist side by side with the Native Authorities, without trying to take over their traditional functions. Mackenzie proposed to group 21 of the administrative districts into 8 counties; he left it to the government to set up other counties later on. If any unit were needed larger than a county, he thought that the existing provinces would do.

The Local Government Ordinance of 1953

The governments in Dar-es-Salaam and London accepted these recommendations. They profited by the lesson they had received in the Gold Coast (Ghana). Dr Nkrumah came to power there in 1951, and one of the first things he did was to abandon the British idea of trying to develop the Native Authorities (the chiefs and their councils) into an effective system of local government. He set up a system of elected local government bodies, though he allowed the Native Authorities to elect some of the members. Tanganyika followed Nkrumah's example. There were in Tanganyika 453 Native Authorities and 29 town councils. The Local Government Ordinance of 1953 provided for three kinds of local government authorities: local, town, and county councils. The local councils were based on the Native Authorities, with some elected members added; the other councils were elected. The government foresaw that it would take some time before the new councils were working smoothly. The local councils were on the whole successful. The county councils were less so; the county area was too big. So an amending ordinance set up an intermediate local government area, the district, and made the district council the principal local government body. The district council took over some of the duties of the central government, and was financed partly from Treasury grants and partly from local taxation.

The enlarged legislative council

The new legislative council met in March 1955. The old council of 15 officials and 14 unofficial members was replaced by a council of 31 officials and 30 unofficial members, with 10 unofficial members from each of the 3 races instead of 7, as the Twining committee had suggested. A ministerial system was begun. Eight of the official members became ministers in charge of departments, and 6 unofficial members (4 Africans, 1 Asian, and 1 European) were appointed assistant ministers, so that they could study the work of departmental administration and be prepared for taking full responsibility later. The governor

ceased to preside at meetings of the legislative council, and was replaced by a Speaker.

About the same time, changes were made in the executive council,
which since 1951 had consisted of 8 official and 5 unofficial members:
3 Europeans, 1 African, and 1 Asian. The number of official members
was unchanged, but the unofficial members were increased from 5 to
7: 3 Africans, 2 Europeans, and 2 Asians. But the council was still a
purely advisory body, whose advice the governor could not be compelled to follow.

Elections and political parties

The most important business facing the new legislative council was to
work out a proper electoral system. It was important, not only because
of what the Twining committee and Professor Mackenzie had said,
but for other reasons.

In 1953 Julius Nyerere, who had arrived back from his studies in
Europe only the year before, was elected president of the Tanganyika
African Association, of which he had been a member before going to
Europe. The TAA at that time was a small body, not very effective,
and too much content with opposing the government without developing much of a policy of its own. Dr Nyerere set himself to transform it
into an effective nationalist movement. In his view, the TAA should
work for African advance of all kinds, and should aim at building up a
Tanganyikan nation. He persuaded the TAA to change its name to the
Tanganyika African National Union, thus putting nationalism boldly
forward as the union's chief aim. But Dr Nyerere did not believe in
racialism. Some of the members of TANU wished to drive Europeans
and Asians out of political life; Nyerere thought this not only unjust
but wasteful, for Tanganyika needed their energy and skill. Some
members did all they could to hamper government work, such as
projects of pest control and community development, simply because
they were being encouraged or carried out by the government. Dr
Nyerere saw no sense in this; it prevented good and necessary work
being done and made government officers dislike and fear TANU.
Dr Nyerere believed that Tanganyika would make faster progress if
TANU cooperated with anyone, of any race, who was willing to serve
the country and its people. As Dr Aggrey used to say, you catch more
flies with molasses than with vinegar.

But Dr Nyerere was as determined as anyone that Tanganyika must
make faster progress towards self-government; and in 1954 he had a
good opportunity of making powerful friends for TANU. In that
year, one of the visiting teams from the Trusteeship Council of the
United Nations came to inspect the work being done by the Tanganyika

government. The visitors met Dr Nyerere and talked things over with him; they went back to New York greatly impressed, and the Trusteeship Council suggested that the time had come for Britain to fix a timetable for Tanganyika's progress towards independence. From then on, Dr Nyerere had many friends in New York, and he visited the United Nations more than once to put his party's views before it.

It is a British characteristic to dislike fixed timetables and target dates in politics, whether for independence or anything else. They know how often unexpected delays occur. Consequently, the British government did not welcome the Trusteeship Council's suggestion of a fixed timetable. It had already made up its mind to push Tanganyika forward towards independence as fast as possible. On the other hand, the British were accustomed to a two-party system in their own parliament, and they found it hard to imagine parliamentary government working successfully with only one party. The British thought highly of Dr Nyerere, but they were not yet sure whether he would succeed in keeping control of his party, TANU.

So the British were inclined to welcome the emergence of a new party, the United Tanganyika Party. This was a party containing members of all three races; 26 out of the 30 unofficial members of the legislative council joined it. The programme of the UTP was not very different from that of TANU. Like TANU, the new party opposed all racial discrimination, and advocated, for example, that all schools should be open to children of all races. The real difference between the parties was that UTP usually supported the government, for it believed that the government was sincerely trying to push ahead with political advances. The UTP however was at a disadvantage. It had no leader who could be compared with Dr Nyerere. It was Dr Nyerere and TANU who had the support of the United Nations. It was natural that TANU, always urging the government to go faster, should win more support among the people than a party which thought that on the whole the government was going fast enough.

The 1958 elections

In May 1957 the legislative council passed a bill to provide for the new elections, to be held in two stages, in September 1958 and February 1959; at each stage, 15 members were to be elected, representing 5 constituencies. Each constituency would have 3 members, one from each race, and each elector would have 3 votes; he would vote separately for European, Asian and African candidates. The United Tanganyika Party was inter-racial, and so (in spite of its name) was TANU. Dr Nyerere insisted that Asians and Europeans should be free to join his party, and that African party members should be ready to vote for them. He once said, 'Let not the world point a finger at us and say that we gained our freedom on a moral argument—the argument of the brotherhood of man—and then threw that argument overboard and began ourselves to discriminate against our brothers on the ground of colour.'

Before the elections the British government in London enlarged the legislative council by adding 6 nominated members, 3 of whom were to sit on the government side and 3 on the representative side. The council would thus consist of a Speaker and 67 members, 34 government and 33 representative. The government side would consist of 15 ministers and assistant ministers (9 official and 6 unofficial) and 19 nominated members; the representative side would consist of 30 members directly elected and 3 nominated members.

When the first stage of the elections was held, TANU won all the elected seats. The UTP, having failed so dismally in this stage, did not contest the second stage. Every one of the 30 elected seats in the council was thus filled by a member (whether African, Asian, or European) of TANU who looked to Dr Nyerere as his leader.

All this political advance had been begun by Sir Edward Twining, who had sent his teams of unofficial members round the country to see how the people could be awakened to an interest in politics. Twining was replaced as governor in July 1958 by Sir Richard Turnbull, who came from Kenya and had seen how keen the Africans there were to make rapid progress. Turnbull's experience in Kenya had convinced him that when the Africans had found a capable leader, the government's best plan was to work with him; there would only be trouble if they hindered him and drove him into opposition. The situation was easier in Tanganyika than in Kenya; it was much easier for a governor to work with Nyerere, who had the confidence of all three races, than with Kenyatta, whom many Europeans in Kenya still regarded with suspicion. The government in London was of the same mind, and supported Turnbull in his efforts to speed up constitutional progress.

Soon after the elections, in May 1959, the governor announced that the 9 ministers would be increased to 12, 5 of whom (3 Africans, 1 European and 1 Asian) would be unofficial. The executive council was not formally abolished, though for most practical purposes it was replaced by this council of 12 ministers. Like the executive council, the new council of ministers was still advisory to the governor, not responsible to the legislature. All 5 African ministers were of course TANU members.

The Ramage committee

The governor then appointed a fresh committee, under the chairmanship of Sir Richard Ramage, to consider what should be the form of the legislature and the executive at the next stage of the country's progress towards independence. The committee consisted of 8 elected and 5 nominated members of the legislative council; it met in May and reported in December. By this time, it was generally agreed that the legislative council ought to have a large majority of elected African members; the scheme of having 20,000 Europeans, 100,000 Asians, and 9,000,000 Africans equally represented in the council was out of date and must be abandoned. This being agreed, the questions remaining for the Ramage committee to discuss were the usual questions, such as who should have the vote; what safeguards there should be for minorities; should elections be held on a common roll or on separate rolls; and what should be the relationship of the council of ministers to the legislature?

The Ramage committee proposed fresh elections for September 1960. The legislative council should contain 71 elected members. Ten seats should be reserved for Europeans and 11 for Asians, the other 50 being open to candidates of any race. It was to be presumed that all these 50 open seats would be filled by African members. In addition to the 71 elected members, the council should have a few nominated members. Voting should be on a common roll. This would mean that an open seat might be contested by candidates of any race, and electors from all three races would vote, each elector having one vote only. In the case of reserved seats, the procedure was more complicated. If for example a constituency was represented by two members, one of its seats being reserved for an Asian, every elector in the constituency would have two votes. He was not compelled to use them both; if he was not interested in the Asian seat he need not vote for any of the Asian candidates. But he could not use both his votes for the African candidate of his choice. This scheme gave African voters a chance of influencing the election of Asian and European candidates for the reserved seats; they might greatly prefer one Asian or European candidate to another. All men and women could vote if they were 21 years old and were literate, or had an income of £75 a year, or had held any one of a list of prescribed positions. This scheme would raise the electorate from 60,000 to over 1,500,000 electors.

The Ramage committee proposed that the council of ministers should have a majority of elected unofficial members. The question whether the council should be made responsible to the legislature was left undecided. But clearly a council of ministers most of whom were TANU members would be very much affected by the views of an overwhelmingly TANU legislature. The council might not be legally responsible, but it would tend in practice to behave as if it were.

Dr Nyerere was chairman of the Elected Members Organization, and it rested with him to say whether the elected members should accept the Ramage proposals as a step forward, or oppose them as inadequate. Nyerere said that he would have preferred universal adult suffrage without these qualifications of literacy or income or status; but he urged his party to accept the Ramage proposals meanwhile and to work for further advance. For its part, the government was ready to put the Ramage proposals into practice, and the governor, Sir Richard Turnbull, was anxious to see the new legislative council elected as soon as possible.

In December the Trusteeship Council discussed Tanganyika affairs, and recommended Britain to set an early target date for full independence. The resolution was adopted by a strong majority. The British delegate was Sir Andrew Cohen, lately governor of Uganda. He declared that Britain could not support the resolution because she did not believe in setting target dates, but she certainly did not wish to delay Tanganyika's independence and could not vote against the resolution; so he abstained from voting.

The 1960 elections

The new elections were held in August 1960. Dr Nyerere's election programme was to replace the qualified vote by universal adult suffrage, to gain full independence in 1961, and to push ahead with training Africans to replace men of other races. When the elections were held, TANU candidates won 70 of the 71 elected seats; the one remaining seat was won by an independent candidate, a son of the most powerful local chief. Dr Nyerere became chief minister, the governor's principal adviser and leader of government business in the legislative assembly. He formed a cabinet, or rather a council of ministers, consisting of 7 Africans, 1 Asian and 4 Europeans. Two of the Europeans were officials, and all the other 10 ministers were members of TANU.

A few weeks later the governor announced that this council of 10 unofficial and 2 official ministers would completely replace his executive council, which was abolished. The post of chief secretary was replaced by one of deputy governor. The governor and his deputy sat in the council of ministers, and the governor retained responsibility for police, defence and external affairs.

These changes did not quite give Tanganyika full internal self-government, but that state was now very near. Dr Nyerere had nearly all the power of a prime minister. In theory perhaps, the governor might reject the advice of his council of ministers; but in fact, Turnbull and Nyerere understood each other so well and worked so closely together that this possibility could be ignored. Again, the council of ministers was still advisory to the governor, not responsible to the legislature; but with 10 of its 12 members drawn from TANU and occupying elected seats in the legislature, it was not likely that the legislature and the council of ministers would disagree.

Internal self-government

If the council of ministers was in fact responsible to the legislature, there was not much point in preserving constitutional forms which pretended that it was not responsible. In March 1961 a conference was held at Dar-es-Salaam in which the Secretary of State, Iain Macleod, took part. Agreement was quickly reached on all points, many of them mere changes of name to make the name fit the facts. The legislative council was renamed the national assembly, the council of ministers renamed the cabinet, the chief minister renamed the prime minister. The governor, the deputy governor, and the two officials left the council of ministers, which now sat under the prime minister's chairmanship and became a true cabinet, responsible to the national assembly. It was agreed that the governor should remain responsible for external affairs and defence until African ministers could be trained to take over these responsibilities as well. This new constitution, which conferred full internal self-government, came into effect on May 1, 1961. On that day, Dr Nyerere was sworn in as prime minister, and he formed a cabinet of 11 ministers, including 2 Europeans and 1 Asian, all of them members of TANU.

The East African Common Services Organization

Full independence was now very near, and one problem had to be settled before it arrived. What was to happen to the East Africa High Commission, which had been set up in 1948 to provide all British East Africa with common services? The commission consisted of the three governors, with a central executive staff and a legislature. The prime minister of an independent Tanganyika, responsible to the people who had elected him, could not work with British governors who were responsible to the Secretary of State in London. On the other hand, the High Commission was doing useful work; it would be a backward step to abolish the commission and leave each government to do the work separately.

The problem was discussed at a conference held in London in June 1961; Iain Macleod and his advisers met Ngala, Mboya and Gichuru from Kenya, Nyerere from Tanganyika, and Kiwanuka from Uganda. There was not much difficulty, and agreement was reached in a week. The commission of three governors was replaced by a Common Services Organization of three ministers, that is to say, the principal elected minister from each of the three territories. To help them in their work, the three ministers had four ministerial groups, each consisting of one minister from each territory. One group dealt with communications; a second dealt with finance; a third with commercial and industrial coordination; the fourth with social services and research. There was to be a central legislative assembly, consisting of the 12 ministers, with 9 members elected by each of the 3 legislatures, with a secretary-general and a legal secretary, 41 members in all.

The scope of the East Africa Common Services Organization was certainly wide. It included railways, harbours, internal water transport, merchant shipping, civil aviation, posts, telegraphs, telephones and radio-communications, customs and excise, allocations from the revenue pool, public service commissions, universities and other higher education, and inter-territorial research in such matters as control of pests and diseases. It is an impressive list, not unlike the list of functions which are commonly reserved to the central government in a federal state. No doubt some people hoped that the statesmen of East Africa, who fiercely rejected any idea of a federation imposed by Britain, might in time grow accustomed to working together in this way and might voluntarily enter into a federation of their own. But there could be no talk of this until Kenya and Uganda too were independent.

Tanganyika independent
Dr Nyerere took the opportunity of his visit to London to discuss Tanganyika's economic problems, and he discussed them again in Washington. Tanganyika was still a poor country; he summed up the domestic policy of his new government as a 'war on poverty, ignorance and disease'. 'These three enemies,' he said, 'beset us hard.' The World Bank sent a team of economists to help him draw up a three-year plan of development. The first things to be done were to improve agriculture and livestock farming, water supplies, communications, and secondary and technical education. On the eve of independence, only 480 African citizens of Tanganyika had completed twelve years of general education. The World Bank economists suggested that a geological survey should be pushed forward to try to discover new mineral deposits. Tanganyika already produced diamonds, with some gold, lead, and mica; it was known to have large deposits of coal and iron hitherto unworked; it was thought likely that phosphates and columbite might be discovered. The cost of this first three-year development plan was about £24 million, and the British government agreed to contribute about half this sum.

At midnight on December 8, 1961, Tanganyika became a fully

independent state, and a few days later the British trusteeship agreement was terminated and Tanganyika was admitted as a member state of the United Nations.

After independence, Dr Nyerere was able to put out a fuller statement of his policy. First, as to home affairs. His policy here was to push ahead with the development plan; to convert what he called 'old-fashioned Native Authority councils' into 'modern and effective local authorities'; to expand education, especially secondary and higher education; and to Africanize the civil service. In external affairs, his policy was to observe the terms of the United Nations Charter, and to keep in friendly relations with all other states that did the same; to cooperate with other African states in brotherly fashion and to work towards African unity; and to keep up Tanganyika's links with the Commonwealth. He was asked whether he would work for an East African federation; he replied that there could be no talk of such a federation until Kenya and Uganda too were independent and had governments responsible to the people.

Tanganyika's smooth progress
Tanganyika had made amazingly quick progress towards independence. No newly appointed unofficial member who entered the legislative council in March 1955 could have expected that in less than seven years the country would be fully independent, with a cabinet responsible to an elected legislature. It all happened smoothly and peacefully. How was it that the poorest country in East Africa was the first to achieve independence?

It was partly because Tanganyika (though hard beset, as Dr Nyerere said, by poverty, ignorance and disease) was spared some of the problems that afflicted Kenya and Uganda. There were European coffee and sisal planters in Tanganyika, but there was nothing like the solid block of Europeans in Kenya's White Highlands. Governor Twining had no difficulty in finding European unofficial members of the legislative council who welcomed the idea of having equal numbers of Asian and African members sitting alongside them. Again, Tanganyika had very little problem of tribal jealousies, compared with Uganda and Kenya; and she had no problem at all of powerful kingdoms like Buganda, with written agreements which blocked the normal path of constitutional development. Dr Nyerere's only problem was to control his party and to convince the governor that they could do business together.

Thus in some respects Dr Nyerere had an easier task than Mr Kenyatta or Dr Obote. No doubt also he was helped by being so highly thought of in United Nations circles. But that help may not have been as important as has sometimes been suggested. The United Nations was constantly urging Britain to speed up independence for Kenya and Uganda and other colonies, as well as for Tanganyika. Britain's reply was always the same: 'Yes, we are anxious to give this colony its independence; but how can we until we have settled this special problem?' In Tanganyika there were no special problems: only the general problems of poverty, ignorance and disease.

Nevertheless, without Dr Nyerere, Tanganyika would not have made the rapid progress it did. It was his achievement that he brought his party under control; that Europeans and Asians came to give him their confidence and serve under him; and that British governors and Secretaries of State decided that he was a man they could trust and work with.

Having given Dr Nyerere full credit for his great achievements, let us not forget what is due to two British governors: to Sir Richard Turnbull, who made the critical decision to back Dr Nyerere, and to Sir Edward Twining before him, who determined that the people of Tanganyika must be awakened to a sense of political responsibility, and that at all costs Britain must not give the appearance in Tanganyika of backing the chiefs and the conservative people and of distrusting the educated men and their hopes of national freedom.

Chapter 13

ZANZIBAR FROM 1893 TO INDEPENDENCE

When Sultan Ali died in 1893 there were no more sons of Seyyid Said left alive, and there was a dispute over the succession. Three men were involved: Hamed, son of Sultan Thuwain of Oman; Khaled, son of Sultan Barghash; and Hamoud, who was son of another brother, Muhammad. Hamed, as son of the eldest brother, was the rightful heir. Khaled tried to seize the throne by force, but he was kept back by British troops, and Hamed succeeded peacefully. Three years later he died, and Khaled again saw his chance. He was now the rightful heir, and he was the head of a party among the Arabs who wished

Zanzibar to be again independent. He thought it unlikely that the British would accept him as Sultan, so he used force: at the head of a small body of his supporters he seized the palace and declared the British protectorate ended. But the warships arrived and called on him to surrender; he refused, and the ships shelled the palace. Khaled saw that the game was up. He left the ruins and sought shelter in the

8 THE SULTAN'S PALACE AT ZANZIBAR

German consulate. The consul took him down to the beach and put him on a boat for Dar-es-Salaam, and his rival Hamoud was proclaimed Sultan.

The anti-slavery decree of 1897

All this made it plain that the British were the masters in Zanzibar. The British and Foreign Anti-slavery Society thought that this would be a good opportunity to get rid of the sultanate altogether; why should not Britain annex Zanzibar and make it a colony, and then slavery could be altogether abolished? But the government refused to take this drastic step. It allowed Sultan Hamoud to take his throne, but in 1897 it persuaded him to make a new decree about slavery which, it thought, would remove the worst evils of the system. The new decree said that the courts would 'decline to enforce any alleged rights over the body, service, or property of any person on the ground that such a person was a slave'. The decree was carefully drafted so as to comply with Islamic law in giving freedom to anyone who desired it, and the government would pay compensation to the owner of any slave who claimed his freedom. The effect of the decree was that no one need remain in slavery unless he chose: all he had to do was to claim his freedom, and his master was compelled to grant it.

The anti-slavery society was delighted. Now, they said, we shall see all the slaves in Zanzibar and Pemba and the coastal strip claiming their freedom. The society was greatly surprised to find that in the first year only about 2,000 slaves claimed their freedom out of 50,000 or more, and the number did not greatly increase as time went on. The reason was that many of the slaves found themselves worse off as free men. As slaves, they were valuable property, and it was worth the master's while to look after them, especially as he could no longer buy fresh slaves to replace them. If they were free, and came to work for wages, the master had no special interest in them. The relationship was then purely a matter of business, a colder and more impersonal affair than the relationship between a good master and his slaves. We may guess that those who claimed their freedom were the slaves of bad masters; slaves with good masters were happy enough as they were. So there was no great social upheaval, as there might have been if all slaves had been compelled (as the anti-slavery society wished) to become free wage-labourers.

When Sultan Hamoud died in 1902 he was succeeded by his son Ali bin Hamoud, who was at school in England. Ali was seventeen, and had been so long in England that he spoke English better than he spoke Swahili or Arabic. He stayed there to finish his schooling, and his first minister, the Englishman A. S. Rogers, became regent. The government took this opportunity to tighten its control over Zanzibar. In 1903 it appointed a financial adviser, and in 1906 a secretary for finance and trade, and an attorney-general. The government was becoming more like the usual type of colonial administration.

The consul-general

All this time, the British consul-general in Zanzibar had been responsible not only for the islands but for the whole of the British East Africa Protectorate. By 1902 the railway had been built to Kisumu, and the first British settlers were arriving in the protectorate; mainland affairs were taking up more and more of the consul-general's time. So in 1904 the consul-general in Zanzibar was relieved of any responsibility for affairs on the mainland, and was able to devote all his attention to Zanzibar matters. From 1906 onwards he was in a position very much like that of a colonial governor. He had to supervise the increasing numbers of British officials. In 1908 the law courts were placed under the supervision of British judges. Next year the final step was taken towards the abolition of slavery: a decree of 1909 announced that no compensation would be paid for slaves set free after 1911.

Edward Clarke became consul-general in 1909. He was a man of great energy and a first-class administrator, and he set himself to modernize the administration of Zanzibar. He introduced financial reforms. He began a large programme of draining swamps and building roads, which diminished malaria and enabled crops to be carried to market in carts instead of in head-loads. He built hospitals and schools; he had the food markets inspected, the streets cleaned, the rats killed. When he died in 1913 he had done a great deal to make life in Zanzibar more comfortable for everyone.

All these improvements were carried out by greatly increasing the British staff. Sultan Ali, though well educated in England, found himself left with less and less to do, and he felt his position unbearable. He spent more and more of his time away from Zanzibar, and in 1911 he left it never to return; he abdicated the throne and was succeeded by Khalifa bin Harub.

Zanzibar under the Colonial Office

Clarke was the last consul-general. Zanzibar was now completely under British control, and on July 1, 1913 the Foreign Office in London handed over responsibility for Zanzibar affairs to the Colonial Office. The post of first minister was abolished, and the duties of first minister and consul-general were combined in the new post of Resident. Zanzibar was to be directly administered, and the Resident was to be under the authority of the governor of British East Africa (Kenya);

no authority whatever was to be left to the Sultan. Sultan Khalifa however protested against this, and the Colonial Office agreed to set up a protectorate council of three officials and three unofficial members. The Sultan was to preside, but he was not to appoint the members; all six were to be appointed by the Resident with the approval of the governor of British East Africa. In practice, no doubt, the Resident would consult the Sultan when drawing up the list.

Edward Clarke's improvements were only the beginning; many more were needed. In 1914 the population of the protectorate was about 197,000. There was very little education for Arabs and Africans apart from the Koranic schools; there were a few government primary schools with a seven-year course, and there was one small mission secondary school. The Indians were better off; they ran some schools for their own children, and in 1909 they founded the Euan Smith Madressa, named after one of the early British consuls; it began as a primary school, but its founders hoped to develop it into a secondary school. In 1916 the government began giving grants to mission schools, and the Euan Smith Madressa was one of the first grant-aided schools. One of the missions was training a few primary school teachers, and in 1923 the government opened its own teacher training college, with only seven students. A new government commercial course was more popular; it had twenty students in its first year. In the years after the war, education made slow progress. In 1927 it was reckoned that nearly five per cent of the Arab and African children were attending school, and nearly twenty years later, at the end of the second world war, this figure had increased to 15 per cent. The Indians were better educated; as early as 1931 it was found that nearly all Indian children went to school. The Indian community paid for its own schools; the Arabs and Africans depended on the government and the missions.

Meanwhile, Zanzibar was developed more and more on colonial lines. In 1923 the Sultan's law-courts were (as the official report put it) 'closely approximated to the British Courts', and the right of appeal was provided to the East African Court of Appeal and to the Judicial Committee of the Privy Council in London, just as if Zanzibar were a colony.

In 1926, the regular colonial system of government was introduced, with executive and legislative councils. The legislative council consisted of 8 official and 6 nominated unofficial members: 3 Arabs, 2 Indians, and 1 European. No African member was nominated until 1946; a second was added the next year. There was no talk of elections.

EDUCATION AND LAND

Between the two wars, the two problems which mainly worried the British officials in Zanzibar were African education and African land. The two were connected. The prosperity of Zanzibar depended mainly on the clove crop. The cloves were grown partly on large estates owned by Arabs, partly on small African peasant plots whose owners added to the income from their own crop by the wages they earned by working on the estates. But the hard-working and well-educated Indians were steadily investing their money in land, and both Arabs and Africans were becoming frightened of them. In 1933 the government estimated that during the previous eight years, Indians in Pemba alone had gained from Arab and African owners 35,000 coconut trees and 237,000 clove trees; in Zanzibar too they were making similar large gains. The government feared that if this went on, the Indians, who already controlled most of the trade, would control most of the land as well.

There were three things which the government might do to protect Arab and African interests. It could push ahead with education, so as to enable Arabs and Africans to compete better against the Indians. It could give financial help to poor people to enable them to acquire land of their own. It could make a law to check the alienation of land. The government tried all three of these ideas. Education was expensive, but by 1935 the government had provided a four-year middle school and a boys' secondary school, and two town schools with an eight-year course. Until money became available under the Colonial Development and Welfare Acts, Zanzibar like other colonies found it difficult to finance a programme of educational expansion.

The government started a land settlement scheme; it provided land holdings of from one to five acres, and carefully picked the most suitable men from the long line of applicants. The tenants were to buy the land by instalments spread over several years. The scheme was helped by being started at a time when clove prices were high, so that the tenants found it easy to pay the early instalments.

Meanwhile the government took drastic action to check land alienation. The Land Alienation Decree of 1934 provided that land was not to be sold to anyone but an Arab or an African without the Resident's approval; land might be leased to Indians or Europeans, but not for longer than twenty years. There were in fact no European settlers in Zanzibar; the Indians were the problem, and they objected strongly to the new decree. But the decree remained in force.

The Resident and the British officials were facing a difficult problem in the multi-racial community of Zanzibar. The Arabs had always been the masters, and like the European settlers in Kenya, they wished only to be left alone to run their estates as they pleased. The Africans were treated as a lower class; they wished to improve their position, but were hampered by lack of education. Both Arabs and Africans were threatened by the competition from the Indians, and it seemed to the British that they would be failing in their duty if they allowed the Indians to take over all economic power in the protectorate. Whatever the British did to check the Indian advance would bring them trouble from India; whatever they did to help the Africans would bring about trouble with the Arabs. When people feel their economic position improving, they begin to demand political power, and no Arab in Zanzibar wished to see political power in African hands.

After the second world war, the government was able to do more to help the Africans with money obtained under the Colonial Development and Welfare Acts. As in other colonial territories, it set up a ten-year development programme. As regards education, the aim of the programme was to raise school attendance among Arab and African children from 15 per cent to 40 per cent of the child population, and to make big improvements in secondary education and the training of teachers. By 1954 there were over 11,000 children in primary school and 600 in secondary school. For higher education, students from Zanzibar had to go to Makerere or to the newly established Muslim Institute at Mombasa. The government was spending 13 per cent of its own money on education, plus almost as much again from CDW money. In 1958 a Higher School Certificate class was opened in the government boys' secondary school.

Local government

The development of local government was another part of the government's plan. Under the Sultan's government, the administration had been centralized: the village headmen had been officials of the central government. The British hoped to be able to develop local councils. The District Administration and Rural Local Government Decree, which came into force at the beginning of 1948, gave certain legal powers to local councils wherever the people were able to elect them. One village council had already come into existence before the decree, and by 1952 there were six others, administering the affairs of from 2,500 to 12,000 people.

POLITICAL AND CONSTITUTIONAL AFFAIRS

All this encouragement of African development led to friction between the Africans, who felt themselves climbing towards more prosperity, and the Arabs, who felt their old dominant position threatened. In 1951 the government's annual report for the first time hints at trouble: 'Latterly,' it says, 'the time-honoured amity between communities has known some unfortunate exceptions.'

At that time, the unofficial membership of the legislative council was still 3 Arabs, 2 Indians, 2 Africans, and 1 European. During 1951 there were some discussions about introducing some system of elections, but no agreement was reached.

In June 1954 matters came to a head. Though a small country with a population of about a quarter of a million, Zanzibar had more than twenty newspapers, most of them small and short of money. The weekly paper *Al-Falaq*, owned by the Zanzibar Arab Association, was prosecuted for one of its articles; the paper was suspended for a time and its presses were confiscated. Feeling ran high, and the Arab leaders decided to adopt a policy of non-cooperation with the government. They refused to go on with the discussions about elections, and they refused to sit on the legislative council and other committees. Their non-cooperation continued right through 1955; in December of that year, one Arab from Pemba agreed to resume his seat on the council, but he was murdered.

The government carried on its work without Arab help. It invited Mr Coutts, who was at that time Minister for Education, Labour and Lands in Kenya, to come to Zanzibar and advise on a scheme for elections. He came in 1956, and the Arab Association refused to meet him; but when the Arabs saw his recommendations, the Association agreed to take them as a basis for discussion, and the Arab members resumed their seats in the legislative council.

The Coutts proposals

The existing council was too small to have room for elected members. It was enlarged by the Councils Decree of 1956. The council was now to consist of 4 ex-officio members and 9 other officials, and 12 representative members, thus following the usual British formula of an official majority of one. The Resident continued to preside.

Under the Coutts plan, 6 of the 12 representatives were to be elected on a common roll, the other 6 nominated. The vote was to be given to all men of 40 or over, and to younger men with certain qualifications; men of 25 could vote if they were literate in English, Swahili or Arabic, and possessed property worth £150 or an income of £120 a year. No women were to vote. This was a very restricted electorate as far as the Africans were concerned; the literacy and property qualifications kept most of them off the roll. The Arabs were usually literate in Arabic, and most of them had enough property to qualify for the vote. No wonder the Arabs were prepared to accept the Coutts proposals.

The Legislative Council Elections Decree of 1957 divided the country into six single-member constituencies for the election of six representatives, and in July of that year the first elections were held. There was much tension between Arabs and Africans, but there was no disorder on election day. After the elections, however, feeling rose high. Many Africans complained that they had been evicted by their Arab landlords for voting the wrong way. It was plain that political feeling between Arabs and Africans was to be one of the country's main troubles in the future.

The Blood constitutional proposals

Meanwhile, the British pressed on with further constitutional changes of the kind they were making in other countries: all of them tending to increase the political power of the majority of the population, that is, of the Africans. In March 1959 they arranged that the three unofficial members of the executive council should have the beginnings of ministerial powers: each of them should take a special interest in one group of government departments. In April, two more unofficial members were added to the executive council.

The legislative council too was changed: the nominated members were reduced from 6 to 4 and the elected members increased from 6 to 8, the total membership remaining the same. In that same year 1959, the minimum age for the vote was reduced from 25 to 21; the vote was given to all men of 30 (instead of 40) even without literacy; and it was given to women on the same terms as to men. The electorate was thus more than doubled, and by far the greater part of the increase was among the Africans.

The government thought that the next step in Zanzibar's constitutional progress should be a mainly elected legislature and a full ministerial system. In April 1960 Sir Hilary Blood was appointed as a commissioner to advise the government how to achieve this aim without weakening the Sultan's position. He proposed that the legislative council should contain 22 elected members, with 3 senior officials sitting ex-officio, and 5 nominated unofficial members: a total of 30. The executive council should consist of the 3 ex-officio members, with a chief minister and 4 ministers from the elected members of the legislative council. All effective power would thus be in the hands of the elected members. The Resident should cease to preside at the legislative council, and should be replaced by a Speaker. The Sultan should remain outside politics, and should follow the advice of his chief minister.

Political parties

The Blood proposals were accepted and put into effect, and new elections were called for January 1961. Three political parties were formed to contest the elections. The Afro–Shirazi party was led by Mr Abeid Karume. It stood for the African interests against the Arabs; it drew its name from the tradition that some of the earliest settlers in Zanzibar, centuries before, had come from Shiraz in Iran. The Zanzibar and Pemba People's Party was a breakaway group from the Afro–Shirazi. Its leader was Mr Muhammad Abdul Rahman Babu. Its policy was to speed up independence, to push ahead with more secondary education, and to set up a cooperative marketing organization for the all-important clove crop, which would replace the existing Clove Growers' Association. In fact, the ZPPP claimed to be merely a more impatient and extreme wing of the Afro–Shirazi. Such splits between the moderate and the extreme wings of a nationalist party have occurred in other African colonies, notably in Ghana, Senegal, and Zambia.

Lastly, there was the Zanzibar Nationalist Party, led by Sheikh Ali Muhsin. The ZNP denied that it was an Arab party; but most of the Arab voters preferred it to either of the other two parties.

When the elections were held in January 1961, they passed off quietly,

9   CHEERING THE AFRO–SHIRAZI PARTY AT ZANZIBAR

but they revealed a weakness in the Blood constitution. The Afro–Shirazi party won the election by the narrowest possible margin. A victory by one vote in Chake–Chake over the ZNP candidate gave them 10 seats; the Nationalists won 9, the ZPPP 3. After the election, the ZPPP candidates divided, two of them supporting the Nationalists and one the Afro–Shirazi. The voting strength in the council was thus 11 Afro–Shirazi and 11 Nationalists; neither party had a majority and effective government was impossible. The legislative council hastily passed a Bill empowering the Civil Secretary to act as head of a care-taker government; another constituency (making 23 in all) was created on Pemba; and fresh elections were called for June.

During all this turmoil, Sultan Khalifa bin Hamoud died after a reign of 49 years. He was succeeded by his son Seyyid Abdullah bin Khalifa.

The June 1961 elections

The June elections were a disaster. The election campaigns were bitter. The Afro–Shirazi spokesmen said that the Nationalist party was an Arab party, and moreover was opposed to the idea of an East African federation, which was then much favoured by African leaders both in the protectorate and on the mainland. The Nationalists retorted that they could not be an Arab party when only four of their candidates were Arabs; and they accused the Afro–Shirazi party of widespread intimidation. In two constituencies the Nationalists went so far as to boycott the election. In many places there was severe rioting, not only during the voting but afterwards. Arab shops were looted and Arabs murdered; altogether 66 people were killed and over 300 injured.

The British government appointed a commission of inquiry. It reported that the Afro–Shirazi leaders believed that the Nationalists were going in for 'large-scale cheating, double-voting, and impersona-tion'; but although they honestly believed this, the commission thought they were mistaken. All the disorders began in the same way, by Afro–Shirazi supporters trying to force Nationalist voters away from the polling booths and prevent them from voting. Both parties were unwise in their election campaigns: the Afro–Shirazi in appealing to all African voters on racial grounds, the Nationalists in appealing for support on religious grounds. Above all, said the commission, the newspapers were to be blamed: their fiery articles excited the people too much.

Since there were some 240,000 Africans and only 45,000 Arabs, it was perhaps natural for the Afro–Shirazi to fight the election on racial grounds, for voting was on a common roll, and an election fought on purely racial grounds would give them a heavy majority.

It is clear from the results that many Africans must have voted against the Afro–Shirazi party. Nearly everyone turned out to vote: 94 per cent of the total electorate. The Afro–Shirazi and the Nationalist parties won 10 seats each, the ZPPP 3; the Afro–Shirazi leaders were bitter at this result, for they had secured over 1,000 votes more than the other two parties together, and yet they had fewer seats.[1] The alliance of ZNP and ZPPP formed a government, with Sheikh Muhammad Shamte Hamadi of the ZPPP as chief minister and five other ministers, all from the ZNP.

After the election, the Afro–Shirazi leaders decided to boycott the meetings of the new legislative council in protest, and when the council met on July 6, the ten Afro–Shirazi seats were empty.

The Lancaster House conference

As the Lukiko of Buganda found, boycotting the meetings of the legislative council is a weapon as apt to damage the user as to damage his opponent. All political parties want power, and there is no political power in empty seats. After some months of the boycott, the Afro–Shirazi men agreed to visit London with their opponents to discuss further steps towards independence.

A constitutional conference was held at Lancaster House in March and April 1962. It was not very successful, for the two parties were far apart in their views. The Afro–Shirazi delegates wanted full adult suffrage, without literacy or property qualifications, and to this the ZPPP–ZNP delegates agreed. But the ZPPP–ZNP delegates would not accept the other demands of the Afro–Shirazi party: the lowering of the voting age from 21 to 18, an all-elected legislative council of 31 members, and fresh elections before the grant of internal self-government. The ZPPP–ZNP delegates would accept a council of 31 elected members, but they wished to add four nominated members, two from each side.

The Secretary of State, Mr Maudling, said that as the two parties in Zanzibar were so far from agreeing, he could not yet fix a date for internal self-government, much less full independence. He accepted

---

[1] The electoral system used in Britain and Zanzibar (and other African countries) does not by any means give a party seats in the legislature in proportion to its votes. This can be illustrated by an example. Suppose there are two parties in an election, and that in each constituency 51 per cent of the electors vote for party A and 49 per cent for party B. Then party A will win all the seats in the legislature, and party B, though it had 49 per cent of the total number of votes, will have none. In practice, things do not give such an extreme result, but the system always gives the victorious party a bigger majority of the seats in the legislature than of the votes in the election. Various electoral systems have been proposed which would avoid this result, but Britain has so far been content to keep the old system.

the proposal that the literacy and property qualifications for the vote should be abolished, this being the one point on which government and opposition were agreed. He promised to appoint a commissioner to fix the size of the new legislative council and to delimit constituencies. Sir Robert Arundell was appointed as commissioner, and he gave pleasure to the Afro–Shirazi men by recommending the council they wanted, to consist of 31 elected members without additional nominated members.

This concession to the Afro–Shirazi party was soon balanced by a concession to its opponents. The Afro–Shirazi party demanded that fresh elections should be held before internal self-government was granted. But the Secretary of State thought it likely that fresh elections would bring about much the same result as before; so he granted internal self-government in June 1963, and the elections were fixed for early July.

The July 1963 elections
The election results showed that the Secretary of State was right. There were 8 additional seats to be contested; the Afro–Shirazi won 3, the ZPPP 3, and the Nationalists 2. The alliance between the Nationalists and the ZPPP still held firm, and it held 18 seats against the Afro–Shirazi 13, compared with 13 against 10 two years before. The Afro–Shirazi party won large majorities in the towns, and again it won a majority of the total vote, 54 per cent. But in elections it is seats, not votes, that count. In Pemba the Afro–Shirazi lost four seats by narrow margins. If it could have won those seats, the Afro–Shirazi would have had 17 seats and its opponents 14, and there would have been an Afro–Shirazi government.

There are questions to be asked about these election results which we cannot yet answer. The Arabs themselves had demanded elections on a common roll. Since Africans outnumbered the Arabs by about five to one, why did the Afro–Shirazi party not gain a bigger majority of the votes, and the seats? What was the true policy of the ZPPP, and why did it ally itself with the Nationalists instead of with the Afro–Shirazi?

As it was, the Secretary of State was bound to accept the argument of the victorious ZNP–ZPPP government that the majority of the assembly was behind it, as it had been two years before, so that there was now no reason for putting off the grant of full independence. A second Lancaster House conference was held in September to discuss the details and work out the new constitution. The prime minister attended with six other government delegates, and Mr Karume with four others from the opposition. It was agreed that the Sultan was to continue as head of state, and should be able to nominate his successor; but he must always follow his ministers' advice. The opposition had one great fear: that the government might use its majority in the assembly to make changes in the constitution even before independence day, especially in the direction of limiting the political rights of Africans. This fear was removed when the conference agreed that the assembly should be summoned merely to enact the revised constitution, and should have no power of amending it. The conference also agreed that future assemblies might amend most of the constitution by a simple majority, but that the clauses which defined the rights of the citizen and the rights of minority groups could be amended only by a special procedure. There must first be a two-thirds majority in the assembly in favour of the amendment; then a new assembly must be elected, and the new assembly too must pass the amendment by a two-thirds majority.

Sultan Abdullah bin Khalifa died a week before the July 1963 elections after a reign of less than three years, and was succeeded by his son Seyyid Jamshid bin Abdullah.

Independence
Zanzibar became independent at midnight on December 9, 1963. It was a night of great rejoicings. But some foreign observers noted that the rejoicing crowds were mainly composed of Arabs, and it was the Arab quarters of the towns that were brightly illuminated. The African quarters were much darker, and many members of the Afro–Shirazi party were heard to complain that Zanzibar was now supposed to be free, but that freedom ought to mean freedom not only from British colonial rule, but also from the Arabs.

Chapter 14

EDUCATION IN THE COLONIAL PERIOD

The plans which Britain made for constitutional progress would be ineffective unless she educated the African people to manage their countries successfully after they had achieved independence.

There were difficulties in developing education in East Africa. It was a region of great distances and poor communications, and the development of education and other social services was hindered, until the Colonial Development and Welfare Act of 1945, by the British government's rule that no grants for such purposes could be made from the British Treasury. The revenues of the colonial governments, as we have seen, might rise one year and fall the next, and however anxious the governments might be to spend money on education, they sometimes did not venture to build a much-needed school for fear that they might not be able to supply it with staff and equipment.

Another difficulty was that so many different languages were spoken. The British thought that a child should begin its schooling in the mother-tongue, and that the use of English should come later. But there were so many mother-tongues in East Africa that it was impossible to apply this policy effectively. Much primary education was given in Swahili, and this was reasonably satisfactory in Tanganyika, but not elsewhere. In Buganda there was trouble when the government tried to introduce Swahili as the language of instruction in primary schools; the parents insisted that their children should be taught in Luganda.

It was largely for reasons of language that the East African governments began providing separate schools for African, Indian, Goan, Arab and European children; in Kenya there were even separate schools for English-speaking children from Britain, and for Afrikaans-speaking children from South Africa. When the numbers of Asian and European children grew, the expense of providing separate schools for them was a hindrance to the expansion of African education. But the hindrance became serious only in the later years. In the last year or two before independence, all schools were opened to pupils of any race.

Western education was introduced by the Christian missionaries, but from the beginning of the colonial period the colonial governments recognized that they had a responsibility for African education, even if for the time being they had not the money or the staff to do very much. The East Africa Protectorate had 61 mission schools in 1906, with 2,200 children, an average of fewer than forty children to a school. These small schools were usually run by a European missionary, perhaps with one or two African assistants whom he himself had trained; all the children came from near-by villages, so that the school had no language problem. A good teacher is more important than buildings or equipment; and such small schools as these, each run by an experienced teacher in close touch with his pupils, can give a sound education. This was the pattern of education in Kenya in those early days; only a few children went to school, but their education was sound as far as it went. In 1908 the country was visited by an 'educational expert' from India, Dr Fraser, who came to help the government to draw up a 'central general scheme of education'.

In 1919–20 the Kenya government was running a few small schools of its own: three for Europeans with 286 children, two for Indians with 308, and two for Arabs and Africans (one at Mombasa and one at Machakos) with 139 children. At that time, the government had little knowledge of the mission schools for Africans; it reported merely that there was a 'large number' of them. Next year it estimated that perhaps 30,000 African children were attending the mission schools, and in 1922 it increased its estimate to 'some 50,000'. In 1922 the government picked eleven of the African schools and gave them a grant of £10,896. It commented that 'the vastly preponderating numbers of Africans present the greatest educational problem'. Next year, 1923, it gave for the first time the number of African schools: there were in all 939 schools, with 43,000 children. These 43,000 children had 238 European and 1,326 African teachers, an average of fewer than 30 children to a teacher; thus, the quality of the education was being fairly well maintained.

By this time the European settlers were becoming more numerous, and, as we have seen, they were much concerned with the problem of finding labour for their farms. Many of them found that they could attract Africans to work for them by providing schools on their land for the African children. In 1924 the government said it was 'satisfactory to be able to report the united effort being made by all sections of the European community for the improvement of African education'.

In Uganda, thanks to the long-established position of the missionary societies, education began earlier than in Kenya, and for many years the government did not find it necessary to open any schools of its own. The first secondary school was opened at Budo in 1904, and in 1906 Budo received its first government grant of £100; in that year there were 107 mission schools in Uganda with over 12,000 pupils. Most education at that time was being given in Luganda; only Budo and three or four other schools used English at all. In 1920 the educational system had greatly expanded; there were then over 70,000 boys and 45,000 girls in school, though most of them did not stay long enough to finish the primary school course. In 1922 the government opened its first school; this was Makerere, which began as a technical school, but which the government hoped would one day develop into a university college.

After the first world war the British government had a new sense of its colonial responsibilities, and in Uganda the opening of Makerere was the beginning of a programme of energetic expansion. In 1924 the government set up its own education department and began a five-year programme of school building with a budget of nearly £100,000, its annual grant to the mission schools was increased to nearly £11,000. In 1932 Makerere was training African teachers and medical, veterinary, survey and agricultural probationers. Two years later it opened a three-year general arts course.

This development of Makerere helped secondary education in Kenya. The first Kenya school to go beyond the primary level was the Alliance High School, which was opened as a junior secondary school in 1926. By 1936 the Alliance High School and one Catholic secondary school were preparing their pupils for the Makerere entrance examinations. It was not until 1940 that the Alliance High School provided a four-year course leading to the Cambridge Overseas School Certificate. That year saw the appointment of its great headmaster Carey Francis, who did so much for education in Kenya until his death in 1966.

In Tanganyika, the British followed their usual custom of leaving the missionary societies to provide most of the schools, and of using the government education department mainly to supervise the work of the mission schools. The poverty of the Tanganyika government forced it to maintain this policy. It reported to the United Nations: 'The whole pre-war educational system dissolved in 1914, and when the first British director of education was appointed at the end of 1920 he worked practically alone until 1924, devoting his energies to the training of some teachers and to re-establishing a few village schools with the aid of the surviving African vernacular teachers trained prior to 1914.' Tanganyika education was badly hit by the slump of the 1930s. The director of education retired in 1931 and his post was left for a time unfilled; the superintendents of education were reduced from 40 to 25 and similar cuts in staff were made elsewhere; the grants to the mission schools were cut by 10 per cent.

In all three territories the growth of African education followed the same pattern. Before 1914 there were only a few thousand African children in school, but the education they received was good as far as it went. Between 1919 and 1939 the numbers of children in school increased greatly. In spite of the difficulty caused by the slump, the governments did what they could to supervise and assist the work of the missions, but they could not altogether maintain the quality of the education being given to the increased numbers of children. The missionary societies found themselves short both of money and of staff, so that there were fewer missionary teachers available than there had been before 1914, and the governments could not afford to replace the lost missionary teachers with government teachers. After the second world war, money became available for education under the

Colonial Development and Welfare Acts, but even with this assistance the governments had great difficulty in providing for the hundreds of thousands of children now flocking into the schools. In Kenya there were 129,000 African children in school in 1938 and 207,000 in 1946; in Uganda the attendance rose from 170,000 in 1951 to 275,000 in 1956.

All the same, the Act of 1945 gave the colonial governments new hope. Kenya's ten-year development plan, for example, budgeted for an expenditure of £15,500,000, of which £2,400,000 was for education. In 1949 the Beecher committee recommended among other things that sixteen new secondary schools should be provided as quickly as possible, and fourteen of them were opened and at work within two years.

One of the main problems was to provide qualified teachers for these thousands of new pupils. A great increase in the training of teachers was another recommendation of the Beecher committee, and between 1946 and 1958 Kenya increased its staff of qualified teachers from under 2,000 to over 10,000. The De Bunsen committee, which in 1953 drew up a plan for the improvement of African education in Uganda, was impressed with the problem of wastage. Children stayed at school too short a time to gain any permanent benefit from their schooling. It was reckoned that a school life of four years was the shortest that would enable a child to become permanently literate in his mother-tongue. The De Bunsen committee estimated that in Uganda three boys out of four, and three girls out of ten, attended school at some time or another. But not more than one child in twelve stayed at school for this minimum period of four years, and not more than one in 500 stayed for twelve years and entered for the School Certificate examination. The biggest problem was not to get children to go to school but to get them to stay there.

This problem was met at all levels. For several years after it first opened, the Alliance High School remained small, for parents found that after one or two years at the school their boys could get good jobs, so they took them away and sent them to work. The secondary schools and the institutions of higher education would remain starved of students until more children could be persuaded to complete the primary school course.

Part of the difficulty was that so many uneducated parents did not understand what the schools were doing. As their children became educated, they entered a world into which their parents could not follow them. With this difficulty in mind, a Colonial Office committee produced a report in 1944 on what it called mass education. There were many ways, it said, in which village people might make their lives fuller and more comfortable if they were shown how: in matters of health, agriculture, housekeeping and child care, and in literacy. This idea of mass education (or community development, as some called it) was taken up by the governments, and all over East Africa development teams and literacy campaigns began working. The East Africa High Commission set up an East African Literature Bureau, which produced quantities of cheap reading material in English and in several African languages. Adult education was further helped by the department of extra-mural studies which was set up at Makerere.

10 COMMUNITY DEVELOPMENT

Community development assistants being trained in Kenya

East Africa's system of higher education came into being as a result of the Asquith commission of 1944 and of the financial help given under the Colonial Development and Welfare Acts. The De La Warr commission had already recommended that Makerere should be developed towards university status, and in accordance with this Makerere became an independent college in 1939. Universities in Britain are not controlled by the government. The British government thought that university institutions in Africa must similarly be free from government control, but it was important that they should earn the respect of universities in the rest of the world. For this purpose it invited all the British universities to set up a joint council to advise and help the young African university colleges. The council helped them by lending staff; by setting up committees to ensure that, even if their syllabuses differed from those in British universities,[1] the standard of their examinations was as high as in Britain; and by helping them to plan their development. The British proposal was that East Africa should have a federal university, with separate colleges in the different countries, all the colleges being joined in one federal council. For a few years the federal university should be closely associated with the University of London until its academic reputation was secure and it could safely become independent.

The British took the first steps to put this plan into operation. Makerere College was raised to the status of a university college in 1950. In October 1956, the Royal Technical College of Nairobi was opened, with 215 full-time students; it was raised to the status of a university college in 1961, and became one of the colleges of the proposed federal university in July 1963.

The university college of Dar-es-Salaam was opened in October 1961. Until then, students from Tanganyika had been going to Nairobi or Kampala for higher education; but Dr Nyerere explained that his government's educational expansion would soon increase the number of students sixfold, and there would be no room for them in the other two colleges, so it was an urgent matter for Tanganyika to provide a university college of her own. The buildings cost nearly four million pounds; £850,000 were given by Britain, and nearly a million and a half came from the United States.

After independence, the three governments decided to abandon the British idea of a federal university and to establish the three institutions as three separate universities. The three universities were established in 1970, Makerere then having over 1,500 full-time students, Nairobi not quite so many, and Dar-es-Salaam nearly a thousand.

[1] For example, it is right that biology should be illustrated in British universities from British animals and plants, but in African universities from African. In history, geography and some other subjects there is room for an African and a British syllabus, different in content but of equal value.

Chapter 15

EAST AFRICA IN 1970

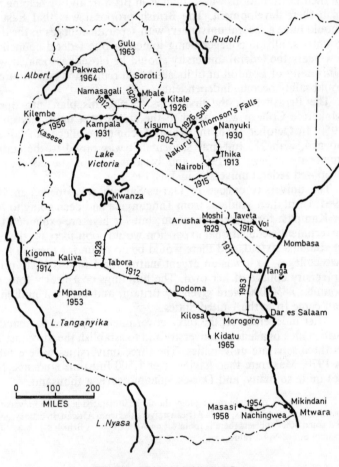

EAST AFRICAN RAILWAYS

The dates of completion are given. One or
two short lines cannot be shown, such as
that from Kampala to Port Bell and from
Kisumu to Yala and Butere, the latter
finished in 1931

When the independence celebrations in East Africa were over and the cheering crowds had gone home, the national leaders went back to their offices to face a number of problems, some of which the British had not been able to solve and which they now inherited; others arose for the first time now that their countries were independent and had to stand alone. We may group these problems under five heads.

1. POLITICAL PROBLEMS INHERITED FROM THE COLONIAL PERIOD

Much of the history of East Africa in the last ten years is the story of the way in which the East African states have sought an answer to questions which used to trouble the colonial governments.

Zanzibar and Tanzania

The government of Zanzibar which achieved independence in December 1963 came to power through an election in which it gained only a minority of the votes, but won a majority of the seats in the assembly. Little more than a month after the independence day, the Nationalist Party government was overthrown. On January 12, 1964 the city of Zanzibar was attacked by a force of 600 men. There were no troops in Zanzibar, only police. The attackers were well led; they seized the radio stations, the Sultan's palace, and the government offices. The police stations were quickly captured, all but one, which resisted for a whole day. The Sultan escaped to Dar-es-Salaam and Europe.

The Afro–Shirazi leader, Mr Abeid Karume, became president of the new republic. One of his ministers was Mr Muhammad Abdul Rahman Babu, who was at one time secretary of the Nationalist Party. In June 1963 Mr Babu resigned from the Nationalist Party, and founded a new party which he called the Umma Party. Soon after independence, early in January 1964, the new government banned the Umma party, and Babu retired to Dar-es-Salaam.

Mr Babu himself said that the banning of his party was the final injustice which sparked off the revolution; and he returned to Zanzibar as soon as he could and allied his party with the Afro–Shirazi. But the revolution had other causes. One was the fury of the Afro–Shirazi party at finding itself excluded from power although it had obtained 54 per cent of the votes in the recent election. Another cause was the hatred felt by the Africans for their Arab rulers. There was growing unemployment, partly because the world market for Zanzibar cloves was shrinking. It was rumoured too that the Sultan was planning to introduce Egyptian officers to train an army and maintain himself in power. The fury of the revolution was directed against the Arabs and the Asians; there was much killing, looting and imprisonment, and the surviving Arabs were reduced to poverty. The power was held by a revolutionary council of about thirty members. At the end of January 1964 the council declared Zanzibar to be a one-party state. The ruling party was to be the Afro–Shirazi party, and Mr Babu brought his Umma party to join it.

The Arab question was thus drastically settled. What was to be the position of the new republic in world affairs? Kenya and Uganda recognized the new government at once, Tanganyika only a few days later. The Soviet Union and some other communist countries were equally prompt. But Britain, Canada, Australia and the United States were slow; they all recognized the new government together, six weeks after the revolution.

On April 23, 1964, Tanganyika and Zanzibar came together by an act of union, to form the United Republic of Tanganyika and Zanzibar. Dr Nyerere was to be president, and there were two vice-presidents, Mr Kawawa for Tanganyika and Mr Karume for Zanzibar. Zanzibar was to have its own regional government, and it seemed as if the central government would have very little power there. Soon afterwards, all British officials in Zanzibar were dismissed, and an American communications station was closed. The United Republic changed its name to Tanzania at the end of October 1964.

Four years after the act of union, Mr Karume said that the constitution of Tanzania, which gave Zanzibar internal self-government, would continue indefinitely.

Politics in Uganda

There were two important problems in Uganda still unsettled when the British flag was hauled down: the problem of the 'lost counties', and the larger problem of Buganda's place in an independent Uganda. Dr Obote declared that Uganda would be developed as a one-party socialist state, and that he would hold a referendum in the two counties of Buyaga and Bugangazzi so that the people there could choose whether the counties should stay in Buganda or become once more parts of Bunyoro. This talk of a referendum angered the Kabaka Yekka Party; it withdrew from the coalition government and joined the Democratic Party in opposition. Nevertheless, in November 1964 the referendum was held; 13,600 people in the two counties voted for union with Bunyoro, 3,500 for union with Buganda, and 112 for remaining as a separate district under the central government.

When the figures were announced, there was rioting in Kampala, and Mr Kintu resigned as katikiro. Dr Obote proposed to transfer the two counties to Bunyoro, but the president of Uganda, who was also Kabaka of Buganda, refused to sign the necessary papers. The Buganda government applied to the High Court for a ruling that the referendum was invalid, because 9,000 Baganda had moved into the two counties since the Molson commission two years before, and these people had not been allowed to vote. The High Court rejected the application, and Buganda then appealed to the Court of Appeal; but Dr Obote transferred the two counties to Bunyoro at the beginning of 1965, before the Court of Appeal had given its decision.

So this was the end of the 'lost counties' problem. The prime minister had rejected the Buganda government's position and had acted without the consent and cooperation of the president, the Kabaka. Anyone could foresee on independence day that the compromise which placed the Kabaka of Buganda at the head of the federal government, with a federal prime minister who came from the north, would be a difficult arrangement to work. This affair of the 'lost counties' referendum was the first important occasion on which the two men had been openly at variance.

Dr Obote was clearly a determined leader, and his position was becoming stronger; at the end of 1964 the leader of the Democratic Party and five of his members crossed the floor of the assembly and joined the government. The government then had 67 members and the opposition 24: Kabaka Yekka 14, Democratic Party 10. There was one independent member.

In February 1966 there was serious trouble. It began when Mr Daudi Ocheng, a member of the Kabaka Yekka party, accused Dr Obote himself, two of his cabinet ministers, and some others, of corruption. Dr Obote was away from Kampala on tour in the north of the country; but as soon as he came back to Kampala he suspended the constitution and appointed a commission of inquiry into Mr Ocheng's allegations. Five ministers who were supposed to have given Mr Ocheng his information were imprisoned. Dr Obote said that during his visit to the north, he had learned that persons holding government office had asked foreign countries to supply troops to help to overthrow the government. Who these persons were, he did not at first say; but on March 2, 1966 he himself took over the duties of the president and the vice-president, and next day he declared that it was the president himself, the Kabaka, who had asked for foreign troops. The Kabaka replied that he had certainly asked for foreign troops, but not to overthrow the government. On the contrary, he had heard reports that there was a plot to overthrow the government, and he had asked for troops to protect it.

This reply did not satisfy Dr Obote. On April 15 the assembly adopted, by 55 votes to 4, a new constitution which abolished the federation and transformed Uganda into a unitary state with a strong executive president. Dr Obote himself was sworn in as president the same day.

This was a direct challenge to the Kabaka and the Buganda government, and it was at once taken up. The Kabaka brought an action in the High Court, seeking a declaration that he was still president of Uganda. The Lukiko went further, and demanded that the central government should at once leave Buganda territory; this would mean abandoning both Kampala and Entebbe. Dr Obote's reply was to declare a state of emergency. On May 24 the army attacked the Kabaka's palace on Mengo hill and captured it after heavy fighting; the Kabaka escaped and eventually reached Britain. The judges of the High Court ruled that the new constitution was valid, and thus the Kabaka was no longer president of Uganda, as he claimed to be.

The opposition of the Buganda government was now crushed, and Dr Obote proceeded to abolish the privileged position which Buganda had held so long. All four kingdoms ceased to exist, the rulers of

11   MODERN AFRICA: THE POWER STATION AT OWEN FALLS ON THE NILE

Ankole, Bunyoro and Toro (but not the Kabaka) receiving pensions. Ankole, Bunyoro and Toro became administrative districts in the new unitary state, and the kingdom of Buganda was divided into four new administrative districts. The Lukiko was dissolved, and some of its members were detained under the emergency regulations. In 1968 the ruling party, the Uganda People's Congress, was all-powerful, with 83 seats in the assembly against only 6 held by the Democratic Party. But the state of emergency was still in force.

This then was the end of the Buganda agreement, which for so long had hampered the British in their efforts to make Uganda a unitary modern state. When the agreement was made, the north had hardly come into the British view. It was left for the man from the north, Dr Obote, to undo the work both of Johnston and of the Muganda conqueror Semei Kakunguru. Dr Obote survived an attempt on his life, and his position was strengthened when the Kabaka died in London in November 1969. But in February 1971, while Dr Obote was out of the country, his government was overthrown by a military coup led by General Amin.

Politics in Kenya

African politics in Kenya during the colonial period had been much concerned with tribal jealousies; KADU was a union of several tribal groups against the dominant Kikuyu. These jealousies did not die when Kenya became independent.

Things began well. In December 1964, Kenya declared itself a republic, and the prime minister, Mr Kenyatta, became president. The leader of KADU, Mr Ronald Ngala, dissolved his party, and he and his followers crossed the floor of the assembly and joined the government. 'We consider the cause of Kenya', said he, 'to be greater than any of our personal pride, gains, or losses. This is one of the times when we must be prepared to sacrifice our political dignity for the peace and harmony of Kenya.' In this way, Kenya became, by general agreement, a one-party state.

The peace and harmony of Kenya still depended, however, on good feeling between the tribal groups, and especially between the two biggest groups, the Kikuyu and the Luo. This good feeling was greatly helped by the close alliance between President Kenyatta and Mr Tom Mboya, who was a Luo. The vice-president, Mr Oginga Odinga, was also a Luo, but he was not nearly so much identified with the official policy of neutrality or non-alignment in foreign affairs.[1]

In March 1966 KANU held a party conference at Limuru, and

[1] For the policy of non-alignment, see page 264.

abolished the post of deputy president of the party, which was then held by Mr Odinga. Mr Odinga's reply was to leave the government and form an opposition party called the Kenya People's Union. The government replied by carrying through the assembly a constitutional amendment which provided that members of KANU in the assembly who left the party must resign their assembly seats and seek re-election. They were elected, said the president, as members of KANU. If their constituents still wanted them when they were no longer members of KANU, very well; but the constituents must be given an opportunity of saying so. In June, 30 by-elections were held accordingly; 21 were won by KANU and 9 by Mr Odinga's party, the Kenya People's Union.

The government felt that it needed still further powers to maintain order. In June 1966 it passed a Preservation of Public Security Act, and next month the assembly gave its approval to regulations, issued under the Act, providing for a curfew, control of people's movements, and detention without trial. About the same time, other constitutional amendments provided that the president of Kenya should be elected by a popular vote instead of by an electoral college, and that no independent candidate should stand for election to the assembly: all candidates must be members of a recognized party. In December 1966, yet another constitutional amendment abolished the senate and gave Kenya a single-chamber assembly. The House of Representatives was enlarged by adding 58 new seats; 41 of them were allotted to former Senators, and 17 were filled by by-elections. The enlarged assembly contained 175 constituency members and 12 specially elected.

These measures tended to weaken Mr Odinga's party, the Kenya People's Union, and in August 1968 it suffered a heavy blow. Local government elections were being held, and no fewer than 1,800 KPU candidates were disqualified because of some irregularity; the KANU candidates for these seats were declared to be returned unopposed.

All this time the strength of the government appeared unassailable. It rested on the alliance between the Kikuyu, led by President Kenyatta, and the Luo, led by Mr Mboya. Mr Kenyatta was not merely the Kikuyu leader, he was the national leader, and as such he had no rival. But Mr Mboya was a much younger man, and—provided the Kikuyu would accept a president who was not one of themselves—he seemed a likely candidate to succeed to the presidency when Mr Kenyatta retired. But on July 5, 1969 Mr Mboya was murdered in Nairobi. The Luo at once broke out into rioting against the Kikuyu. After this rioting, Mr Oginga Odinga was detained under the emergency regulations, and his party was banned. A Kikuyu man was arrested and convicted of the murder, and the president appointed two other Luo men as members of his cabinet. But the incident showed that the jealousy between the two biggest tribal groups was a problem still unsolved.

The Asians in Kenya

The days were long past when the Asians had competed with the Europeans in Kenya for the political control of the country. Although political power in Kenya had passed into African hands, the Asians still had great economic power: nearly all the retail trade was in Asian hands, and so were a great many of the big business and industrial firms. Asian firms tended to give employment to Asians rather than to Africans, and there was much African ill-feeling on this account.

When Kenya was a British colony, its people, of whatever race, were 'citizens of the United Kingdom and colonies'. When it became independent, under an African government, the Africans of Kenya gave up this status and became citizens of Kenya; but it was part of the independence settlement that the Europeans and Asians should be allowed to choose whether to become citizens of Kenya or to retain their British citizenship. Three years after independence, the Kenya government announced that it would give preference to Kenya citizens over those who had chosen to remain foreigners. In 1967 an Immigration Act was passed, which provided that after December 1 of that year, all European and Asian residents in Kenya who were not Kenya citizens must apply for permits to live and work in the country; these permits could be renewed every year, but would be granted only if no suitably qualified Kenya citizen was available to do the work. This was not a racial law. It gave no preference to African citizens over other citizens, but gave preference to all Kenya citizens, whatever their race, over non-citizens.

The Immigration Act hit the Asian community harder than the European. The European community in Kenya had always been smaller than the Asian, and many of those who did not wish to accept Kenya citizenship had already left. There were still 190,000 Asians in Kenya, of whom 70,000 had accepted Kenya citizenship. The remaining 120,000 saw that in a year or two they would have to leave Kenya, and they began to make hasty preparations for going to India or Pakistan or Britain.

Thus Kenya remained a multi-racial state; but the government had got rid of the really difficult problem of race: the problem of racial minorities who were in the habit of appealing to the governments of Britain or India to protect their interests against the government of Kenya.

The Frontier Problem
African frontiers are artificial. They were settled by agreement between the different colonial powers. They took no account of tribal boundaries, and often took little account even of geographical features. On the whole the newly independent African states found it convenient to preserve these frontiers, however unsatisfactory. They realized that if they once began making alterations they might find themselves in danger of splitting into smaller and smaller units. But the frontier problem did sometimes make itself felt. The most serious case in East Africa was the northern frontier of Kenya. The northern frontier province is an arid region, inhabited by nomadic peoples and their herds. During the colonial period, more and more Somali herdsmen had come into it. There was constant quarrelling between Somali and Kenya peoples over the use of water-holes for their animals, and a good deal of fighting took place. When the independent republic of Somalia came into existence, the Somalia government claimed the whole of the province, saying that a majority of the inhabitants was now Somali. President Kenyatta refused to give it up, and in June 1966 he broke off all trade relations with Somalia because of the constant border fighting.

A year later, the Organization of African Unity[2] tried to settle the dispute. President Kaunda of Zambia acted as mediator, and in October 1967 President Kenyatta met the prime minister of Somalia at Arusha in Tanzania. There the two men signed an agreement to end the fighting and the emergency regulations, and to set up a committee of Kenya, Somalia and Zambia representatives to draw up a final settlement of the problem. The committee reached agreement early in 1969. The disputed province remained part of Kenya, but Kenya and Somalia returned to a peaceful relationship; they agreed to cooperate in development projects, and Kenya undertook to propose that Somalia should be admitted to membership of the East African Community.[3]

2. PROBLEMS OF EXTERNAL AFFAIRS

The Congo
The Belgian Congo became independent in 1960. The Belgian colonial administration was efficient in some ways, but it had done nothing to prepare the country for self-government. Very soon after inde-

[2] For the OAU, see pages 263, 264.
[3] For the East African Community, see page 263.

pendence, tribal jealousies tore the country apart. The southernmost province, Katanga, declared itself independent of the rest of the Congo. Since this province was the Congo's copper-belt and still contained large numbers of Belgian mining men and other settlers, the newly independent government at Leopoldville (Kinshasa) declared that Katanga's declaration of independence had been arranged by Belgium. The country lapsed into civil war. There was much discussion in the United Nations and elsewhere over who was to blame. The United Nations sent a military force to help the central government to restore order.

This brought problems to the Congo's neighbours. Floods of refugees crossed the border into East Africa (especially Uganda). At one moment there was trouble between the Uganda and Kenya governments over a shipment of arms which was imported by Uganda through Mombasa. The Kenya government declared that the arms were not intended for Uganda's own army, but for one of the leaders in the Congo civil war. Kenya was neutral in the civil war, and would not allow her territory to be used for such a purpose. The matter was quickly settled in a friendly way, but it showed how easily difficulties could arise.

Rhodesia

There was no disagreement in East Africa over the Rhodesian question. The British colony of Rhodesia had a strong body of European settlers, and had enjoyed nearly complete internal self-government ever since 1923. The only limitation was that the government in London retained the power of vetoing any Rhodesian law which did not apply equally to all races. This power of veto had never been used. From 1953 to 1963, Rhodesia was joined with its neighbours Zambia and Malawi in a federation. When Zambia and Malawi became independent in 1964, Rhodesia also asked for independence, but the British government refused to grant it unless the minority European government would give much more political power to the African majority. The Rhodesian government refused this condition, and in November 1965 declared itself independent. The government in London said that this was an act of rebellion, and consequently the Rhodesian prime minister, Mr Ian Smith, and his colleagues were no longer the lawful government of Rhodesia.

Shortly before Rhodesia's declaration of independence, the Organization of African Unity held a meeting to consider the situation, at which several resolutions were passed. One resolution called on Britain to take all steps (including the use of armed force) to put down the Smith government. Another said that if Britain decided to recognize

Rhodesia's independence under the Smith government, all member states of the OAU should consider breaking off relations with Britain. Other resolutions urged member states to use armed force against Rhodesia if Britain refused to do so, and to help the African people in Rhodesia to set up a government of their own.

When Rhodesia declared herself independent three weeks later, not only did the British government refuse to recognize Rhodesia as independent, but it brought various kinds of economic pressure to bear on the Smith government. But it would not use armed force. Tanzania was so indignant with Britain over this that she broke off diplomatic relations, and did not restore them until July 1968. Kenya and Uganda agreed with Tanzania that Britain should have used armed force against the Smith government, but they did not think it necessary to break off relations with Britain on this account.

3. PROBLEMS OF AFRICAN UNITY

Disagreements between independent states make it harder to achieve African unity, which everyone so much desires. One of the strongest advocates of African unity was President Nkrumah of Ghana. He constantly urged that as long as African states remained politically separate, there would arise all kinds of economic and political differences between them which would make real unity impossible. The only way was to bring about political union first. Putting the matter in East African terms, Nkrumah would argue that no treaty of economic cooperation was sufficient; Kenya, Uganda and Tanzania should agree to unite into one East African region under a unitary form of government. The East African leaders did not agree to this, though they did consider setting up an East African federation. At one moment indeed, President Nyerere announced that if Kenya and Uganda were willing to join with his country into one state, he would be willing to serve under anyone who might be chosen as head of the combined state. But his offer was not accepted.

Shortly before Kenya and Uganda became independent, the three leaders met and agreed in principle to set up an East African federation at the end of 1963. But they did not do so. They held a further conference in April 1964, and Dr Nyerere then said that Tanganyika, the poorest of the three countries, was suffering under the existing arrangements. Industry tended to develop near Nairobi and Kampala, not near Dar-es-Salaam. He would like to impose duties on imports from Kenya and Uganda so as to encourage his own country's industry. Kenya and Uganda opposed this, and the conference set up a committee to draw up a scheme of federation. The committee agreed on a system of import quotas, and agreed also that Kenya and Uganda should encourage industry to settle in Tanzania. But it failed to agree on the difficult political problem of which powers should be held by the federal government and which should be held by the three state governments. So the proposed federation came to nothing.

The East African Community

Meanwhile, the Common Services Organization remained in being, and the three governments continued their discussions. In June 1967 they reached an agreement. They would set up an East African Community, a kind of economic federation without political links. They would not discriminate against each other's manufactures. There should be no customs duties on the frontiers: the whole region should become a free trade area. All three countries should impose the same customs duties on imports from outside the Community. If one of the three made a trade agreement with a foreign country, it should see to it that the other members of the Community should be able to share the benefits of the treaty. The administration of the Community should be decentralized; for example, its headquarters should be at Arusha in Tanzania, whereas the Post Office and the Development Bank would be at Kampala. The Community came into being on December 1, 1967. The establishment of the Community enables the most highly industrialized country of the three, Kenya, to give economic assistance to the other two: an arrangement which in the long term should increase the prosperity of the whole region, Kenya included.

The Organization of African Unity

The East African Community was a regional organization, and it had to be fitted into the all-African body, the Organization of African Unity. The OAU was founded at Addis Ababa in May 1963, and its permanent headquarters and secretariat remain there. Tanganyika and Uganda joined as founder-members; Kenya joined in July 1964. Dr Nkrumah of Ghana would have liked the OAU to have troops and other means of enforcing any decision it reached, but the OAU has not so far developed in this way. In 1970 it still remained merely a consultative body, in which African governments met to discuss their common problems. Such discussions are valuable. They have helped African governments towards agreement on such problems as Rhodesia, the Congo, and the Nigerian civil war. The OAU has no force behind it save the force of public opinion; which, as education spreads in Africa, will become more and more powerful.

One of the earliest achievements of the OAU came in January 1964, when in all three countries of East Africa there occurred mutinies among the troops. All three governments asked for British help, and in a very short time the mutinous troops were disarmed and disbanded. The trouble was most serious in Tanganyika, where there was some rioting, and President Nyerere felt that he still needed foreign troops for some time longer. But he would rather have African troops than British, so he asked the OAU to help, and the OAU arranged for the British troops to be replaced by Nigerians. The Nigerian troops stayed in Tanganyika till September; then the danger was over and they returned home.

4. THE PROBLEM OF NON-ALIGNMENT

On one important matter the OAU and its member states are agreed. Africa wants to have nothing to do with the quarrel between East and West, between communism and capitalism, between the United States and the Soviet Union. African governments do not wish to commit themselves entirely either to the system of free enterprise and the profit motive, or to the doctrine of the class war.

It is a difficult attitude to maintain, for both the East and the West are anxious to enlist the African countries on their side. Both are willing to give economic assistance, but both hope that by doing so they will win over the African governments. But Africa wishes to remain neutral, to align herself with neither side. She needs help from overseas, but will not accept help which is given on political conditions. This African attitude is called the policy of non-alignment. It was well expressed by President Kenyatta in December 1964. He said,

'I shall fight with all my strength against anyone, any group or any country, that may be tempted to undermine our independence. It is naive to think that there is no danger of imperialism from the East. In world power politics the East has as much design on us as the West, and would like us to serve their interests. . . . To us, communism is as bad as imperialism. What we want is the Kenya nationalism which helped us to win the struggle against imperialism. We don't want somebody else's nationalism.'

5. NEO-COLONIALISM AND THE PROBLEM OF POVERTY

Africa is in no danger now from old-fashioned imperialism. But African leaders greatly dislike what they call neo-colonialism. Their countries are poor, and still depend largely on their exports of raw materials: coffee, cotton, copper, sisal and the rest. They still need to import large quantities of manufactured goods, and to employ large numbers of technical staff from overseas. They complain that they have to sell their raw materials at prices which are fixed in London and New York, prices over which they have no control. If the merchants in these world markets would pay more—even only a little more—for African raw materials, it would make a great difference to African prosperity. The African leaders feel that the old political colonialism is dead, but that this economic colonialism (neo-colonialism as they call it) is still very much alive.

The grievance is just, but it is not easy to devise a remedy. Neo-colonialism is not a system deliberately invented. It is a natural result of the system of world trade whereby all prices are determined by supply and demand: when something is scarce or is badly needed, its price is high; when something is plentiful or not much needed, its price is low. Every African village market is run on this system. The price of all food crops goes up as the dry season advances and comes down when the new season's crop arrives; the price of fish comes down when the fishermen have made a good catch. In matters of world trade, Africa's difficulty is that nearly everything she produces can also be produced elsewhere. Africa supplies the non-communist world with nearly all its diamonds and cobalt, and most of its cocoa, chromium, and palm-oil. African sisal is important, and so are some African metals, such as gold, copper, manganese, lithium and columbium. But African groundnuts, tin, cotton, and coffee form only a small part of the total world production. There are other kinds of fibre to replace sisal, and other kinds of oil which could be used instead of groundnut and palm-oil. Thus, if the supply of all African products ceased, it is only in diamonds and cobalt that the world would find itself seriously and permanently embarrassed; the other things it could supply in time from alternative sources. Africa's bargaining power therefore is weak. The demand for African products comes mainly from Western Europe and North America, for it is there that the wealth, the financial skill, and the manufacturing industry are at present concentrated; and it is there, consequently, that prices are determined. A century hence, things may be different. The communist countries may come to equal or surpass Western Europe and North America, and world trade may be run on a different system.

The fundamental problem—poverty
Africa's fundamental problem is poverty. Much of East Africa is too dry for farming and too full of tsetse-fly for cattle. Taken as a whole,

the region is thinly peopled, and (as far as we know at present) is not well supplied with minerals. Yet, East Africa's contact with the modern world has taught her people to desire the comforts that are brought about by modern industrialization. Roads, railways, schools and universities, hospitals and factories are expensive. They can be provided only out of the profits made by trade and industry. For many centuries, Britain was a poor country, living first by exporting wool, and later by exporting woollen cloth. It was not till the nineteenth century that she developed a large industry in iron, steel, textiles and machinery; she was able to do this because she discovered large deposits of coal (which provided power) and of iron close together.

East Africa does not have this good fortune. Power is being provided by hydro-electric plants on the Tana and the Nile, and elsewhere. But power is only one of the requirements for establishing a successful manufacturing industry. Other requirements are readily available raw materials, and a ready market near the factory. Manufacturing industry is best begun with local raw materials and with products that can be sold near home. It would be unwise, for example, for Kenya to use the Tana river electricity to run a factory for making railway loco-motives, for most of the steel and other materials would have to be imported, and East Africa does not need many new locomotives a year. This may come later; but to begin with, more useful manufactures are cement, cigarettes, beer, tinned meat and milk and fruit; all these can be made with local materials and sold in East Africa. Other ex-amples are copper wire for the electrical industry, sacks made from Tanzanian sisal for Kenya's coffee beans, and cotton cloth and leather shoes, which can all be made from local materials and will save imports from abroad.

Meanwhile, East Africa is still receiving overseas aid. Tanzania has a treaty with China, under which China will build a railway to Zambia to bring Zambian copper out to a Tanzanian port. The Soviet Union has provided Tanzania with schools, hospitals and factories. Britain too has helped; when President Nyerere broke off diplomatic relations with Britain because of Rhodesia, he said that Tanzania had received £30 million worth of aid from Britain since independence, more than from any other country. Kenya and Uganda too have received aid from Britain and from the communist countries also.

The control of overseas capital: the Arusha Declaration

In addition to overseas technical aid which is received through govern-ments or through the United Nations, the East African governments naturally hope to attract private capital from overseas to develop their industries and increase their trade. But this involves a danger: large

12 A CROWD CHEERING THE ARUSHA DECLARATION

foreign firms might come to control too large a share of the economy, in the way that the Asians of Kenya did until 1967.

Independent African governments, not only in East Africa but in other parts of the continent, try to guard against this danger by what they call African socialism. They take control of essential resources and services, of the use of land and minerals and water supplies, and they run such services as railways, posts and airfields. Foreign firms wishing to establish businesses in Africa are welcome, but they have to submit to certain controls or conditions: for example, they may be required to train Africans for responsible technical or managerial positions, or to appoint Africans to the board of directors. African socialism was explained by President Nyerere in 1967. He said that foreign money could be used to undermine the nation's independence. Tanzania therefore must manage without the sort of development that requires large investment of capital from overseas. National leaders, such as members of the assembly or of TANU, must be farmers or workers, not shareholders or landlords or company directors. This speech of February 5, 1967 is known as the Arusha Declaration, because it announced an economic programme which had been drawn up by the president and approved by a meeting of the TANU executive a few days earlier at Arusha. The government, continued the president, would place the major means of production under the control of the farmers and workers of Tanzania; these 'major means of production' would include land, forests, minerals, water, oil, electricity, transport and communications, banks, insurance, and all big industries.

In the next few days, the Tanzania government nationalized all the banks and insurance companies, eight flour-milling companies and eight import–export companies; in addition, it took over a majority holding in the shares of six industrial companies. The staffs of these firms became government servants, and the government promised to pay full compensation. Kenya and Uganda, though approving of African socialism, did not immediately adopt such a thorough-going programme of socialist measures.

East Africa is changing fast. It has changed almost out of recognition since 1870, when Livingstone was wondering whether the Lualaba river flowed into the Congo or the Nile, when slaves were being freely bought and sold in Zanzibar market, and when Mackinnon was planning the first steamship service between Zanzibar and Aden. East Africa is now part of the modern world, and the world of 1970 is largely the result of the efforts and the mistakes made by the peoples of Europe. The world of 2070 will be very different; it will be deeply influenced by the contribution made by the peoples of Asia and of Africa.

Appendix I

QUESTIONS AND EXERCISES

Chapter 1

1 Why did Europe take so little interest in East Africa between 1700 and 1860?
2 What effect did the opening of the Suez Canal have in East African affairs?
3 How far is it correct to speak of the East African empire of the Sultans of Zanzibar?
4 Explain why Buganda and Bunyoro became enemies, and illustrate your answer by a sketch map.

Chapter 2

1 Why did Britain show so little interest in East Africa before 1887, and so much afterwards?
2 What was the importance of (a) Baker, (b) Gordon, (c) Stanley in bringing European influence into East Africa?
3 What effect did the introduction of Christianity into Buganda have on the position of the Kabaka?
4 Describe Sultan Barghash's difficulties in dealing with (a) the British, (b) the Germans.
5 The Sultan of Zanzibar had two possible methods of opening up East Africa: he could work either through Kirk and Mackinnon, or through Mirambo and Tippoo Tib. Explain why both possibilities failed.
6 What were the events that led up to the Berlin Conference?
7 How far was the British government responsible for the failure of the IBEA Company?
8 Explain Kabaka Mwanga's difficulties in Buganda.
9 What were the different motives that led the European powers to partition East Africa?
10 Draw a map to illustrate the journeys of (a) Karl Peters, (b) Emin Pasha.

Chapter 3

1 Explain the main differences between the German and the British system of administration in East Africa.

2 Describe the causes and the results of the Maji-Maji rising.
3 Describe Lugard's work in Uganda and show its importance.
4 Write the life story of Kabarega of Bunyoro.
5 What was the importance of the work of Semei Kakunguru?
6 What were the results of Sir Harry Johnston's administration in Uganda?
7 Why did the IBEA Company have so little success in governing the interior of Kenya?
8 What was the importance to Uganda of the frontier changes made by the British? Illustrate your answer by a map.
9 All early European travellers feared the Masai, but the Masai gave the British very little trouble. Why was this?
10 Why did the British before 1901 give so much more attention to Buganda than to Kenya?

Chapter 4

1 Why were the Germans in East Africa so successful in resisting greatly superior allied forces in the 1914–18 war?
2 What is a currency crisis? Explain why a currency crisis occurred in East Africa after the war, and describe its chief symptoms.
3 How did the British government's position in Tanganyika after 1919 differ from its position in Kenya and Uganda?
4 What were the chief causes of the economic depression of 1929–35, and how did the depression affect East Africa?
5 Why did Mussolini attack Ethiopia, and why did his attack arouse so much indignation?
6 Why was the League of Nations so ineffective in preventing the Italian conquest of Ethiopia?
7 What new developments occurred after the 1914–18 war in European thinking about colonies?

Chapter 5

1 Describe Sir Charles Eliot's hopes for the future of Kenya, and explain why they were not fulfilled.
2 What good, and what harm, did Lord Delamere do to Kenya?
3 Describe how the White Highlands policy came to be accepted by the government in London.
4 What were the main objects of the European political associations in Kenya?
5 What were the main differences between the Crown Lands Ordinances of 1902 and 1915?
6 Draw a map of Kenya and mark on it the land which has enough rainfall (a) for cattle, (b) for agriculture. What proportion of

Kenya is suitable for (a) agriculture and cattle, (b) cattle only, (c) neither?

7 'The Masai agreements were not in themselves bad; the bad thing about them was the hesitating way in which the government carried them out.' Do you agree with this?

8 What were the main differences between the Masters and Servants Ordinances of 1906 and 1910?

9 How far is it true to say that the Kenya government had one labour policy, the Kenya settlers another?

10 What examples can you give of the way in which Christian missionaries in Kenya became involved in politics between 1919 and 1945?

11 What were the results of the Carter Commission?

12 What were the purposes of the Resident Natives Ordinance of 1918 and the Native Registration Ordinance of 1920?

Chapter 6

1 What was the Kenya government's general policy in organizing the administration by the regulations and ordinances of 1897, 1902, 1912 and 1924?

2 Explain the importance of the common roll and the communal roll in a multi-racial country.

3 Describe the events leading to the Devonshire White Paper of 1923 and give its main terms.

4 Show the importance of Harry Thuku in Kenya politics, and the results of the Kenya government's treatment of him.

5 What arguments can you suggest in favour of the movement for closer union in the 1930s? Why did the movement fail?

6 Trace the beginnings of political activity among the Kikuyu, and describe the early activities of the Kikuyu Central Association up to 1939.

7 Describe the importance of the following in Kenya affairs:
(a) Lord Moyne, (b) the Hilton Young commission, (c) Lord Milner, (d) the Kakamega gold-field, (e) the Wood–Winterton proposals, (f) the Devonshire White Paper.

Chapter 7

1 Why was Uganda's problem of European settlement less serious than Kenya's?

2 Describe the beginnings of the Uganda cotton industry.

3 What was *mailo* land, and why were there differences as regards *mailo* land between Buganda and the other states?

4 What were the causes of the Bataka movement of 1918?

5 Describe (a) the occasions, and (b) the underlying causes of the disagreements between the Buganda and the protectorate governments before 1945.

6 Describe the policy of Sir Philip Mitchell and Sir Charles Dundas towards Buganda, and explain why it failed.

7 Why was Martin Nsibirwa murdered, and what were the results of his death?

Chapter 8

1 Describe the labour policy of the Tanganyika government in the 1920s.

2 How did the Tanganyika government incur criticism from European settlers in East Africa?

3 What was Sir Donald Cameron's plan for developing Tanganyika?

4 Describe the beginnings of African politics in Tanganyika.

5 What were the difficulties facing Sir Horace Byatt, and how far did he succeed in overcoming them?

Chapter 9

1 How did the war of 1939–45 affect (a) the economic position, (b) the political situation in East Africa?

2 What was the importance to East Africa of (a) the United Nations, (b) the Colonial Development and Welfare Acts?

3 Describe the Colonial Office's general policy for constitutional development in East Africa.

4 Describe the British policy of indirect rule, and explain why it proved a hindrance to constitutional progress in East Africa.

5 What was the British government's purpose in establishing the East Africa High Commission, and why was the idea of the commission unpopular in East Africa?

Chapter 10

1 Explain why education developed slowly in Kenya before 1939.

2 Describe the educational policy of the Beecher commission.

3 How far is it true to say that the British government granted Kenya her independence only because it was frightened by the Mau Mau?

4 Why did the African leaders reject the Lyttelton and Lennox-Boyd constitutions?

5 How far is it true to say that African political parties in Kenya began as tribal organizations?

6   Describe the Kenya land problem from the points of view of (a) the Kenya government, (b) the Africans, (c) the Royal Commission on Land and Population.
7   What were the principles of the Swynnerton scheme?
8   Explain the importance of (a) the Native Lands Registration Ordinance and (b) the Land Control (Native Lands) Ordinance.

Chapter 11

1   How was the Asquith Commission important to East Africa?
2   Compare the Bataka Federation of 1946–49 with the Bataka movement of 1918.
3   Why did the Lukiko dislike the protectorate government's constitutional proposals?
4   What was Sir Andrew Cohen's importance in Uganda's development?
5   What brought about the disagreement between the governor and the Kabaka?
6   Why were the 1958 elections a failure?
7   Describe the beginnings of political parties in Uganda.
8   What was the importance of (a) the Namirembe recommendations, (b) the Wild committee, (c) the Munster commission, (d) the Molson commission?

Chapter 12

1   How was Tanganyika's progress towards independence helped by the United Nations?
2   What was Sir Edward Twining's contribution to Tanganyika's development?
3   What effect did Dr Nyerere have on the Tanganyika African Association?
4   Compare the United Tanganyika Party and the Tanganyika African National Union, and explain why UTP failed.
5   Explain the importance of the Ramage committee.
6   How far did Tanganyika's 1960 constitution fall short of full internal self-government?
7   Explain why the East Africa High Commission was replaced by the East Africa Common Services Organization, and point out the main differences between the two bodies.
8   What steps were taken after 1961 to remedy Tanganyika's poverty?

Chapter 13

1   What were the stages by which the slave trade and slavery were abolished in Zanzibar?

2 What did Zanzibar owe to Edward Clarke?
3 Describe the measures by which the administration of Zanzibar was made to conform to the regular colonial system.
4 What was the land problem in Zanzibar, and what steps did the British take to solve it?
5 Compare the Coutts plan for Zanzibar with the 1956 constitution for Kenya.
6 Describe how the Coutts plan was amended by the Blood plan, and point out the weakness in the Blood constitution.
7 What was the importance of the common roll in Zanzibar politics?
8 Why was the newly independent government of Zanzibar so quickly overthrown?

Chapter 14

1 What were the chief difficulties preventing the rapid expansion of education in East Africa before 1939?
2 Show how education in East Africa was helped by (a) the 1939–45 war, (b) the Colonial Development and Welfare Acts.
3 What was the importance to East African education of (a) the De La Warr commission, (b) the Asquith commission, (c) the 1944 report on mass education?

Chapter 15

1 Explain the problem of the 'lost counties' in Uganda, and say what steps (a) the colonial government and (b) Dr Obote's independent government took to solve the problem.
2 What were the events that led to the exile of the Kabaka in 1966?
3 Describe the changes which Dr Obote made in the Uganda constitution after 1966.
4 How did President Kenyatta's government strengthen its position after 1966?
5 How did events in the Congo affect East Africa after 1960?
6 How far is the East African Community a substitute for the proposed East African Federation?
7 What are the main problems facing the Organization of African Unity?
8 What is meant by the African policy of non-alignment?
9 What difficulties do the East African governments meet when trying to establish manufacturing industries?
10 What dangers do the East African governments fear in accepting external aid, and what steps are they taking to guard against the dangers?

Appendix II

THE CENTURY OF CHANGE:
HOW THE YEARS WERE SPENT

The periods into which the century may be divided are illustrated by the sectors into which this circle is divided. The year 1870 is at the top, and the circumference is divided into five-year periods, proceeding clockwise until the year 1970 too arrives at the top.

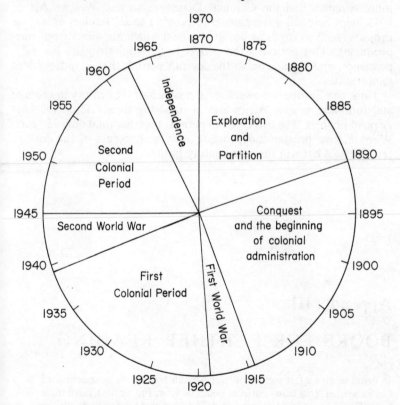

The century may be divided into seven periods. From 1870 to about 1890 is the first period, that of exploration and partition. The second period, from 1890 to 1914, is the period of conquest and of the beginnings of colonial administration. Then comes the first world war, from

275

1914 to 1918. From 1919 to 1939 we have what may be called the first colonial period. There is no more fighting, but there is much political activity, especially in Kenya. The colonial governments are poor, partly because of the general world poverty which resulted from the war, and partly because of the British theory which prevented the government in London from giving direct financial help to colonies except in extreme necessity. Economic development in this period is therefore slow. The fifth period is that of the second world war, from 1939 to 1945. The sixth may be called the second colonial period. It is a period of much greater prosperity and faster economic development; prices of colonial products are high and so colonial governments have more revenue, and the Colonial Development and Welfare Act of 1945 helps colonial governments to provide social services as well as projects (such as roads or power stations) which are directly revenue-producing. This period is the period of national struggles for independence, and it leads on to the seventh period, that of independent nation states.

Thus, the European powers spent nearly half the century in groping and fumbling in East Africa and in imposing their rule on the East African peoples. The two colonial periods together total only 38 years. When Kenya became independent, only seven years of the century remained. What will the next century hold?

Appendix III

BOOKS FOR FURTHER READING

In order to give a fair picture of East African history, we have consulted books written from many different points of view, and we have listed them here. They are not of equal value, and we do not recommend them all; but from this list we have made a small selection of books which the student can safely consult.

Donald L. Barnett and Karari Njama: *Mau Mau From Within*

Michael Blundell: *So Rough a Wind*
Richard Coupland: *East Africa and Its Invaders*
Richard Coupland: *The Exploitation of East Africa 1856–1890*
Charles Dundas: *African Cross-Roads*
Peter Evans: *Law and Disorder*
Muga Giceru: *Land of Sunshine—Scenes of Life in Kenya Before Mau Mau*
L. B. Greaves: *Carey Francis of Kenya*
Waruhiu Itote: *Mau Mau General*
Frederick Jackson: *Early Days in East Africa*
Elspeth Huxley: *White Man's Country—Lord Delamere and the Making of Kenya*
Kenneth Ingham: *A History of East Africa*
N. S. Carey Jones: *The Anatomy of Uhuru*
J. M. Kariuki: *Mau Mau Detainee*
Jomo Kenyatta: *Facing Mount Kenya*
Jomo Kenyatta: *Suffering Without Bitterness*
Frank Kitson: *Gangs and Counter-Gangs*
D. A. Low and R. Cranford Pratt: *Buganda and British Overrule 1900–1955*
Fred Majdalany: *State of Emergency*
Tom Mboya: *Freedom and After*
Philip Mitchell: *African After-Thoughts*
G. H. Mungeam: *British Rule in Kenya 1895–1912*
Oginga Odinga: *Not Yet Uhuru*
The Oxford History of East Africa, volumes 1 and 2
D. H. Rawcliffe: *The Struggle for Kenya*
W. McGregor Ross: *Kenya From Within*
C. T. Stoneham: *Mau Mau*

We have used also the annual reports issued by the governments of Kenya, Uganda, Tanganyika and Zanzibar in colonial days, and the Report of the Kenya Land Commission (the Carter commission) and the Report of the Royal Commission on Land and Population in East Africa of 1953–55. Much of the recent history of East Africa can be studied in contemporary Press reports, and we have made much use of the full digests of the Press given in *Africa Diary* and *Keesing's Contemporary Archives*.

To the student who has begun with our book and wishes to know which book to read next, we recommend:

Kenneth Ingham: *A History of East Africa*
The Oxford History of East Africa, volumes 1 and 2
Richard Coupland: *East Africa and Its Invaders*
Richard Coupland: *The Exploitation of East Africa 1856–1890*
D. A. Low and R. Cranford Pratt: *Buganda and British Overrule 1900–1955*

These are all books written by professional historians trying to present a balanced picture, whereas some of the books given in our longer list do not pretend to do more than relate the authors' personal experiences or give their personal points of view.

INDEX

The most important references are printed in **bold type**.

10.00
B &T